THE ENDLESS HOUR

THE TRUE STORY OF A HAUNTED SOUL

THE
ENDLESS
HOUR

JESSE BATTLE
WITH WILLIAM GREENLEAF

theendlesshour.com

WinePressPublishing
Your Book, Defined. Since 1991.

WinePress Publishing (PO Box 428, Enumclaw, WA 98022) functions only as book publisher. As such, the ultimate design, content, editorial accuracy, and views expressed or implied in this work are those of the author.

The author of this book has waived a portion of the publisher's recommended professional editing services. As such, any related errors found in this finished product are not the responsibility of the publisher.

Unless otherwise noted, all Scriptures are taken from the *Holy Bible, New International Version®, NIV®*. Copyright © 1973, 1978, 1984 by Biblica, Inc.™ Used by permission of Zondervan. All rights reserved worldwide. www.zondervan.com

Scripture references marked KJV are taken from the *King James Version* of the Bible.

Scripture references marked NASB are taken from the *New American Standard Bible*, © 1960, 1963, 1968, 1971, 1972, 1973, 1975, 1977 by The Lockman Foundation. Used by permission.

Illustrations by Jesse Battle.

Cover Photographer Dwight William.

ISBN 13: 978-1-4141-1723-2
ISBN 10: 1-4141-1723-X
Library of Congress Catalog Card Number: 2010901620

CONTENTS

Part I: Imagination. Creativity. Dreams.

1. Unspoken Words 1
2. Forever and a Day 17
3. In a Moment's Time 23
4. It's Romper Room Time 35
5. Sunday 45
6. The Significance of One 57
7. For Some It's Summer 61
8. Likeness of Red 71
9. Batman 81
10. Change 87
11. Transcend 97
12. Beyond the Unknown 107
13. Solitude 115
14. Blue Sky 121
15. December 133

Part II: Vision. Life. Hope.

16. The Story 143
17. Romantic Rebel 151
18. Garden of Denial .155
19. White Knight 163
20. The Confrontation 167

21. A Beautiful Day 169
22. The Visitation 175
23. Sanity. 181
24. Labyrinth 185
25. Vision. 191
26. Silent Lucidity 197
27. Unveiled. 205
28. The Mission 211
29. Revolution Begins 219
30. Last Seven Days 225
31. Rise and Fall. 233
32. Master of Deceit. 243
33. Rain 249
34. Whispering Wind. 257
35. Regeneration 263
36. Chosen 1959 269
37. Alone 277
38. Babylon 285
39. Freedom. 291

PART I
IMAGINATION. CREATIVITY. DREAMS.

CHAPTER 1

UNSPOKEN WORDS

AS HIS EYELIDS slowly opened, an orange ball of fire descended from the sky. He heard an explosion, followed repeatedly by others. Screams and angry yells echoed through the air. Tires screeched, and cars crashed on contact. Footsteps pounded the pavement like thunder. Frantic faces filled with fear cried with apprehension.

Inside his jacket, he felt the heavy weight of steel. He braced the gun with both hands and pointed it in front of him. Quivering with excitement, he fired six consecutive shots, the bullets leaving trails of smoke.

"Jesse! Get in your room and pick up your toys."

Hearing his mother's voice, Jesse got up slowly, standing above his toy soldier. He bent over and picked it up. The small plastic green figure stood about two inches high, with immovable parts: his warrior and hero.

Longing to continue his adventure, he stared at the other soldiers from a distance. His childlike mind fought the transition back into reality, the soldiers' words still on his lips.

"Ahhh, I'm hit! Don't think I'm going to make it. They got me! Oh no! I've... I've got to get up!"

Escaping back into his imaginary world, he bent over to place his green playmate among the others.

"You'd better be picking up those toys and cleaning your room," came his mother's voice again.

Five-year-old Jesse looked around in a daze as he returned to the present. Annoyed with the interruptions, he frowned and stood up slowly.

Looking down at his clothes, he made sure that his short-sleeved red-print shirt, blue jeans, and white canvas sneakers were still meticulously neat.

Although he resented having to give up his adventure, he knew that his mother meant business, so he headed toward that dreaded place. Emerging from behind the living room sofa, he walked in the direction of his room, passing the empty kitchen. Then he stopped, took four steps backward, and slowly crept across the kitchen floor. Approaching the gigantic refrigerator, he struggled with the handle but managed to open the door. He peered inside.

There it was, wrapped tightly in plastic: his favorite snack, watermelon. Jesse plunged into it. The plastic covering presented a problem at first, but in no time Jesse had it out of the way. He stuffed one handful after another of cool sweetness into his mouth. The melon's juice dripped down his face and onto his shirt. It didn't take long before he had managed to get the juice all over himself and the floor.

Spotting a pitcher of Kool-Aid®, he wanted a glass. He tried to reach the pitcher by standing on his toes, but couldn't. He quickly put his plan into action. Moving a chair from the kitchen table, he pulled it toward the refrigerator. He couldn't seem to get the chair there fast enough.

Through the open window, the sun cast rays of warmth upon freshly washed dishes. Jesse grabbed a glass from the drain board in the sink. After climbing onto the chair, he poured and slurped down the Kool-Aid® so quickly he hardly had time to taste it before pouring a second glass. After wiping his face with his hands and shirt, he shut the refrigerator door, leaving sticky wetness sliding down the handle.

Moving as quickly as he could, Jesse placed the dirty glass back with the clean dishes. He was grabbing paper towels when he heard the latch on the screen door. He froze as he listened to the familiar footsteps coming toward the kitchen. He wiped his shirt with the paper towels before throwing them in the garbage. Quickly pushing the chair back to the kitchen table, he tried to camouflage himself in the chair. *I'll make myself invisible*, he thought.

A mood of a man walked through the kitchen door, six-foot-three-inches of unrest, with eyes dark and intense. Happiness seldom lingered there, Jesse knew, and a magnitude of tension always followed him. His steps thundered like an earthquake, causing the floors to shake and Jesse's fragile body to tremble. Andre Battle was his name.

Wiping the sweat off his forehead, Andre opened the refrigerator door, never noticing the little boy sitting perfectly still. After realizing he didn't have a glass, he removed one from the sink. He poured himself a glass of Kool-Aid®, drank it hard and fast, and wiped his mouth. He was about to close the door when something caught his attention. His eyebrows shot up like alarms going off.

"Grace!" he shouted, his thin face scowling in anger. "Why is this kitchen such a mess? The watermelon in the refrigerator is uncovered, and it looks like someone stuck their hand in it!"

Jesse's father slammed the door shut and went hunting for his wife. Jesse held his breath. He felt powerless to say something in his mother's defense. Filled with fear, he was unable to speak. The rage he heard in his father's voice paralyzed him. He knew his dad was going to be mean to his mom.

Jesse climbed out of the chair and peeked around the living room doorway, watching as his father found her rolling up the vacuum cord. Grace looked up at him with her gentle brown eyes, not intimidated by his yelling. The expression on her face was a look of sadness— sadness equal to weariness. A quiet woman, she didn't speak much. When she spoke, it was with a voice of instruction. When love and affection were needed, she offered them.

"Woman, can't you hear?" his father demanded. "Answer me!" He stood supremely above her. The tension inside him made his lean, muscular body seem larger than life as he towered over her petite, plump form. He was like a volcano ready to erupt.

Grace continued to look at him as if deciding the best way to handle the situation. Her energy had to find somewhere to go as her hands worked steadily, rolling up the vacuum cord.

"A man works hard and can't even find a clean glass in the house," Andre growled. "The Kool-Aid® was almost gone. And why is it every time I come home, the kitchen is a mess?"

"I just washed the dishes," his mother said firmly. "It seems the harder I work and try to please you, the more you complain. What is it that makes you so unhappy? I do my best, and yet you still show no gratitude. What's happened to you?" His mother looked tired. The light in her eyes had become increasingly dim.

"Who are you talking back to?" he barked.

The violent eruption of the volcano was at hand. Jesse waited for his father to vent his uncontrollable anger. He felt even more nervous and afraid, while still attempting to maintain his powers of invisibility.

He heard someone knocking at the door. His parents didn't seem to notice. Then the screen door slammed, and their neighbor Janice walked in. Jesse liked Janice, a short, stout woman with a light complexion. She kept her hair in a short afro. She often commented that his mother was a good, respectable woman, and how her children were always kept clean and well taken care of. According to her, the other children in the neighborhood looked as though they were raising themselves, with their hair unkempt, their clothes filthy, and their faces unwashed.

"Grace, are you all right?" Janice called out. She touched Jesse on the head as she passed by and went to his mother. Janice put her arms around her while glaring at Andre with distaste written on her face.

"What do you mean, is she all right?" Andre demanded. "And what are you doing in my house?" Jesse knew his father didn't like women like her, who "didn't know their place and how to stay in it," as he often said.

"You heard what I said," Janice said, her voice rising. She didn't seem intimidated by him.

"Get the hell out of my house," Andre commanded. "I'm the man here. Who do you think you are?" He took a step toward Janice.

"Man?" Janice said in an outraged voice. "What makes you think you're a man? I hear that word so often. I must ask myself, do you know what that word truly means? Well, let me explain to you what a man is. He is someone who has gained self-knowledge of his own nature, abilities, and weaknesses. A man is self-reliant, supporting women, rather than being manipulative and cunning and feeding on women like leeches. Having respect for oneself and others shows another quality. In order to gain respect, you must show respect. A man is endowed with courage. He uses that courage to instill strength and confidence in others."

Infuriated, Andre barked, "I'm tired of listening to your crap."

Janice shot back, "Are you aware of your responsibilities as a man?"

Andre looked at her in disbelief, his body rigid and tense.

"You must make someone else feel inferior because of your own inferiority complex," Janice continued. "When no one subjects themselves to your irrational way of thinking, you use physical force. You think you win with fear, but you lose. Love and hate are the same to you." Janice leaned her face closer to his. She now stood only inches away as she glared directly into his eyes. The tension between them reached its peak.

Jesse felt his heart pounding in anticipation of what might happen.

"You obviously don't know what a man is," Janice said, "so you definitely have no idea what a husband is. If you did, you would never let your children see you yelling and beating their mother, who is supposed to be your sacred wife."

His father replied in a chillingly calm voice, "I've had enough of your mouth. If you don't get out of my house, I'll have you regret the day you were born."

Not intimidated by this threat, Janice turned and saw the audience standing in the doorway. Jesse jumped as he noticed that his older brother, Eric, and sister, Leah, had joined him. They looked frightened, and Leah's eyes were glazed with tears.

"Get in the kitchen, and don't be all day about it!" their father yelled at them with a wave of his hand.

The children dashed into the kitchen, one almost knocking the other over.

"Come with me, kids," Janice said, following behind them.

"Get out of my house!" their father roared, rushing at Janice from behind like a lion ready to pounce on its prey.

Janice ignored him. "Grace, I'm going to take the children with me," she said, continuing to walk toward the kitchen.

Their father raised his arm to strike Janice.

"Andre, no!" Grace screamed, barely holding his arm back with both of hers. "Please, no."

For a moment, he seemed bewildered. He gawked at his wife for a brief second and snatched his arm from her grip with his familiar stubborn, ugly resolve.

Janice glared at Andre for a moment longer. "Come on, children," she said, her voice trembling. She picked up Jesse and led Leah and Eric toward the front door, ignoring their father's ranting and raving.

"You'll pay," she yelled back over her shoulder as she crossed the street. "By God Almighty, you'll pay. Whatever you sow, you shall reap. God don't like evil."

Jesse's heart raced as he looked over Janice's shoulder at his father, whose voice was filled with outrage as he shouted above Janice's voice. He shook his fist wildly in the air.

Jesse heard his mother's voice. "Andre, please calm down."

"Who are you telling to calm down? What goes on here is my business. I'm the man here!"

Jesse heard distant screaming and shouting inside the house. He also heard the sounds of furniture hitting the walls, glass breaking, and his father's voice yelling above it all. Jesse could tell blows were being laid between the shouts of anger. With what measures Andre chose to place upon Janice, it was doubled to his wife.

Screams of torment could be heard. Jesse's small frame ached with hurt as he stared at their house. If only he were a warrior, he could help his mother. But he wasn't, and for now, all he could do was watch over Janice's left shoulder as she carried him across the street. It was a moment he would never forget.

"Don't worry, kids," Janice said, trying to sound cheerful. "Everything's OK. We can go have some ice cream."

The tears now flowed from Leah's eyes; Eric looked solemn.

Janice placed the children on the couch in the living room. Jesse sat on the floor.

"Here, you can play with these things while I get the ice cream," Janice said in a warm, friendly voice.

Leah and Eric looked somberly back at Jesse as Janice left. Leah's hair, which had been parted in the middle as usual and pulled back into ponytails, was now mussed. Her tall, thin frame hunched over as she wiped away her tears. Eric, with his dark complexion and close-set eyes, resembled their father. His coal-black hair, like Jesse's, was cropped short. He looked older than his years today.

Jesse gazed down at his own hands, lying limply in his lap. He had inherited his mother's lighter skin tone—"like cocoa-colored taffy," she had once said. He was small for his age and wondered if he would ever grow up to be a big man like his father.

The three sat quietly together, while Jesse let his mind wander.

Hours later, Grace arrived to pick up her children. She looked shaken, as though she had been crying. Her right cheek was bruised and swollen. As always, however, she maintained her poise.

"Thank you, Janice," she said softly.

"You're quite welcome," Janice replied.

"Are you all right?"

"Everything is OK now."

Grace and the children left the house, with Janice looking out from her porch protectively. Things were quiet when they got home. Andre was sitting in the kitchen, contemplating. He didn't even acknowledge that they had come home. Grace ushered the children to their rooms. The house was quiet and subdued. The stillness of nightfall was stifled by silence and tainted with fear.

That night, Jesse's pillow was wet with tears. His tiny heart felt sadness, and his eyes became weary as he dozed to sleep.

In the morning, the house was a different place, as if the events of the previous night hadn't happened. Jesse's mother arose as she customarily did and began her day, seeing about her family. His father sat in the living room with Jesse and his siblings, watching television, while their mother was in the kitchen. There was another side to his father, a side that sometimes tried to shine through even if it didn't stay long. Saying sorry wasn't something he could do.

Their mother was cooking bacon, which popped and burst with a mouth-watering aroma. Soft mounds of grits and scrambled eggs also filled the room with scent. She called them in to eat. The table setting was complete, everything put in dishes and steaming hot. Their father, now in a good mood, walked up to the kitchen table and playfully pushed Eric on the back of the head.

"Big-head boy," he said, chuckling a bit. "Your nickname ought to be Hook." He smiled thoughtfully, sitting down.

Eric smiled, too, but he didn't say anything.

"And you," Andre said, looking over at Leah. "A girl should have a soft name. Grace, what do you think about…Rain, for Leah?"

Their mother set a steaming plate of bacon, eggs, and grits before him. "Rain is nice," she said while serving the children.

They all sat down together and ate until they became full of her cooking.

Andre sat back, satisfied. "Little man, we'll give you something…Tiny Tim? Naw, we'll just call you Tim, that's different enough."

Jesse just looked at him, unconcerned about the entire issue of nicknames. He wanted to play in his own world.

Grace stood up and started to scrape the excess off the plates. She then instructed the children to pick up their toys before going outside to play. Quietness surrounded the house that day.

Jesse really only had one day to play and rest: Saturday. Sunday was for church. Many things might fade from his memory as he got older, but never Sunday morning.

Waking, Jesse opened his eyes and saw Eric still asleep, his head turned this way and his arms that way, his mouth wide open and lopsided. Jesse lay still trying to ignore the constant rhythm of his brother's snoring.

"Wake up."

Jesse turned to see his mother standing over him. She was always awake before everyone else. Never once had she looked tired, and she always had a bright smile to greet them. The sun was shining through the window behind her, creating an angelic glow. She always looked beautiful, and never seemed to have as much as a hair out of place.

"Go wash your face and brush your teeth," she told him as she moved to wake up his brother, who, when Jesse left, was still fighting her off in his sleep.

"This bed is wet!" his mother said as she pulled the bedspread from the bed.

"The bed's wet?" his father asked, coming down the hallway. "Which one of you wet the bed?" He started to unbuckle his wide black leather belt to deliver the usual punishment.

"Jesse did it," Eric said quickly.

Jesse was just about to brush his teeth when he heard his father call out his name. Dutifully, he came.

His father stared at him through narrowed eyes. "What are you doing wetting the bed? You're too old to be doing that."

Before Jesse could respond, Andre began interrogating him with a barrage of questions. Jesse stood before him confused, not knowing what to say in his defense. Grace stood aside, looking on thoughtfully as the two boys stood side-by-side in front of their father. Eric had been excused and Andre was about to proceed with the thrashing.

"By the time I'm finished, I guarantee, you won't wet the bed again," his father said while raising the belt to strike.

Jesse trembled with fright, feeling helpless to defend himself.

His mother quickly spoke. "Andre, wait, check his underwear."

"Come here, boy," his father said to Jesse and checked him for dampness. The side of him was wet, but his underwear was not.

"Eric!" he commanded.

Completely wet. He was the culprit.

"Go on and finish getting ready for church," Andre told Jesse abruptly. "Come here, Eric." He motioned to Eric to follow him.

"No, Daddy, please!" Eric pleaded, knowing that he was going to receive the punishment he had almost escaped.

Jesse lingered in the hallway and listened as Eric was dragged into the living room.

"First, you lie to me," their father said, and Jesse heard the snap of the belt. Eric cried out. "Who do you think you were trying to fool? I wasn't born yesterday." He gave Eric another and another. What seemed to last an eternity, lasted five minutes.

Then their father yelled, "Go get ready for church and get out of my eyesight."

Eric, his face wet with tears, passed Jesse in the hallway on the way back to the bedroom. He rammed into Jesse and shoved him into the wall. "Punk!"

Back in his room, Jesse saw that his mother had laid their clothes out neatly. He started to dress in the heavily starched clothes and was halfway dressed when his brother returned. Eric didn't hit him again, but he kept giving him dirty looks.

Their mother appeared back in the room with a hairbrush and Royal Crown Pomade. She placed a glob of the sticky substance on the back of her right hand, then combed and parted Jesse's hair while oiling his scalp. She took the remainder and smeared it onto his face, making circular motions. He felt as if his face were being covered by an octopus. She rubbed the pomade around until Jesse looked like a shiny copper penny.

Starched, greased, and clean, it was time to leave for church. The ride to church seemed to take forever. Nobody talked much. Eric stared ahead and turned periodically to give Jesse mean stares that he wasn't aware of until he turned his head. Jesse stuck out his tongue and turned away.

Jesse hated the routine of going to church. All the younger children had to go downstairs to the bowels of the church: the basement, where Sunday school was held. He'd rather stay with his mother instead of going there. When they arrived at the church, everyone was around outside, talking and laughing with each other. It seemed as if a thousand hats floated around above him. The women were always stylishly dressed in brocade dresses and pearls, hats adorned with decoration, and high-heeled shoes. The smell of different perfumes engulfed him. The men just looked like giants, most of them with booming laughs and firm handshakes.

The stairs were an annoyance. Jesse had to be dragged up the huge, speckled granite steps because he could never keep pace. His legs simply weren't long enough.

Leah always took Jesse and Eric down to the basement's entrance. The dim light was too weak to brighten the entire area, so Jesse carefully watched his steps. He sat with all the little kids as the Sunday school lesson began. He didn't understand many of the lessons, although he tried. He didn't like being around the other kids. He wanted to go off by himself, so he just waited impatiently until the lesson was over. That day, his collar was too tight around his neck, so he kept trying to loosen it, and the starch in his pants was making him itch. The teacher kept giving him looks as he fidgeted, but he couldn't sit still.

When class was finished, all the kids went up the dark, winding staircase. Jesse carefully looked at the intricate designs in the wood grain as he walked up. All the other kids with boundless energy always rushed past him while he was observing his surroundings.

Their mother waited in the same area every Sunday for her children, to lead them to their seats for church service. In the pew, Jesse's feet never reached the floor; they always dangled. He swung them back and forth due to boredom. Church was always crowded, so they would have to squeeze together tightly wherever they sat.

While Grace said hello to some of the other members who had come to sit beside them, Eric reached over Leah and hit Jesse. Jesse reached over and hit him back. They did this until Leah threatened to tell. She didn't have to, because Grace always knew what was going on.

"Jesse, come and sit on this side of me," she said, patting the space on her left.

The service began. Everyone sat like straight arrows, with undivided attention, except for Jesse. He constantly leaned over and looked around at all the faces. He wanted to move freely and couldn't stand to be confined.

Soon, the sun began penetrating the stained-glass windows. The gospel choir, adorned with colorful robes, stood and sang. Jesse noticed several of the people, including his mother, stood and clapped. Then the moment always came, the Altar Call. The music became slow and mournful. People with tears and sad hearts walked to the front of the church and gathered around the altar, bowing their heads.

His mother walked up front this day, effortlessly gliding down the center aisle, her eyes fixed on the altar. Jesse could tell she was dispirited. Even though he was a child, he knew something was troubling his mother deeply. He felt her heart hurting, and it hurt him. All he knew of her was caring, love, and guidance. When she came back from the altar, she sat beside him. She looked at him and smiled slightly, then turned her attention back to the service. He noticed she appeared to be relaxed and at peace. Grace had received an answer she had been seeking for some time, and from that point on, she had the strength to make a change.

Jesse continued to dangle his feet and look around. Finally, when church was over, he was happy. Back down the giant stepping stones. Back to being swallowed up in a world of adults and their boring environment and conversations. Everyone was saying goodbye, and some even hello. He was grateful it was over.

It was a dark, angry night. The summer wind whipped and beat anything with which it came in contact. The rainstorm had cooled things off from the heat of night. Jesse was in bed when he heard pounding on the front door and his father's thundering voice.

"Grace!" his father yelled. "It's me, Andre. Open the door!"

"Andre, it's late," Grace said.

"Just open the damn door!" he said angrily.

Several weeks had passed since his mother and father had separated. His father had gotten his own apartment nearby. They had rarely seen him during that time.

Now, hearing his father's voice, Jesse tensed, lying in his bed like a board. As his father pushed open the door and came inside, Jesse heard their exchange.

"What? Now I'm not good enough for you?" Andre demanded. "You act as though you weren't even going to open the door."

"Andre, please don't. Just leave!"

"You don't tell me to go! Where are my boys?"

"They're asleep."

Jesse heard his father's heavy footsteps coming down the hall, while his mother followed behind, protesting. Then his father burst into the room, slamming the door against the wall. He stood there dripping wet, his clothes plastered to his body.

"Come on, boys," he said loudly. "Get up. You're going with me."

"Andre," Grace said, her voice pleading, "please stop. Jesse, Eric, go back to sleep."

"I said get up!" he yelled angrily, pulling the sheets back. He grabbed Jesse first, scooping him into his arms and lifting him out of the bed.

His mother reached for him. "Give me Jesse!" she cried.

"Get out of my way, woman!" He slapped her hard with his spare hand.

She slammed against the wall with the force of the blow, which echoed through the house.

"You!" Andre said in a cold, emotionless tone. "Do not tell me what to do. You think you're so independent now. You think you can whip me. I'll kick your..."

His voice trailed away as she rose up. She looked at him with so much hatred, he looked away.

"No! Give me Jesse," she screamed.

Andre pushed her hard, still being the stronger power. Then he picked up Eric and started for the front door. Both Jesse and Eric were upset and crying.

Jesse felt the rain soak him as his father carried him outside. Their mother reached the car just as their father placed them inside. On the top of the car, the heavy raindrops made rapid pattering sounds. Other cars sped by in the storm, causing gushes of water to splash against them.

Jesse could barely see through the darkness as his father struggled to place him in the car. Headlights moved in both directions, the vehicles only a blur to Jesse. Then he heard an eerie, piercing shriek. Jesse turned his head and saw a black shadow darting across the street between the cars. Then he heard a deadening thud.

Everything seemed to move in slow motion. The moment became like a silent movie. Jesse no longer heard the thunderous rain, vehicles passing in the night, or blowing horns. He turned again and looked out the back window. Through the rain on the window, he could barely see his mother on her knees.

Within seconds, the downpour of rain became heavier. The rain soaked her, leaving her clothing and body drenched. She struggled to stand but couldn't. She let go screams of pain and anguish as she clenched her fists helplessly. Slowly, she made it to her feet, her body bent and swaying. She took a step, lost her footing, and slipped back into despondency.

Jesse's father started the car and drove off. He turned the corner sharply, the car swerving almost out of control. He sped the car down the slick expressways like a madman, mumbling as he drove, not saying anything coherently. He seemed unaware of his children in the back seat, shivering and crying with fear. Headlights from other cars zoomed in, lighting the entire vehicle, giving it an ominous glow.

They pulled into a narrow driveway, and their father opened the car door for them to get out. He ushered them through the rain and into the house, but not before they were soaking wet again. He took them to a room in the back of the house, cold and confused.

"Get in the bed and go to sleep," he said gruffly as he left the room.

Jesse looked around the empty room. The walls were shabby and dirty. The bed was unmade; the blanket and sheets lay on the floor. The carpet looked as if it had never been cleaned. Eric picked up the covers from the floor, threw them on the bed, and climbed in.

"Come on," he said. "He might come back in here and beat you."

Jesse scrambled under the covers. The bed smelled horrible. In fact, the entire house had a stench to it.

They lay still. Jesse stared at the ceiling, uneasy and uncertain how to accept what was happening, wondering if they would see their mom and Leah again. As the night grew long, he eventually drifted off to sleep.

It seemed as if they had just closed their eyes when they were being awakened again. Jesse heard voices, and men in blue uniforms came into the room with his father. Picking up Eric and Jesse, the men took them home.

Jesse was relieved to be in familiar surroundings again. His mother was there with a tear-stained face. She took him and his brother into her arms, then bathed and dried them with a mother's care. Relief and gratitude showed on her face.

"OK, now you two get into the bed," she said softly, smiling at them.

Eric ran to bed, but Jesse walked slowly through the living room. In the dark, he saw a light flickering in the corner of the room. Like a magnet, he was drawn to it. He drifted closer and closer toward the light, as if in a trance.

On the television screen, violence had erupted. Screams of anger and terror came from a crowd of people moving through the streets. He saw a woman fall, and within seconds, men in uniforms began beating her with clubs and pulling at her clothing. Helplessly, she was dragged along the concrete curb.

Jesse's heart pounded wildly like the drumming of the Congo, out of control.

On the screen, another boy was pinned against a wall, screaming, while two enormous, ferocious animals growled viciously like wolves, barking and snapping their teeth at him. The German Shepherds seemed on the verge of breaking away to devour anyone in their path.

Women searched for any kind of protection, with babies and children in their arms. People rushed frantically for places of safety. In the background were flames, overturned vehicles, explosions, sirens, burning storefronts, and shattered windshields. People's mouths hung open, while making no sound. Many victims turned to retaliate.

More zookeepers in blue uniforms appeared by the hundreds, with stern faces and cold, steely eyes. They moved in unison with menacing accuracy, their hands gripping clubs. Some wore hard hats. Huge leather belts hung around their waists, with heavy pieces of metal in their holsters.

Suddenly, the fear of the people turned into anger, which led to action. They pelted the uniformed men with rocks, bottles, just about anything. Some uniforms retreated back to their cars, while others continued their attack on the crowd. More police cars were turned over and set ablaze. Many of those in uniform now displayed frantic faces.

A voice came through the television set: "As you can see, the situation is out of control. The National Guard will obviously be called in if order cannot be established. This is total mayhem."

Fury rose in a burst of flames as a police car and a helicopter caught ablaze. More and more fire trucks arrived as the flames of hate and aggression grew. People were being hosed down by firemen. The force pinned some against the buildings, while others fell through storefront windows or to the pavement. Some other substance was sprayed on the people, who now rebelled completely, like wild animals escaping from their cages. Busloads of police arrived to help the uniformed survive in the jungle.

Though outmatched against the fire hoses, dogs, clubs, and guns, the people tried to maintain dignity and respect. Nevertheless, they were overcome by those in authority. What had started as a defiant demand for respect had turned into a massacre. The people were being slaughtered. Screams muffled by sirens continued as blood flowed along the street curbs.

Jesse continued to watch as the people were beaten down with repeated blows. He saw people running, screaming, and holding their heads, trying to stop the flow of blood.

His mother walked by with laundry in her arms. "Jesse, I thought I told you to go to bed," she said.

Mesmerized by what he was witnessing, Jesse barely heard his mother's voice.

"Jesse, go to bed now!" she said again, this time pulling him by the hand as he stood still, transfixed.

For a moment, she stopped pulling at him. He looked up at her and saw that her eyes had turned to the television screen. She clasped her hands over her mouth, aghast.

Then she murmured, "I know I've done the right thing. I know it." She turned to Jesse, her face wet with tears. "There is power in prayer, Jesse. You remember that. Now go to bed."

Not knowing what his mother meant, Jesse turned around and took the steps of a child. His feet moved forward, but his mind stayed back.

For a long time, he lay awake in bed with nameless faces passing through his mind. Sleep refused to lay by his side. Even when he did finally sleep, he could still see their faces and hear their cries.

Jesse had witnessed the horrors of the summer riots of Rochester, New York, on July 24, 1964. When he was older, he learned that there had been riots in several other cities at this time.

There were mixed stories of how the riot began. Those in authority had their version. Extensive looting and vandalism had taken place on Joseph and Clinton Avenues. City, county, and state police officers were needed to control the people, with the help of the National Guard. By July 30, 1964, the unrest had simmered to a halt. Many people were hospitalized, and four people had died. More than five hundred arrests were made.

The black population had grown in Rochester between 1940 and 1960, with people looking for better jobs and opportunities. What they found was quite the contrary. Blacks were often denied good jobs and housing solely due to race. Police brutality was common. Often, officials ignored the cases brought by blacks, who were discouraged by the system of bureaucracy. Meanwhile, whites in the same area lived lives of leisure, feeling well protected by those whom they trusted.

To some, there were no racial problems; there was no police brutality or discrimination, because it was all swept under the rug. It all went unnoticed, even when the pot began boiling over.

Nevertheless, years of pain had mounted into tension, which exploded into anger. The people wanted true freedom from their oppressor and had not received it. They had spoken softly first, through the voice of the law. They had made statements that America did not want to hear. In a reasonable tone, they had asked for equality and justice, but time and time again, their cries went unheard. They had cried out for freedom and equality to a system that said they didn't even deserve rights as human beings. The people grew tired of being manipulated, oppressed, and ignored by the government. The anger, hatred, and words turned into action. The hurt and the pain formed the unspoken words of the silent majority.

CHAPTER 2

FOREVER AND A DAY

FOR A PERIOD of time after the riots, Jesse and his siblings were not allowed outside. Eric and Leah often agitated each other and caused commotion within the household. Their mother was constantly scolding them and setting them back on track.

"Mama," Leah said one morning at breakfast, "is Daddy coming back home soon?"

Their mother paused and looked at Leah, as if startled. "Your father is not coming back to live with us anymore, Leah," she said quietly.

"Where is he going to live?" Leah asked.

"He's gonna live in a big black hole," Eric said tauntingly.

"Eric!" their mother said sharply. "Be quiet."

She turned to her daughter, whose saddened expression echoed what Jesse felt inside. Eric triumphantly chewed on a piece of bacon with a grin on his face. Jesse looked down at his plate.

"Is he still our daddy?" Leah asked.

"Just because he doesn't live here anymore doesn't mean he isn't your father," said their mother. "He will always be your father."

"I told you, Eric," Leah said with relief on her face, even though she tried to act tough about it.

Their mother turned to her oldest son. "Eric, why would you say something like that?"

"Because I don't want him to be my daddy." Eric refused to look at his mother, with a stubborn look set on his face.

"He's still your father," she said, having the last word.

"Why can't we go outside?" Eric whined. "It's boring in here with nothing to do."

"Maybe tomorrow," she said firmly. "But not today."

Eric fell quiet. Considering the look his mother was giving him, he knew not to push his chances any further.

The next day, their mother ventured out to the grocery store. Leah and Eric didn't want to go, so Janice stayed with them until she came back. With a child's spirit, Jesse followed his mother, joyous to be out of confinement.

Their street had suffered little change during the riots, but when they turned onto Joseph Avenue, Jesse saw the aftermath. Broken glass crunched underfoot as he and his mother slowly walked along the sidewalk, stepping over mountains of debris. Burned storefronts, collapsed buildings, and boarded-up homes surrounded them. Other areas looked like empty, bombed shells. Abandoned and overturned cars sat in the middle of the street. The smell of ashes hung in the air, days after the catastrophic nightmare. People walked solemnly, lost and disoriented, not knowing where to begin to clean up the damage.

The store was packed with people coming in to replenish their cupboards after having spent many days inside their homes. The air filled with conversation as people opened up about their feelings for the first time after what had happened. Most were upset, somber, and agitated.

Jesse's mother quietly got the items she needed and made her way to the front of the store to check out. A group had congregated at the checkout line in a heated dialogue. The lines were so long, talk seemed the natural thing to do, and somehow it soothed the misery.

"I don't know how much more I can take," said an old man who stood bent over. "It hurts me inside, watching our people destroy their neighborhoods and themselves. It gives me a sickening feeling inside my gut." He hesitated a moment, then continued in a quavering voice, "Why do we keep trying to fit into a country that doesn't accept us and never will? I ask myself this one question over and over: why do whites hate black people so much? I mean, what is the real truth?"

"Lord, have mercy!" said a stout, middle-aged woman, interrupting the old man. "When are we going to stop disrespecting ourselves? In order to gain respect, you must respect yourself first. And I do agree with you—when are we going to stop destroying our own? When?"

"Our own?" replied a tall, contentious man. "What do we own?" He answered his own question. "We don't own anything. Right now, my only concern is to protect our families and children. They come in here with their dogs and weapons, beat us, hose us down, and when we fight back to protect ourselves, they call us violent. They beat us down like animals and go back to the suburbs to their wives and families. For centuries, they have systematically destroyed and robbed us of our wealth, power, and royal past. The system they have set in place is a continuous attempt to keep us from finding our true place in modern-day history!"

"Did you see the way the policeman hit that woman holding her baby?" another interjected. "She was only trying to get him out of all that mess, and they said she lunged at them. How come what our eyes see and what they interpret are two different things? Anybody with a heart could have seen what that woman was doing. They don't want to see, and those that do are too afraid to speak up."

"What kind of world is this," the old man said, "where women and their children are treated like dogs and it goes unpunished? They even laugh in the courtroom whenever something comes to trial, if it ever gets that far. They can do whatever they want to us, and there is nothing we can do to fight back, unless we want to be killed." He heaved a sigh of despair. "Nothing is ever gonna change."

"Well, if it ain't never gonna change," a heavyset woman said, "black folks need to stop destroying their own and accept it."

The tall man looked at her with disgust. "I'll never accept that I'm less of a man because of my color."

"Hello, Grace," someone said.

Jesse turned to see Cora, who lived two doors down from them.

"Hi, Cora," said his mother.

"How're you doing?" Cora asked, reaching for a pack of chewing gum from the counter.

"I'm all right. I ran out of everything and had to come to the store."

"Yeah, me too." Cora's eyes looked far away. "Just don't seem real, do it?"

"No," Grace said, shaking her head sadly.

"My nephew is up there in the county hospital in a coma. They don't think he'll come out of it. My poor sister is a wreck. They had to sedate her. I'll take some food over there and try to help out with the kids while she's in the hospital. I just don't understand how a policeman could beat down a fourteen-year-old boy. His father is talking about going to see Fred Payne—you know, the black lawyer. I just shook my head when he said he was going. I've always heard if you want a good lawyer, get a Jewish lawyer, because Jewish lawyers will defend black people. Black folks say they win most of their cases and even get more than what they would have settled for."

Cora came closer and said with a stern look, "See, that's one thing about black folks. They'll either do a half job, or when they get a degree or a little status, they have no problem turning their backs on their own people. Money talks, and I just don't know whether it would be wise for him to go see Mr. Payne or not."

"It can't hurt to try," Jesse's mother said softly.

The caring in her tone must have sparked something in Cora's heart. "No, it can't!" Cora said, her tired eyes brimming with tears. "But I want somebody to tell me what sense it made for that to happen to him? He didn't have no gun; he wasn't a threat. He was trying to get his smaller brother off them streets just like most of them other folks. The police beat him down in front of his mother, while the other cops held her back, screaming and kicking."

Everyone had fallen quiet as they listened to Cora's pain.

"I wish they could know what it feels like!" she continued bitterly. "I'm sick of this. I'm sick of them hurting us!" She shook her fist upward in hopeless anger. She started to sob uncontrollably, and Jesse's mother put her arms around her and held her tight.

"Everything got worst when they brought out them dogs," the old man said, shaking his head sadly. "Even dogs get treated better than black folks."

The walk back to their house was worse than the walk to the store. Grace's eyes were moist, and Jesse just couldn't help going over in his mind what those people had been saying. Though he had limited understanding, he knew pain. Something drastic had happened to those people, and this was the result of it: ruined streets and heavy hearts.

Jesse felt warmth on his face and looked up. Sunlight streamed through the clouds. The light fell on one particular area, as though predestined. That was when Jesse noticed, amongst all the rubble, that the church still stood. Stone by stone, it was the same, untouched by the riots. It served as a source of strength for its people. The cross perched atop the steeple glowed in the path of sunlight, giving off a warm, golden radiance against the azure-blue sky. It told them that God saw and that they were not alone. He was watching over them.

Still, it seemed as if the sign went unnoticed by many. People walked around lost in grief. Others retained strength in their inner beings, yet had no power to change what had happened. What could they do? They could only pick up the broken glass that reflected their broken spirits, board up their destroyed windows like they boarded up their hearts, and sweep out their streets like they swept out their hopes for change. Helplessness and despair would take them back to the prison of their environment.

Grace picked up Leah and Eric on the way home. The kids were given permission to sit on the porch. Their mother gave them each a Popsicle® and strict instructions not to leave the porch area. So they sat in a row, the three of them licking their Popsicles®.

As Jesse licked his Popsicle®, he counted the vehicles passing by, one after another. Eventually, growing bored, he looked for something to amuse himself. In the distance, he noticed something dark and stiff lying lifeless along the curb. His eyes strained as he leaned forward on the steps, trying to make out the mysterious shape.

Suddenly, he remembered that murky, thunderous night when headlights were moving in both directions and vehicles were just a blur— the night his father had taken him and his brother from his mother. He remembered the piercing shriek he had heard and the shadow moving between the cars, then the dead sound.

Now Jesse saw the carcass of a black cat. It lay along the curb, stiff and hideous. Its mouth was drawn open and its body mangled, its eyes decayed. Jesse leaned forward and slowly lowered his Popsicle® from his mouth. His eyes studied the dead cat, killed needlessly. Nobody cared; nobody had tried to make it right.

"Jesse, your Popsicle® is melting all over the place!" Leah yelled.

Jesse turned to look at his sister and then at his Popsicle®, which had almost melted away. The syrup had gone between his fingers, covered his hand, and streamed over his elbow onto his clothing. Jesse gave his sister a distant stare, as if in a trance. He looked afar, letting his mind drift. Gradually, the clouds gathered and blocked out what was left of the sunlight.

CHAPTER 3

IN A MOMENT'S TIME

JESSE STOOD AWKWARDLY in the corner of the school room, try-ing to take in all the commotion surrounding him. Full of vitality, the other children couldn't keep still, laughing, giggling, and running back and forth. A toy car zoomed across the floor and crashed into a wall.

"All right!" yelled a little boy nearby.

Jesse had tried desperately to fit in but couldn't. Slowly, he bent over and picked up some bright wooden building blocks at his feet. He tried to build something, but it wasn't interesting. In fact, it was downright boring. Yet he wanted something to keep him occupied in this room of activity. He would have much preferred to take his toy soldiers on another adventure, but he hadn't been able to bring them.

On this early September morning, his mother had awakened him with a smile on her face. It was almost like getting ready on Sunday morning. After a hot breakfast, she had brought him here to this place. She talked with him briefly and assured him that everything would be just fine. Then, waving, she backed away and left, still wearing that different smile. Jesse didn't know why she was so happy; this place definitely was nothing special.

Jesse looked up when he heard an adult voice. Mrs. Ellis was her name. She was cheerful and charming. She wore a long, bright dress with vibrant colors that matched her personality. She had golden hair, blue eyes, and a Colgate smile. Her personality seemed right out of the Walt Disney Mickey Mouse Club.

"All right, children!" she said, pulling them from their world of paradise.

Several small faces looked up at her.

"Settle down," she said firmly for the remaining children who were still moving about. "Please line up on the side of the room, and when I call your name, I want you to take a seat."

School was now in session.

"Aaron Brown…" she called out, seating the children alphabetically. Jesse found himself at the front of the class, where he sat stiffly. Later that day, the children all stood in a circle and held hands. They sang joyous songs that matched the atmosphere. Jesse looked around at the happy faces.

One little girl's pigtails flopped around in the air as her head bopped from side to side. She yelled out the songs, trying to sing the loudest. She often looked to the teacher for approval and seemed encouraged by her smiles.

When the singing stopped, they sat on the floor, staying in the same circle to play the game Duck, Duck, Goose. The teacher had selected a student to walk around the circle of children. When the student was ready, he would tap his classmates on the head, while yelling, "Duck, duck… goose!" The child chosen as the goose would chase the other student around the circle, trying to tag him before returning to a sitting position in the circle.

Silly game, Jesse thought, happy when no one tapped him. Why were they playing this game, anyway? This had nothing to do with the reality he had seen on the television. He had witnessed destruction, not singing, happiness, or any part of that "Mary Poppins" world. So he decided, since he hated doing all these things, he would fake it. He felt alienated in the fairy-tale bliss of that place, and when it was time to go home, it suited him just fine.

At home that evening, after Grace fed the children, they had to do their homework. Eric and Leah finished quickly. Since Jesse didn't have any homework, his mother had him work on his ABC's. He sat at the table reciting: "A B C D E F G H I…I…I."

His mind kept failing him. The more he tried to concentrate, the harder it became.

His mother turned from the sink, where she was washing dishes, and said, "Try again."

After three more attempts, his mind drifted away. Jesse reached across the table and gripped one of his green toy soldiers in his small hand.

"Jesse!" she said sharply, taking the toy soldier out of his hand.

Jesse jumped.

"Education is very important. It should be taken seriously. Without a good education, you won't be able to get anywhere in life. You shouldn't be playing around. You'll have plenty of time for that later. Now, try again."

He started again slowly, looking at the soldier his mother had placed back on the table. He knew better than to touch it.

"A B C…" Jesse started again and successfully completed the entire alphabet from A to Z.

"Good!" his mother said, smiling broadly as she walked by him. "I knew you could do it." She continued out of the kitchen.

As soon as she was gone, Jesse confidently began reciting the alphabet, but just as he started, his memory failed him once again. His mind gave way to wandering. Noticing the music playing from the radio on the counter, he hummed along with the song as he reached to pick up his toy soldier for another adventure.

In a moment's time, fall had turned into winter. December had arrived. In the months that had passed, Jesse had gotten into the routine of dealing with school. Every day after class, he met Leah at the bottom of the hill behind the school for the walk home.

To Jesse and many of the other children, the hill seemed like a giant mountain. Humongous. It stood wide and high.

School had let out early that day, and, as usual, children were swarming around the hill. Scores of kids would meet there after school to do one thing: slide. Soaring down the hill wasn't just an event. It was a wild, exhilarating, breathtaking odyssey. Children came down the hill on wooden and plastic sleds, jumbo-sized truck tire tubes, even old bed mattresses—just about anything they could find for participation. Amusement was in the air; there seemed to be no end to their recreation.

Jesse watched the action while he waited for his sister to arrive. Soon, however, impatience took over, and he found himself climbing the hill behind the other kids. Jesse made his way up the hill with difficulty, lagging behind the bigger kids. Snow mixed with sleet left a slippery coating of ice, which made footing difficult. Some children slipped while climbing and slid back to the bottom, then struggled to make it back to the top.

When Jesse reached the halfway point, he was exhausted. It seemed as if he were climbing Mt. Everest, but still he kept climbing steadily with a look of determination on his face.

Once at the top, Jesse looked down the hill, which seemed even larger to him from above. He then looked over and saw a cluster of kids forming together. Everyone was getting ready for the game called "the dare." The kids buzzed around, ready for action. Jesse hesitantly crept over to see what all the commotion was about. Once in the area, he looked over the edge again. This time he saw a narrow, icy path that went straight to the bottom. Kids were lined up on both sides of the path, taunting, cheering, and laughing. At the top, the older kids pushed the smaller ones out of the way.

In front of him, one of the older boys was getting ready to take the dive on a piece of cardboard to the bottom of the hill.

"Chicken," somebody yelled out. "You ain't gonna do it!"

The boy didn't answer him; he just jumped on the cardboard and whooshed down the patch, yelling and whooping. The kids cheered as he went down. One after another, they jumped on top of the boy for a ride down the path. Some mistimed their jumps and hit the hard ice. By the time they reached the bottom, they were all piled up on top of each other. They rolled off one at a time. The boy stood up from the cardboard and pounded his chest in victory with a Tarzan yell. He had survived the pounding and the weight of the kids' bodies on the way down.

Jesse watched with fascination as they all lined up again for the next daring ride to see who would take the challenge.

Jesse stood still, peering over the edge.

"Go on!" an older boy said, pushing him forward. When Jesse resisted, he added, "Chicken!"

"Leave me alone," Jesse said.

"Chicken! Chicken! Chicken!" the children chanted.

Their voices grew louder and louder in Jesse's ears. He looked down the hill again and thought he would never back down from a challenge. It would be nothing to him. His little chest swelled up, endowed with a sense of power.

Tough and brave, he inched forward. Momentarily, he hesitated, and fear took over. Then there was the push—the push that sent him sprawling down on the waiting piece of cardboard that served as a vehicle for speed.

From the start, the ride didn't seem bad at all. Slowly he accelerated, and the icy air rushed into his lungs. The cold wind slapped into his face, making his eyes water. "The dare" was the most thrilling ride he had ever taken. Everyone started cheering and jumping on for the ride. Once after another, they piled on his small frame. As he sped down the hill, specks of ice hit his face like spiked barbs. Jesse wondered if he would ever reach the bottom. He couldn't move, couldn't breathe. He heard the shouts, but they were muffled by the weight on top of him. The weight was so heavy, Jesse thought he would pass out. Finally, after being crushed without mercy, he crashed to the bottom.

For a second, everything fell quiet. Then the shouts of whooping joy and laughter exploded around him. The kids jumped off Jesse and raced for the hill to do it all over again.

"You ain't no punk after all!" someone said. He had no idea who it was, because he couldn't move. He lay there face down in the snow, flat. His body refused to get up. He felt as though he had been crushed by a compactor.

"Jesse!"

Weakly, he lifted up his head and saw Leah running toward him. She tried to pull him up. "What are you doing? You must be crazy sliding down that hill!"

Eric stood off to the side, cracking up with laughter. Tears fell from his eyes as he held his belly, unable to form words. He just pointed at Jesse and continued to laugh uncontrollably.

"Help me get him up," Leah said angrily, tugging at Jesse's coat, which had been torn at the zipper. He was covered with snow and shaking. "Get over here and help me!" she shouted again when Eric kept laughing.

"All right." Eric frowned, his laughter turning sour. "Get up, fool!" he said, grabbing Jesse roughly by the arm and pulling himup.

Jesse was so dizzy he couldn't stand. His legs were too weak to function. His entire body was numb and heavy. He looked up at the hill in a daze.

"Come on," Eric said once again, and they literally had to carry him home.

After the riots, Jesse's mother decided they should move. The stagnant reminder of the oppressive darkness remained in that apartment, not only as a result of the riots, but because of their father, too. They all needed a change.

The rent was higher at the new apartment but it was a much nicer place. It was spacious, with immaculate white walls, wooden floors, and a beautiful kitchen. There was also a living and dining room.

Grace was working two jobs and sometimes talked about the bills she was putting off paying. But she assured them that with the money she had managed to save, everything would be OK. For the first time in a long time, their family had peace.

Just past dawn on Christmas morning, Jesse and his siblings woke their mother and opened their gifts. They could not have been happier. Leah received dresses and bracelets, Eric a race car set, and Jesse his G.I. Joe and talking Mr. Ed puppet. Even though times were hard, they hadn't been denied Christmas.

After the two-week Christmas break, it was back to school again. Jesse, Leah, and Eric always walked to school together. Tonya, who lived four houses down, walked with them, too. She was a tall, pretty girl, and all she and Leah ever talked about was boys. Eric usually walked ahead, pretending not to be with them, but he was always within eyesight.

"Did you do your homework?" Leah asked Tonya as they walked slowly.

"I tried, but it was hard," Tonya said. "I only got half of it done."

"Mrs. Myers is going to embarrass you," Leah reminded her, swinging her book bag back and forth.

"So? I don't care," Tonya said. She whispered something in Leah's ear, and they started laughing.

"Curtis is so cute," Leah said dreamily.

"Who? That nappy-headed boy?" Tonya said, her face curling up in distaste.

Jesse thought they were both silly and walked behind them a few steps. All they ever talked about was girl stuff or boys, and he wasn't interested. He shuffled along, not wanting to go to school at all. To occupy himself, he made prints in the snow with his boots.

He frowned as they walked past a parked milk truck. To Jesse, the truck was a stagecoach. So, as Eric, Leah, and Tonya walked on, he climbed on the back of the stagecoach's bumper and held onto the hand rail, just like in the western movies. Before he realized it, the truck began moving down the street.

Yee-haw! Giddy up! Jesse thought. He had only a few moments before his sister noticed his stunt.

"Jesse!" Leah screamed at the top of her lungs. She and Eric ran after him.

Jesse rode half a block before the truck stopped. When it did, Jesse simply let go of the hand rail and stepped down with a smile of accomplishment written across his face. He turned around, and Eric yanked him by the collar.

"You are going to get it now!" Eric said triumphantly. "When Mom gets hold of you, she ain't never gonna stop whipping your butt."

Leah and Tonya approached them at that moment. Leah, out of breath, stopped and squatted over, resting her hands on her knees with her head down. When she caught her breath, she grabbed Jesse by the arm.

"I'm going to tell Mom," she said in a scolding manner. "You're in big trouble!"

Leah held his hand the rest of the way to school and kept a close eye on him. Needless to say, Leah and Eric kept their word once they arrived home from school.

"Mom, he just ran off and jumped on the back of that milk truck," Leah said. "I thought he was walking behind me—"

"He said he didn't care if we told on him, too," Eric added, clearly hoping to get Jesse in more hot water. Eric looked down at him with his chin held high, waiting for him to say something in his own defense.

Grace listened quietly and told Eric and Leah to leave the room. She looked at her smallest child standing before her and sighed. "Stay right there, Jesse."

She left the room. When she returned, she had a belt in hand and proceeded to give him the beating of his life. "I'm afraid the daredevil in you is going to kill you one day," she said as she left, closing the door to his room behind her.

Afterward, Jesse sat alone in his room because he wasn't allowed to go outside. He put his G.I. Joe and Mr. Ed together on the bed and stared at them. He wondered what was wrong with adventure, living on the edge, and taking chances. The way he saw it, there was nothing wrong with it. Jesse placed the Mr. Ed puppet over his hand, using the other hand to support the head. Once he had Mr. Ed's head in an upright position, he pulled the string.

"Hi, my name is Mr. Ed," said a cheerful voice that came from the puppet. Jesse sat staring at the talking horse as he pulled the cord over and over again.

The day was cloudy but warm. Birds chirped in the trees, and squirrels played tag. A robin stood nearby with its chest stuck out proudly. A cardinal sat hidden in the leaves, minding his own business. Spring had arrived.

Jesse was watching television when they got an unexpected knock on the door. Jesse followed behind his mother to see who it was, but stayed at a distance.

As his mother opened the door, Jesse saw his father. His receding hair looked unkempt, and his thin mustache needed trimming. He glanced past her into the living room, where Caesar Thomas sat watching television.

Jesse had met Caesar a few weeks after Christmas, when their mother had introduced him to the family. He was a bus driver and occasionally drove trucks. With his muscular forearms, heavy eyebrows, and booming voice, he was somewhat intimidating. He wore a pencil mustache and short sideburns. Every so often, he would stop by and bring the kids something. He always brought Jesse comic books, which Jesse cherished. Sometimes Caesar would stay long enough to have supper, always leaving before Jesse and the others were put to bed.

"Kids, your father is here!" his mother called out.

Tumbling feet brought Eric and Jesse to the door in breathless anticipation.

"Come to the car," their father said proudly. "I got something for you. Where is Leah?"

"Over at Tonya's," Eric said. "What have you got?"

Their father laughed a little. "Hold your horses," he said as they walked to the car.

"Ahh, man!" Eric exclaimed, seeing the glimmer of the bikes in the trunk of the car.

Jesse's mouth hung open in amazement. "Wow!"

Their father unloaded the two gleaming bikes. One was a rich black and the other a sunny gold. Both had training wheels. Eric and Jesse jumped on them while their father laughed and instructed them how to stay balanced and ride.

"Look, Mom!" Jesse shouted.

His mother smiled at them. She looked on for a few minutes before going back inside.

Their father stayed for a while, giving encouragement and riding tips. Just before he left, he asked his sons how school was going.

"Mostly C's," Eric said.

"Me, too," Jesse said, looking up at him.

"Gotta do better than that. The world is full of average people. You've got to do better to get ahead. Next report card, I want to see some A's and B's, all right?"

Eric and Jesse both nodded. After watching their dad pull away, they looked at each other and ran for their bikes. Eric learned how to ride quickly and got his training wheels taken off. Jesse, on the other hand, had a more difficult time. He hated riding with training wheels. It made him feel like a baby. So, he practiced every day after school and tried hard.

One prideful day, Jesse mounted the bike without training wheels, and this time, he made it! The ride was exhilarating. His chest swelled with pride and happiness. Every day, he got better. Soon, there was no stopping him. After several weeks of practice, he had become a master.

One Saturday evening, Jesse sat on the front porch wearing his favorite cowboy hat, red bandanna around his neck, and pistol holsters. He was bored, with nothing to do, as he listened to his small portable radio. Their house was on a steep hill. His mother didn't know it, but every chance he got, Jesse would race cars down the hill on his bike. She had made the rule of always riding up and down the sidewalk, never in the street. It also was forbidden to go around the corner where she couldn't observe him.

Jesse continued listening to his radio as he missed a passing car. How he hated missing out on a race. So, he sat on the porch, his bike a few feet away, waiting.

He was humming a tune when all of a sudden he saw it coming down the street: a flash of red and the roar of a mighty engine. He jumped up and quickly mounted his bike.

"Hi-ho, Silver!"

In his mind, he was the Lone Ranger, and his bike was his horse, Silver. He could outrun any vehicle that wanted to cross the desert. This was a once-in-a-lifetime race with a motorcycle. His adrenaline was flowing, and his heart was pumping. He started pedaling fast, skinny legs and all, faster and faster as the sun went down, pumping and glaring at the man riding his motorcycle. Planting a stern look on his face, Jesse kept pace with him. Faster and faster. The man in the helmet looked over, smiled, and beeped his horn. With a flip of his wrist, he was gone.

Just like the roadrunner, Jesse thought. "I almost had him!" he said aloud. Then he realized he had been pedaling so hard and fast that now the pedals were just spinning. Jesse was flying. He tried to apply the brake to slow down, but it didn't work. He couldn't stop.

Now what?

The Bullwinkle Show flashed through his mind.

At the end of the block was an open lot with gravel and dirt. Now he had a choice—either head into the street or turn the corner into the lot. He chose the latter. Almost unable to make the turn, Jesse zoomed into the lot at high speed, with gravel and dirt flying everywhere. Bumping along, still unable to stop, Jesse began to panic. At the end of the lot was a small drop. He stuck his feet out, desperately trying to stop. He was skidding, but nothing was stopping his bike.

Finally, his bike hit a log along the concrete base, and he went sailing over the handle bars head first. Everything was quiet until the second crash. Jesse hit the pavement and gravel hard, then continued to tumble and roll into the bushes and weeds. He lay still for a moment.

As the dust cleared, Jesse heard loud sounds of laughter in the distance. Dazed, he lifted his head above the weeds and started to move. The people sitting on their porch across the street were laughing and pointing at him. He stood up slowly, confused and stumbling.

Jesse dusted himself off, adjusted his pistol holsters on his waist, and picked up his bike. He noticed it was almost dark and got worried, because another one of Mom's rules was to be in the house before the street lights came on, and they were now on. Jesse knew he was going to be in trouble if he didn't make it home very soon. He also didn't want anyone to know that he had crashed his bike. He hoped it wasn't broken. Nearby, he found his damaged straw cowboy hat.

"Must have flown off before the crash," he said to himself.

Slowly, he made his way home. His hands gripped the handle bars well above his head. The bike was far too big for him, with its huge, wide tires. During that time they called them "trucks" because they were so gigantic, but his father told him he would be able to grow to fit it. And what did he care? He was just glad to have one.

He paused at the front of the house, taking a deep breath.

"Jesse," he heard his mother call out. "It's dark. Put that bike up and come inside."

He did just that. He put his bike away and walked into the house as if nothing had happened.

"You were supposed to be in before dark," she said with her back turned to him. "If you can't be inside…" Her voice trailed off as she turned around. "Oh, my God!" she screamed. "What happened to you?" When she had gained her composure, she grabbed him.

"Nothing." He looked down at himself for the first time. His clothes were dirty and ripped to shreds. Blood covered the front of his shirt. A twig was embedded in the bottom of his chin.

"Leah," his mother called out, "get the first aid kit!"

She ushered Jesse into the bathroom. She quickly checked him over, finding cuts and scratches, but nothing serious. She applied ointment and Band-Aids to his cuts and took off his ruined clothes. She calmed down as she realized he was OK.

"Boy, you are going to kill yourself yet!" she said with a tired sigh.

CHAPTER 4

IT'S ROMPER ROOM TIME

JESSE WANTED THE new Spiderman comic book. It had become all he thought about. He was at the point where he would do just about anything to turn that thought into reality. It was like a piece of warm apple pie, just baked, with a light and flaky crust. Jesse could almost taste it on his lips, feel it in his hands. That was how much he wanted Eric to loan him a dollar so he could buy the Spiderman comic book.

Eric stood over him like a person in charge, looking at him snidely as he assessed the situation. Having what Jesse needed clearly made him feel in control.

"I don't lend money," he said.

Jesse was saddened by his remark. He slumped down farther into his seat, with his hands folded together.

"I'll tell you what," Eric said. "If you let me hit you upside your head one hundred times with this comic book, I'll give you the dollar. One penny for each time I hit you."

Jesse looked at him, his expression veiled. "That's not fair."

"Who said anything about being fair?" Eric said smugly, raising his eyebrow. "You want a dollar, and I got it. Do it my way, or forget it."

Eric started to walk away. Jesse looked at him solemnly. The new Spiderman comic book was plastered on every newsstand, calling his name. True desire ruled his senses. He could see Spiderman leaping over walls on an adventure. The thought passed through Jesse's mind again and again, itching, nagging. He had to have it. He could take one hundred hits.

"All right," Jesse heard himself say just as Eric was about to walk through the bedroom door.

Eric turned slowly with a Grinch-like grin on his face. He picked up an old comic book of Jesse's and rolled it up tightly.

Jesse braced himself, waiting, his fingers gripping the chair on which he sat.

"Hold your head down!" Eric commanded.

Poised and ready, he began striking Jesse across the back of his freshly shaved head. The loud popping sounds could be heard in the next room. Time seemed to move slowly as the hits continued.

WHACK! Twenty-two… *WHACK!* Twenty-three… *WHACK!* Twenty-four. . .

"Naw, man, I can't take anymore," Jesse said. "That's it!"

"You can't stop now!"

"No, that's it. I quit."

"You won't get your money then…the deal was a hundred."

Jesse thought for a moment. "OK, go ahead."

WHACK!…Sixty-one was no fun… *WHACK!*…Sixty-two struck like a gun… *WHACK!*…Sixty-three was worse than sixty-two… *WHACK!*… Sixty-four stuck to his head like glue… *WHACK!*…Sixty-five, he needed to reconsider what to do.

He hadn't expected it to hurt so much. His head was throbbing as if it were being beaten with a shovel. His eyes were on the brink of tears when he realized it was more than he had bargained for. Feeling dizzy and faint, with his vision blurred and his resolve just about gone, Jesse could barely murmur the two words, "I quit."

"You quit?" Eric snapped.

"Yeah, that's it. I quit. It ain't worth it. You can keep the money."

"Look, all you gotta do is let me hit you upside your head thirty-five more times," Eric said triumphantly.

"Thirty-five?" Jesse considered the number through the pounding in his head.

"Yeah, just thirty-five. But I gotta use another comic book. This one is all torn up, and it's too loose."

"Thirty-five?" Jesse said again, still dazed. "Okay, thirty-five. But there's no way you get to use a new book."

"All right. Put your head back down."

With a wide grin, he proceeded to beat Jesse on the head with the shredded comic book.

By the time Jesse reached one hundred, his ears were ringing. Tears were ready to burst forth like shooting stars from his eyes, but he held them back. He wouldn't cry. He wouldn't let his brother witness his tears. No satisfaction would be granted at his expense.

Eric looked at him closely, waiting for him to cry. Jesse sat staring at the floor, trying to hold back the pain. Eric bent down, turning his head to look up into Jesse's eyes. But he saw nothing, not a single tear.

Eric stood up straight with a disgruntled look and pulled a dollar from his pocket. He then handed it to Jesse.

Hand trembling, Jesse reached for it.

Eric snatched it back, crumpled it, and threw it on the floor at Jesse's feet. "There's your dollar," he said dryly and walked out of the bedroom.

Jesse stumbled over to the bed and sat down. His eyes were so blurred with tears, he could barely see the dollar on the floor. By this time, it didn't matter. It wasn't worth it. He would never consent to something like that again.

❦

Jesse saw a change occur in his mother after Caesar arrived. For a long time now, she had seemed weary, working all the time and keeping their household. When Caesar asked her to marry him, she seemed grateful. Jesse watched with a few members of their families as his mother and Caesar married quietly.

During the year of 1967, Jesse's baby sister was born. She was named Crystal. When Jesse was shown his sister for the first time, he didn't know what to think. He watched her curiously as she lay on the bed all wrapped up in pinks and blues. Jesse stood on his toes, leaned over, and peered inside the opening. To his amazement, he saw radiant dark eyes, ruddy cheeks as round as balloons, and the glimmer of an innocent smile. Her skin was a pale brown. He liked her. In time, he knew he would introduce her to his adventures, but for now he could hear his toy soldiers crying for battle.

It was now late fall. His mother had spoken to them earlier that week because they were moving. Jesse wasn't quite sure what the difference would be, except they would be living in a new home, and he was obligated to get acquainted with new surroundings, which obviously made him a bit nervous. When Grace and the family had moved, she had removed the children from their public school and registered them with the neighborhood Catholic school, Immaculate Conception, which was only a block away from their new home. He had heard his mother and Caesar talking about the expensive tuition. She had said it was expensive, but that she wanted the very best education for her children, even if it would mean working two jobs, which was what many black mothers had to do.

Jesse stood beside his desk along with the other children. He was now entering the third grade. The Catholic school system was quite different from the public school system he had come from. Jesse stood at military attention with arms stiff at his sides. The students had just finished reciting "The Pledge of Allegiance," which they were told had to be done every day before class began. Jesse was confused by the entire process of standing and staring at a red, white, and blue flag hanging on a pole attached to the wall above their heads. He didn't know what the words meant and had difficulty pronouncing some of them. He never could remember the words. He didn't have any idea what "allegiance" meant.

"I pledge allegiance…to the flag…"

The rest was always forgotten or mumbled. He just faked it. It was most embarrassing having to watch the other students to figure out which hand to place on his chest, the right or the left. He never got it right.

Jesse sat nervously amongst his new classmates. Their seats were arranged in straight rows, and the students were placed according to their last names. Jesse always felt uneasy and out of place around the other children. He was shy and quiet.

The majority of the children were black. The other small percent were white. Everyone sat stiffly in their school uniforms. The girls wore white blouses and long, checkered blue and green dresses with white socks. The boys wore navy-blue shirts with dark blue clip-on ties, matching pants, black socks, and polished black shoes. That was the uniform required throughout the school year. Conformity was the goal.

Their teacher, Ms. Lipani, was a rotund woman wearing a bright flowered dress with a short, neat haircut, and she always donned a cheerful smile.

During a particular class assignment, the children were practicing cursive writing. Examples of the alphabet hung on the wall around the classroom. After the class instructions were given, everyone seemed busy at work, having no difficulties, except Jesse. He was having a hard time.

The public school he had attended previously hadn't begun to teach cursive writing, so he had no clue what everyone was doing. He felt dumb, embarrassed, and alienated. The classroom was hushed. By now, fifteen minutes had passed, which seemed like an hour to Jesse. The other students' heads were down as they worked. Ms. Lipani sat at her desk at the head of the class, preoccupied with the material in front of her. Once in a while, a student lifted his head up in thought, staring at the ceiling momentarily before dropping his head again and writing furiously. Jesse looked around the class, hoping to whisper to someone for help, but he didn't know anyone. So, with pencil in hand, he stared at the blank paper on his desk.

"OK, class, hurry along," Ms. Lipani said as she looked up and viewed the class. "You only have five more minutes to complete this assignment."

Jesse raised his hand. His only escape was to go to the bathroom. The word "lavatory" had to be used, not bathroom, and, of course, Jesse had that confused with "laboratory."

"Yes, Jesse," Ms. Lipani acknowledged him softly.

"May I please have permission to go to the lavatory?"

"Yes, you may," she replied, giving him a smile.

Jesse opened the classroom's thick wooden door and quietly closed it behind him to avoid disturbing anyone. Once outside the room, he breathed a sigh of relief. Looking down at the floor, he saw that it was as immaculate as the rest of the school. The marble floor had a sheen, as though it just had been waxed and buffed. *Perfect*, Jesse thought. He looked at his shoes. They were black, laced, with pointed toes. "James Brown shoes," he called them. On the heel, silver metal taps had been attached, which he had pleaded with his mother to have placed there. He felt he had to have some sense of identity. As he walked down the hall, they made a clickity-clack sound.

Clickity-clack…Clickity-clack…

Jesse took a running start and slid down the hall floor, which seemed to him about a mile long. Hands and arms stretched out shoulder-height, standing sideways while leaning back, Jesse slid down the hall, singing.

"Baby…Baby…Baby…I got the feelin'…and I break out…" He mouthed the sounds of the musical instruments in between the words. "Dun…Dun…Dun…Dun…in a cold sweat."

He stopped and launched into a frenzy, shaking his head, pumping his arms, jerking his hips, and shuffling his feet, while pretending to have a microphone in his hand. "Baby…Baby…Baby…I got the feelin'!"

He was imitating the James Brown he had heard and the dance movements he had witnessed James Brown perform. Now it was time for the splits, which he could never bounce back up from the way James Brown always did. Then he spun and came to a halting stop at the bottom of the stairs on his way to the lavatory. Jesse had gotten so caught up with his performance that he had lost track of his surroundings.

As he looked up from the floor, he saw her positioned at the top of the stairs, towering above him. Jesse's eyes widened, and his mouth grew slack. He froze. He didn't even dare breathe. He gulped.

"Oh, no, I totally forgot about her!" Jesse said to himself just above a whisper, hoping she wouldn't hear him. He started to step back, but it was too late. That wouldn't stop her from seeing him, because she always did. Her expression was always the same: solemn. At times, when he didn't think that she was watching, he would look back over his shoulder and see her staring intensely at him. Whenever they met and he looked into her eyes, which was rare, they seemed to penetrate his very soul. He was terrified of her. She haunted him. She never spoke, and everyone else seemed to ignore her and continue with their activities. Normally he ignored her also, but now he couldn't. She was there waiting, and he didn't dare move. *I can't do it. I can't walk by her…What happens if I walk by and she reaches and grabs me and yells my name? Would I scream? I'll sneak by her and not look up at her, and she won't even realize I walked by.* The thoughts whirled in Jesse's mind.

"I can do it…I can do it," Jesse repeated to himself.

He began walking up the stairs one at a time, carefully placing each foot down to avoid making a sound. The closer he walked in her direction, the more profound her presence became. Why was she always out here every time, anyway? His heart pounded harder with each step. Then he froze. He broke down in fear. He suddenly turned, jumped down six stairs, fell, rolled over, and was up in one motion, dashing back toward the classroom.

Clickity-clack, clickity-clack...

Jesse made it back outside the closed classroom door.

"Whew!" he said to himself. "That was close, man! Forget that, I'll have to wait to use the bathroom when I get home. I'm not walking by her, no way. Whew! She almost caught me."

He gathered his composure, straightened his clothing, and entered the class. Ms. Lipani had begun teaching a math assignment. She wrote on the chalkboard and explained the term "infinity" to the students.

"Now, everyone, you should understand with the use of numbers in addition and multiplication, numbers can go on into infinity. In other words, the numbers continue forever. They never end. Again, this term in math is known as infinity. Please write this down in your notes."

Jesse sat down at his desk, perplexed. *Forever?* he thought.

"Another term to write down would be 'infinite,'" she continued. "'Infinite' means immeasurable, unbounded, and unlimited. Everyone here has a mother and father. If that were not so, it would have been impossible for you to have been born. So, your parents brought about your birth. But God, who is infinite, made us in His image. He is the Creator of life. God knew you before you were born. Without God, no one and nothing would exist. God is beyond space and time. His love, mercy, and forgiveness are also infinite. We should always be thankful."

At that moment, the class bell rang, announcing that school had ended.

That evening, as usual after a school day, Jesse did his homework, ate supper, and took a bath. He was allowed to watch television for a short period of time, and by eight o'clock, not a second after, it was bedtime.

On that night, Jesse went to bed somewhat earlier than other nights. As he walked into his room, which he shared with his brother, he noticed something on the bed. He reached and picked it up. It was the Spiderman comic book that he had wanted to purchase earlier. Also lying on the bed was a dollar bill, not crumpled but flat, as though someone had deliberately taken the time to press the wrinkles out of it. Just then, Eric walked into the room.

"Whatcha got?" Eric asked.

"Spiderman comic book!"

"Is it the one you wanted?" Eric asked with a quizzical, but unconcerned, expression.

"Yeah," Jesse said, smiling.

"Well, it's almost bedtime. Mom will be in any minute to check up on us, so we better hurry and get ready to get in the bed."

Eric turned to the closet and looked for his pajamas. Jesse placed the Spiderman comic on top of the stack of his collection, stuffed the dollar into his pants pocket hanging on the bedroom doorknob, and began getting ready for bed.

Jesse and Eric slept in the same bed. Their mother hadn't been able to afford to buy the bunk beds she intended to get for them. Usually, both of them sleeping in the same bed caused problems, to say the least. There was continuous fighting. They could never get along. An imaginary line stretched down the middle of the bed, and if either one touched the other person, it meant trouble. They would hit back and forth until a full-fledged fight broke out. Their mother would come in and threaten to punish both of them if they wouldn't stop bickering. That usually worked.

But on this night, no punches were thrown, no kicks or arguments. They lay in bed on their proper sides, Jesse on the right, Eric on the left. Their mother peeked in the room through the door, and even she seemed surprised. She looked at both of them, shook her head in disbelief, and departed, leaving the door partially open.

For several minutes, the room remained silent until Eric spoke. "Would you like to hear a joke?"

Joke? Jesse thought. This was uncharacteristic of Eric. Jesse had never known him to tell a joke. But still not having gotten over the shock of the Spiderman comic and pressed dollar, he said, "OK."

So Eric began. "There were one hundred chipmunks in a bed. Ninety-nine were fat and huge, and there was one very tiny one."

"How can one hundred chipmunks fit in a bed?" Jesse questioned, turning his head and facing him in disbelief.

Eric slanted his eyes toward Jesse and said, "Believe me, one hundred chipmunks can fit in a bed."

"Well, most chipmunks are small. They're not fat."

"Wait a minute," Eric said, now leaning on one elbow and looking at his brother. "Whose joke is this, anyway? Mine. So let me tell it the way I want to tell it."

Jesse thought for a moment and realized he couldn't argue. He turned his head and continued staring at the ceiling. "OK."

"Thank you." Eric dropped his head back to the pillow and looked up at the ceiling in the dark room, with only a hint of moonlight coming from the window next to their bed. He continued, "The tiny chipmunk was on the farthest edge of the bed and couldn't sleep because he was hanging over the edge." He paused. "Are you listening?"

"Yeah, go ahead."

Eric began to sing a song. "There was one hundred in the bed, and the little one said, 'Roll over, roll over,' so they all rolled over, and one fell out. There was ninety-nine in the bed, and the little one said, 'Roll over, roll over,' so they all rolled over, and one fell out. There were ninety-eight in the bed and the little one said, 'Roll over, roll over,' so they all rolled over, and one fell out. There were ninety-seven in the bed…"

This continued until Eric reached fifty.

Finally, Jesse became impatient with the repeated lines. "How long is this joke?" he asked.

"Just be quiet and listen." From there, he continued, "There were fifty in the bed and the little one said, 'Roll over, roll over,' so they all rolled over, and one fell out…" This continued until only three were left. "And the little one said, 'Roll over, roll over,' so they all rolled over, and one fell out. There were two in the bed, and the little one said, 'Roll over, roll over,' so they all rolled over, and one fell out. There was one in the bed, and the little one said…'Good night!'"

Eric immediately fell asleep and began snoring aloud.

Jesse blinked. He turned and looked at his brother to see if he was actually asleep. To his amazement, he was.

Jesse smiled and thought, *What a dumb joke.*

He continued lying awake, his mind wandering and remembering what Ms. Lipani had spoken about—infinity and God. His mind tried to understand "forever" as it soared out beyond the galaxy and stars. *Numbers don't stop. They go on forever and ever… There's no end… and God! Wow!* he thought. "God made me? I'm sure glad you made me a boy rather than a girl," he spoke aloud to God, weighing the differences. With his hands touching his hair, face, and chest, he now looked up to God and asked, "Who am I? And why am I here?"

Jesse was relieved and thankful to have some form of existence. He couldn't comprehend not having any existence at all. His mind continued to drift further and further in search of answers. Once again, he eventually fell asleep, but his mind never rested.

"So I say to you: ask and it will be given to you; seek and you will find; knock and the door will be opened to you. For everyone who asks receives; he who seeks finds; and to him who knocks, the door will be opened."
—Luke 11:9-10

CHAPTER 5

SUNDAY

S UNDAY MORNING, JESSE found himself back in the basement at church, listening to another Sunday school lesson. He tried to focus but couldn't. Bored, he let his mind drift away and stared around the room instead of listening to the teacher.

The adults joined them at the end of the lesson. Jesse's mother took his hand, and they walked to another stark room where folding chairs had been lined up in neat rows. The chairs faced a gigantic glass box half-filled with water. Stairs led into the box. A young man wrapped in a white sheet stood at the foot of the stairs. Someone assisted him up the stairs and into the box of water. The pastor of the church waited for him in the center of the water.

Many of the people had found seats by then, and Deacon Patterson walked up front to address the crowd. "It is now Brother Benson's time," Deacon Patterson said softly. "Brother Benson was a man of the streets, as you all know—a pimp, hustler, gambler, womanizer—the list goes on. Actually, he spent so much time in jail from a young age, he thought it was his home." Deacon Patterson's voice grew louder. "But several of you remained diligent in speaking God's word to him while he sat in soul food restaurants, pool houses, and on the corner. Many of you were patient, kind, and committed to waking up Brother Benson, even though more times than not, he cursed you out. I'm not allowed to mention some of the things that were said, but I'm sure you all remember.

"But!" he then expressed in his loudest voice. "God is all-forgiving and merciful, so the old Benson of the streets we remember is no more."

After that statement, a few people nodded their heads, and a few amens were said.

Now holding up the Bible to the seated audience, Deacon Patterson said, "It says here in Isaiah, chapter one, verse sixteen, that God wants us to wash ourselves clean of wickedness and to quit our evil ways. Now verse eighteen. Here, God says no matter how deep and horrible you feel your sins are, He can cleanse you. But you need to allow Him to help you. He wants to talk things over with you. God is pleading with you. Please don't turn away from Him." He closed the Bible. "Through your hard works and the grace of God, Brother Benson has been saved through the Holy Spirit. All thanks and praises to our Lord and Savior Jesus Christ."

The people applauded and shouted with praises to God.

"Thank you, Jesus. You are merciful!"

"Praise Jesus!" a woman shouted, and others responded, joining in.

The young man stood at the top of the stairs above the audience with his head bowed, eyes closed, and tears streaming down his cheeks.

"So, now," Deacon Patterson said, "Brother Benson has been cleansed by the precious blood of Jesus. By asking God for forgiveness and accepting Jesus, his sins are washed clean. Our final step now is baptism by water."

"Amen," someone shouted out happily.

Everyone seemed cheerful, clapping their hands at this joyous event.

Jesse looked on with anticipation.

Minister Chapman had joined the pastor and the young man being baptized in the tank. The pastor and the minister positioned themselves on each side and held his arms.

"In the name of the Father, the Son, and the Holy Ghost…"

They laid him back in the water and brought him up.

"Thank you, Jesussss…" someone shouted out.

"Praise God, do you hear me! Praise Him! That's right!"

Brother Benson stood in the tank, hands folded in prayer. Looking up, he stated three words with such heartfelt feeling that everyone must have known he was grateful. "Thank you, Jeeeesus!" He broke down and continued crying.

Jesse looked around, still confused. His mother smiled at him but remained silent.

After a few minutes, everyone headed upstairs to the main church area. Jesse obediently followed his mother up the narrow staircase, moving slowly as they stopped to talk or say hello. People spoke in whispering tones as though what they had to say was confidential and couldn't be heard by anyone else.

When they made it to the top of the stairs, Jesse stood in the aisle while his mother continued speaking to a few relatives and friends. Though there was plenty of activity going on around him, Jesse couldn't hear it. He was occupied with looking at the building's interior. The domed ceiling was so high, Jesse imagined that if helium balloons escaped from his grip, even they would never reach the top. He had never seen ceilings that high anywhere. The ceiling stretched down to the colorful stained glass windows. The windows seemed to fill the entire wall on both sides of the church. Beams of sunlight cascaded through them with a shine that set a jubilant mood among the congregation.

A balcony in the back was used only when there was a full house, and they were headed in that direction on this Sunday morning. Attached on the wooden balcony in the center was a clock, and Jesse always noticed it. There was nothing special about the clock. It was circular, with black numbers. The hour, minute, and second hands were also black, just like the one in his third-grade classroom. Jesse still wasn't quite efficient at telling time, but something about this clock always demanded his attention.

The wooden pews stood straight and hard, with precisely crafted carvings. Jesse looked at the red carpet beneath his feet. There were four aisles, one on each of the far ends and two down the main center of the church, which led to the altar. In the front of the church was a section for the choir and seats on the stage for the important people, who always sat obedient and attentive. In the middle of the stage, seemingly above and separate from everything and everyone else, stood the podium, where in time the pastor would ascend.

Jesse noticed an elderly man sitting along the aisle in the pew, near the front middle section of the church. He didn't look like any other person in the church. His clothes were ragged and didn't fit him well, the coat oversized, the pants too short and exposing his soiled white socks, which barely reached above his ankles. His skin was dirty, hair mussed and unshaven. He sat upright, as if waiting to receive or hear something that he had to give his full attention to.

Jesse turned his head to watch members of the church marching down the aisle like kings and queens of yesteryear, regally attired in high heels, big hats, pearls, colorful dresses, deep purples, blacks, browns. They wore jewelry of all sorts and carried different types of bags and purses. The men wore shining patent leather shoes of all colors, thick watches, rings, and fat ties that followed the curvature of their stomachs. There seemed to be more women in the church than men, which was strange, since Jesse knew men were supposedly in charge of the household, leading the flock.

The church was full to capacity and beyond, but no one would sit in the pew with the white elderly gentleman. Still, he sat tall and was not affected by the obvious effort to avoid him.

Jesse's mother led them up the middle aisle. She then looked at the middle pew where the gentleman sat. She glanced toward the gentleman and with a smile said, "Good morning."

He nodded and kept looking forward. Grace sat down beside him. There was whispering all around and disgusted stares. Jesse knew they were talking about the man because he was different. He heard someone whisper behind him, "Now they're coming in the church. They want to control everything. We can't even have our church to ourselves."

Why did they feel that way? That man wasn't bothering them. He hadn't done anything to them. They were always talking about someone, and it wasn't nice, either. Their prideful attitudes and expensive, fancy clothes were all they seemed to think mattered.

Jesse looked ahead at the stage area, carpeted in red with matching velvet seats and runners. Men in robes sat on the far right of the podium with solemn expressions, unmoved by the gospel choir behind them singing and clapping.

Several songs rang through the church and neighborhood. With each song, the volume became louder. The people and choir tapped their feet, swaying side to side, some raising their hands above their heads with eyes closed in praise. The women were the most involved.

While the choir continued singing and shouting in joy, Pastor Barron made his regal entrance. He wore a long black robe with a white shirt and black tie underneath. The front chest piece of the robe was velvet, and a velvet strip circled each of his wide sleeves. The hem of the robe fell just above his black shoes. He walked up to the enormous wooden podium, where a gigantic book sat with a gold ribbon hanging from the pages. He stood with no expression, surveying the crowd until the choir finished singing and everyone was seated.

Jesse stared in awe at the book that sat on the podium. What was in that book that only the pastor could read and understand? What was in the book that made everyone in the church change in personality, sit in silence, and become humble and attentive? What was in the book that gave the pastor so much control and power? Jesse wanted to walk up to the stage, pull himself up to the podium, and peer into the enormous book. Would his face be illuminated with light? Would he fall back off the podium, awestruck? What was in the book?

When Pastor Barron began his sermon, his voice started in a low, slow tone, stretching his words as though dragging them along, stressing certain syllables and emphasizing his statements. Jesse soon became bored and started looking around yet again. He stared at the huge, colorful stained glass window on the wall. The design in the window depicted a Caucasian male figure in a red and blue robe with long hair and a beard, sitting beside a large rock with his arms and hands placed upon it. His eyes stared upward with a light shining upon him, as if he were in darkness. Jesse knew the image was a depiction of Jesus, but why did he look as though he had the weight of the world on his shoulders? Why did he look so sad, praying in that dark place?

"Now today, this day," Pastor Barron said, his tone growing louder, "I'm going to preach about God's will, faith, works, and Samson."

When Jesse heard the name Samson, even he sat at attention. What little he knew of Samson was from movies he had seen on television. He understood Samson was strong like Superman, Hercules, and Tarzan. Most important of all, Jesse knew Samson was a warrior, a true warrior for God. Now he wanted to hear more about this warrior, so he anxiously waited, giving the pastor his undivided attention. He didn't even kick his heels.

The pastor continued speaking as he turned the pages of the Bible. "There are many among you here today who still believe that only believing in God is enough. Well, I'll tell you something. Only believing in God is useless, unless you do what He wants you to do. It is written that faith without action is dead! It's easy to believe in God, but it takes effort to do His works, to do His will."

"Preach it!" someone yelled from the back rows.

"If some of you would take the time and turn to James of the New Testament, chapter two, you don't have to read it now, but I'd like you to mark it in your Bibles and read it when you get home.

"Now, turning to Matthew, chapter seven, verse twenty-one, it clearly states that everybody running around saying, 'Lord, Lord, praise Jesus,' is not going to enter heaven. Only those persons doing the Father's will shall enter the kingdom of heaven. Stop fooling yourselves!" He looked around at the audience. "Jesus Christ accomplished God's will, and everyone in this church has a will by God to accomplish. What is yours? Have you thought about it? Turn your books to Matthew, chapter sixteen, verse twenty-seven. Here it says that God will reward you according to your works!" His voice rose to a shout, and he was sweating profusely. "What are your works? You can't obtain works by just running your mouths and believing. Talk is cheap!"

Jesse heard a few amens. Some people gave hesitant nods of approval. As the pastor continued, Jesse couldn't understand what he was saying due to his rambling style and grunting and shouting. But Jesse sat on the edge of the bench, dutifully waiting to hear the name "Samson," open-eyed with anticipation.

After forty minutes, the audience was full of participation, shouting, "Praise the Lord," "Hallelujah," and "Preach it." A few people fanned themselves, clapping and waving their hands. The place was becoming heated. Jesse noticed a woman behind him who seemed to be mumbling to herself.

"Now, Samson had a will to be fulfilled by God," the pastor continued, "and he knew what it was. But! Samson had a problem like many of you here today among us!" The pastor was at his highest peak. He jumped up and down and paced back and forth. The audience encouraged him with their clapping and shouting. Some even stood, as if in a trance. All along, Jesse stayed focused, now even more eager after hearing Samson's name mentioned again.

"Many of you lie deep in sexual sin!" the pastor thundered while slamming his fist on his throne.

"Oh, Jeeeesus!" a woman yelled. Someone else screamed.

"Stop fooling yourselves!" he continued. "Many of you who are married here have girlfriends. You have no shame, and even boast about it amongst your friends!" He opened the Bible and continued shouting with even more fervor. "The passage speaks about those who claim the name of Jesus Christ but are still caught up in lust, fornication, and adultery. No sin damages the body more than sexual sin. For those who are saved, the Holy Spirit dwells inside you. Stop polluting yourselves. God has paid a great price for your sins. Your body is no longer yours, but belongs to God. So now, use your body to give glory back to God, not filth. God states, 'Be holy, for I am holy.' You all know homosexuality is forbidden, but if you have further questions, continue your reading in Romans, chapter one, verses eighteen through thirty-two, at home. But for now, I'll continue."

Some of the men seemed stunned, while the church was now on the verge of frenzy, especially those who were prominent church members.

The pastor went on preaching at a quickened pace, as if driven by outside forces. "The scriptures tell us that a person is a slave to whatever controls him. So, when we receive freedom from Christ and fall back deep into sin, we are worse off than before. You would have been better not knowing Christ than being saved. In scripture, there is an old saying that a dog returns to his vomit, and a cleansed pig returns to the mud again. That's an example of those who return back to their sins."

At that, a middle-aged man jumped up from his seat and angrily stormed out of the church in disgust, letting the doors slam behind him. The ushers stood at a distance.

The pastor threw more fuel on the fire. Some became restless and began looking around the room. Others clenched their teeth and stared straight ahead. Some even dropped their heads in shame.

"You women are just as bad. Lust was Samson's weakness, and the same with Solomon and David." The pastor, now drenched in sweat, attempted to use a handkerchief to dry his face while gulping down a glass of water which had been sitting on the wooden table next to him.

Jesse didn't understand the word "lust." Jesse did hear two other names, though: Solomon and David. Maybe they were superheroes, too, he thought, still anxiously waiting to hear about "the warrior, Samson," among all the commotion.

"Praise God!"

"Preach it!"

"Don't stop now!"

"I would be ashamed if I were some of you," the pastor shouted, "lying in sexual sin with your boyfriend. The word 'fornication' doesn't cross your minds. And then you come to church to give an offering to the Lord with praises and thanks, not giving a thought of what you did last night."

Now walking over to the Bible, he flipped open a page that wasn't marked and read, "Isaiah, chapter one, verses ten through sixteen." As he spoke, he skipped some verses and seemed to preach on those that directly pierced their souls. As some might put it, he laid down the law. "God calls those now having fallen back into sin, men and women of Sodom and Gomorrah. He says he is sick of your praises and worship because you still refuse to turn from your detestable sins. He says you present yourselves as holy, but you're flawed. You pray with hands outstretched to heaven, but you're phony. It's all for show. Because of your stubbornness, he won't even listen to your prayers!"

The place exploded into hysteria. Two women jumped up, simultaneously screaming and waving their arms with their eyes shut. Male ushers rushed to aid and contain them to keep them from hurting themselves and others. Many women cried openly. Others started shouting and jumping up and down, hollering, "Jeeeesus!"

Another woman ran the length of the church toward the pastor on the stage. She had to be controlled by the deacons. Three other men bolted down the aisle and out the doors. Another woman fainted. Two women rushed over and covered her up, fanning her furiously. The woman who had been behind Jesse was now on her feet, shaking and trembling, arms outstretched, mumbling even louder and faster. Jesse was certain they had all gone crazy. But to his amazement, others sat still, as though nothing was going on.

The pastor continued, turning the Bible to another chapter. "First Corinthians, chapter five, verses nine through thirteen!" His voice boomed above the mayhem. "This is a letter from Paul condemning immorality in the church. Paul warns you not to involve yourself with evil people. He wasn't speaking of those in the world, but of those Christians in the church who are involved in sexual sin, greed, drinking, and other detestable things. Are you listening, people?" he shouted, leaning over the stage.

The people responded in an uproar, although many remained silent.

"Don't even eat lunch with such a person!" he bellowed over the audience. Hesitating and leaning on the podium as if waiting for a response, he continued, looking over the audience in amusement, "We are the ones to deal with those within the church committing these sins. These people must be put out of the church before they contaminate the rest. How are we to accomplish God's will if we ourselves are drowning in sin? We are here to be representatives of our Lord and Savior, Jesus Christ."

The pastor raised and extended his arms. The sleeves of the robe expanded like wings. With palms open and fingers outstretched, he slowly waved to the crowd until calmness was cast upon the wave of wounded spirits.

The organ player continued playing, but now slowly. Softly and gently, the sounds eased through the pipes attached to the walls. The people's voices now quieted. Everyone sat down, speaking softly. A few still said, "Praise Jesus." The pastor wiped the sweat from his forehead. As his breathing slowed, he continued as if from memory.

"'And now there is one more thing to say before I end this letter.'" The pastor now spoke in a normal, clear voice. "'Stay away from those who are causing conflicts within the church. We should stay especially away from those who teach things that are contrary to the Holy Scriptures.' Romans, chapter sixteen, verses sixteen through eighteen."

He closed the Bible. The pastor always had a way of getting his point across, especially on two occasions, Christmas and Easter Sunday, for those who attended church just twice a year. They were never the same when they left as when they had come.

"Praise God," someone whispered faintly.

Several people filed out of the pews and down the aisle. Others listened to the music as it washed over their pain and sorrow.

Jesse sat in wonderment and disappointment. He still had not heard the pastor speak of Samson, the warrior for God. He was upset that all the grown-ups had ruined it with their acts of frenzy, yelling, and screaming. He sat on the edge of his seat with his head bowed, staring at the floor. To Jesse, what had started as an exciting sermon was a total letdown.

After a while, he turned his head to the left to look at the elderly gentleman whom they had sat alongside, and noticed he was gone.

Do not forget to entertain strangers, for by so doing some people have entertained angels without knowing it.

—Hebrews 13:2

Later, after Jesse returned home from church, he was required to go directly to his room and change his "dress wear" before pursuing any other activity for the day. *Go directly to jail. Do not pass go. Do not collect two hundred dollars.*

It was routine. His mother did not want Jesse to ruin his "dress clothes," which she knew from experience he found easy to do. It was like a curse, for every pair of dress slacks Jesse owned had holes in the right pant leg, exactly where the knee was located. For some unexplainable reason, Jesse always found himself falling to the concrete on his knees, arms outstretched, usually after a church function or during a school session, while chasing someone, running alone, riding a bike or a skateboard, or just plain standing still.

Every time, his mother would ask him, "How did you get a hole in these slacks?" Jesse would look up at her with a sad expression, as if to say, *It is totally unexplainable*, while grass stains, dirt, and gravel covered him.

So, he had to change his clothing before going outdoors, and put on his "play clothes," those pants hanging in the closet with the holes always in the right knee, now with a patch over them. While Jesse was lying on his back struggling to put his pants on, he heard his mother's voice.

"Jesse! Come here, mister."

Whenever a "mister" came after his name, it was a sign that his mother was upset, to say the least. Jesse never said a word; he just showed up. His mother stood in the kitchen area with his aunt, preparing Sunday's supper, which was always prepared special from the other days throughout the week.

"Why were you laughing in church today?" his mother asked. Before he could reply, she said sternly, "You shouldn't be in church laughing."

Jesse stood at attention, wondering if he had grinned.

"Your punishment is to stay in your room today. You won't be allowed to go out and play. Also, put away your G.I. Joe, little army men, and comic books. I want you to sit in your room and think about what you did in church and why."

Jesse never had a chance to plead guilty or not guilty. He was only found guilty as charged, his punishment just. Her key witness, his aunt, claimed that Jesse had been laughing in church. Jesse knew if he spoke now on his behalf, he could possibly receive a stricter sentence. So he continued standing in silence.

"OK, you can go now," she said.

Jesse hesitated, eyes swelling with tears, then dropped his head and headed toward jail.

His aunt said loudly, "Can't have him laughing at a holy man of God. Next thing you know, he'll be mocking the pastor right out in the open. Other children see that, and they'll think they can get away with it, too. The important thing is they learn that the pastor is a man of God. They must respect him. He'll get it straight."

Jesse made it back to his room, and in the distance, he could still hear his aunt speaking. "Pastor Barron sure can preach, can't he? Did you see…"

He closed his bedroom door, slumped down in his chair, and stayed there until he was called for supper.

CHAPTER 6

THE SIGNIFICANCE
OF ONE

THE NEIGHBORHOOD WAS always busy with activity. Speakers had been placed in windows, and "soul music" filled the air. Teenage boys raced up and down the street on souped-up mopeds. Every twenty minutes, Chryslers, Dodges, Mustangs, and Plymouth Dusters screeched past, burning rubber along the streets. Smaller boys, with their Sting Ray bikes, tried their best to imitate their idols on the streets by speeding down the sidewalk on their bikes. Upon reaching the highest peak, they slammed on the pedal brakes, causing the bike to hook and slide in a cloud of dust. Once the dust cleared, their dark black tire burns would be visible on the sidewalk. The boy with the longest mark who had not fallen off his bike during the process was hailed and praised by the onlookers.

If you were fortunate enough, you could also witness someone doing a "bike wheelie" while riding down the middle of the street. The rider hoisted the bike up, arm muscles flexing, while pedaling with only the back tire along the pavement, and the front tire suspended in the air. Others paraded behind on their bikes, not using their hands at all. Teenagers continued riding in packs of three to five on bikes into the late afternoon. Often, two or even three people rode on one bike.

Children ran along the sidewalks with balloons, hot dogs, hamburgers, and sodas in hand, shouting and jumping up and down with glee. Ponytails and braids swung in constant motion as little girls danced along the chalk rainbow drawn on the sidewalk and jumped rope while singing poetry. Someone was always throwing a football, which seemed to spiral through the clouds and go the length of the block. Kids played kickball in the streets and in abandoned dirt parking lots, if they were old enough.

Men were outside working on their vehicles, their prized possessions. They treated their cars better than they treated themselves. Working on a car was an all-day affair. Talk usually revolved around fixing cars, music, the job, or someone else's car. Neighbors mowed their yards or what little grass they had. Mothers tended their gardens with small patches of flowers, plants, and vegetables. Not much grew, but it was something, a sign of hope. Women also sat on porches, rocking and passing around stories and gossip.

Throughout the day, the chimes of the ice cream truck announced its arrival as it came around the corner. All the kids screamed out the announcement and would scatter like dust to retrieve money. The parents watched their children intently from the porches, keeping track of their young protectively.

Live music played from garages and back alleys. Drums, electric bass, guitar, and an occasional horn were the main instruments heard, usually playing what they called "the James Brown beat." Whenever an aspiring band assembled, people gathered to listen, laugh, joke, and groove to the music. If the music met the fans' approval, which usually was the case, they applauded and cheered, saying, "Man, that's bad!"

It seemed as though the music and laughter offered a release from the pressures of the day caused by racism and discrimination and the inability to find work. This was a moment to unwind and be among themselves. "Silence" and "quiet" were two words that never came to visit this neighborhood.

Jesse sprung up from bed very early one particular morning in April. Now that winter had passed, a new beginning had dawned, and he was eager to go out and play. So, he got up early to finish his chores and head outside. Finally, with breakfast done and chores completed, Jesse sought permission from his parents before embarking on a new outdoor adventure.

Caesar sat in the living room with the television on. Jesse approached him with hesitation and excitement, with his request already rehearsed in his mind.

"May I..." he began to say, until he noticed Caesar looking more intently at the television than usual. Jesse abruptly stopped his request and turned his attention to the television.

Someone appeared on the black-and-white screen announcing that Dr. Martin Luther King Jr., the great civil rights leader, had been shot and killed.

As Jesse stood frozen watching the television, a feeling of emptiness crept over him. He knew that Dr. Martin Luther King Jr. was a great man. He had seen his mother watching him give speeches. His face held pain and frustration, but he had a peaceful disposition that couldn't be swayed. King had been stabbed, jailed numerous times, stoned, harassed by police and FBI, and ignored by the government. He received death threats constantly, and was deserted after speaking out against the Vietnam War, but still he marched on for humanity. As Moses had led God's people out of Egypt through the wilderness to the Promised Land, so King had continued his march, unwavering, against all odds. His eloquent style and soothing voice had reached out to many. When King spoke, he pierced the hearts, souls, and minds of the people. He spoke what he felt and felt what he spoke. He was respected and honored by the masses. King was a humble and peaceful man of God.

Jesse turned to walk outside. The streets were empty and quiet, with no cars and no one to be seen. There was one exception. On the bridge stood a man with a horn in hand, blowing his horn over the river, across the sea and beyond, for the world to hear. The horn player stood alone, erect, tall, and proud, blowing in the wind.

Jesse saw a broken-down, deserted bench nearby, hanging on its last nail before falling apart. At least, he thought, it would fall apart, but it didn't. He stood staring at that bench for the longest time.

On a specific day
At a specific time
Dr. Martin Luther King, Jr.
Took a shower here.

On a specific day
And at a specific time
Dr. Martin Luther King, Jr.
Was assassinated here.

On a specific day
And at a specific time
It was all over
All over, until now.

CHAPTER 7

FOR SOME
IT'S SUMMER

JESSE SAT WITH his mother across from Ms. Lipani in the vibrant classroom, glancing around at all the colorful pictures and decor. His mother sat with her hands folded over her purse and her legs crossed at the ankles. Ms. Lipani sat across from them with Jesse's folder in front of her.

"Mrs. Thomas," she began, "when Jesse first transferred from the public school system, we spoke about him being about a year behind in our curriculum."

His mother nodded.

"He's been trying extra hard," Ms. Lipani continued, glancing at Jesse and smiling. "But I feel that he hasn't acquired the basics of this grade, and I'm afraid that if we admit him to the fourth grade, he would fall behind completely and be lost. My suggestion is that Jesse repeat the third grade next year."

"I have noticed he was struggling," his mother said.

"Yes. I feel that if he had the extra reinforcement of next year, he would do fine. We just don't want him to start out struggling and continue in that manner. We don't want him to be discouraged. He has been doing extra assignments and, bless his heart, he tries so hard."

"Extra assignments?" his mother echoed.

Jesse remembered getting up early some mornings to do school work. His mother thought he hadn't done his homework assignment and was trying to complete it at the last minute. She had gotten upset and yelled at him first without asking what he was doing. Another time, she had found him trying to write cursive and hadn't given him a chance to tell her he was doing it for extra credit. She had yelled at him even though he was only trying his hardest to catch up.

"Yes," Ms. Lipani said, pulling out some papers from his folder and showing them to his mother. "He had a good start here, and then, as you can see, his grades started falling…"

Ms. Lipani went over several papers with his mother. The final decision was that Jesse would do third grade all over again.

Although Jesse was glad that his teacher knew he was really trying, he could not help feeling disappointment, emptiness, and rejection. He wondered why he was the only child who would not pass. There were many other children less qualified to pass than he was, especially since they were disruptive and ill-behaved. The question entered Jesse's mind over and over, *Why me?* He had always shown gratitude towards Ms. Lipani, because she was one person who had shown interest in him and the desire that he succeed.

It bothered him, thinking of all the kids who would tease him once they heard he had failed. But as summer began, his worries disappeared.

Jesse woke up early one stifling summer morning, the air in his room thick and damp. He lay in the bottom bunk of the new bunk bed, drenched in his own perspiration, his pajamas clinging to his small frame. The sheets in which he slept were soaked. His heart pounded at a rapid pace. Jesse gripped his clothing. He couldn't find air; his chest tightened at every breath, and his lungs refused to expand. He tried to calm down so he could slow his breathing.

Gradually, he was able to roll over and position himself on the edge of the bed. There he sat in darkness, his frail frame slumped over in the corner, his chest caved in, lungs like deflated balloons. He then slid off the bed and stood, hunched over, eyes slowly opening and closing. He felt ready to faint, but he knew he couldn't allow that to happen. He stood in the middle of the floor, weaving back and forth like a reed in a strong wind. He thought as he stood on the wooden floor in his bare feet, *If only I could move myself toward the direction of the bedroom door.*

Wheezing, he made that first step, then another…and another. He stopped and took a rest before knocking on his mother's door. When she saw him, she immediately took his hand and led him to the bathroom. She gave him his pills from the medicine cabinet with water.

"You're having a bout with asthma," she said. "Come on."

She led him back to his room, changed his pajamas and bed linens, and propped him up on some pillows. Jesse laid his head on the pillow, drained from trying to breathe with such difficulty. He waited for relief to come. In about thirty minutes, he could breathe much better, and within an hour, his breath was calming and soothing to him. Jesse now relaxed, his body limp. He fell back to sleep.

Later that morning, Jesse's father called and told him that he was coming to pick him up and take him for a ride, something he frequently promised but seldom delivered. Nevertheless, Jesse was always excited and never gave up hope. As most children, he thought the best of his father.

Eric and Leah had made other plans and didn't want to go. Jesse finished his chores much earlier than usual. With everything completed, he sat on the porch and waited. He sat there for a long time before Grace called out to him.

"Jesse, your Dad called. He'll be here later, so come inside."

Jesse went in and sat down in his stepfather's goliath leather reclining chair, which seemed like a gigantic marshmallow to him. Sunken in, with his arms on each armrest and feet dangling over the edge of the seat cushion, Jesse watched television.

A man was speaking to a large audience with signs, cameras, and balloons. The crowd was in a wild frenzy of excitement. Jubilance filled the air.

Suddenly, in the midst of the crowd, someone was lying on the floor with a black pool of blood beneath his head. At that moment, it was announced that Robert Kennedy had been shot.

The report said that Senator Kennedy had been shot at the Ambassador Hotel in Los Angeles. He had been pronounced dead on June 6, 1968, at 1:44 A.M. at Samaritan Hospital.

Jesse struggled while pulling himself out of the huge reclining chair. The scene remained etched in his mind. The man with the vibrant smile was now gone.

In time, Jesse returned outside and sat on the steps of the porch. Everyone in the neighborhood was outside, and there seemed to be only one description for the temperature that day: hot.

On that Saturday, it seemed the sunshine reflected their spirits, because everyone seemed festive and happy. Jesse watched as a boy tried to talk to Linda, Leah's friend.

"Come on, girl, you know you like me," he said, trying to appear savvy.

"I told you, Michael, I have a boyfriend," she said.

"What do you see in Curtis? He can't even play basketball. I'm gonna be on the team this year, can't nobody mess wit' me!" He laughed while moving closer to her with his arms open, waiting for a hug.

"Stop," Linda squealed, a smile breaking out in the corners of her mouth while she pushed him away. She walked away, twisting and peering over her left shoulder, her walk obviously exaggerated. Jesse knew she liked that boy.

"On your mark, get set, go!" Poised and ready, two boys on bikes took off down the street, whizzing by Jesse, just as the smell of barbecue rose up and greeted him. His neighbors across the street were slapping a slab of ribs onto the grill. James Brown danced down the street, blaring from windows and backyards, "…And I break out in a cold sweat!" The music and voice of James Brown was electrifying to Jesse's ears. People were walking, talking, and laughing. The neighborhood was busy with activity.

As Jesse sat there, he itched to be a part of something. Instead, he was stuck on the porch because of his asthma. He hated that. Besides, his mother wasn't going to let him run around and play in this blistering humid weather, especially after an attack.

A few minutes later, his mother came outside with a platter full of meat. They were having a barbecue of their own. She knew that he wanted to go out and play. "You can probably go out tomorrow," she said on her way to the backyard. "The food is almost ready."

Jesse became bored, wanting adventure, and what would be better than to sneak to the corner store and buy some of his favorite candy?

The store was right down the street, so it wouldn't take long. He would be back before his mother or anyone noticed he was gone. He heard her go back into the house after giving Caesar the meat. After mentally justifying his actions, Jesse slowly opened the front yard gate, which he was forbidden ever to do. He slowly placed the latch back on the fence and sprinted down the street among the mass of chaos.

At the entrance of the corner store hung a large, hand-painted sign: *Jimmy's Grocery Store.* Beneath that, in smaller, misspelled, and barely legible letters, it read, *Smoked saugases, collad greens, candi yams, watermelon…* The store didn't look like much, but it supplied the people's needs, especially those on public assistance.

Jesse pushed the screen door open and let it slam shut behind him as he stood breathing heavily from his short run. The store was crowded as usual. One shadow cast against the wall didn't seem to belong to anyone.

Jesse stood a minute longer in his white shirt, shorts, and white sneakers. Once he caught his breath, he made a mad dash toward the candy counter. With his hands and face pressed against the glass and eyes filled with excitement, he witnessed the colors of the rainbow. *Life doesn't get any better than this,* he thought. He searched for his favorite candy, but there were so many others demanding his attention. Finally, he saw it, and a smile broke out on his face.

All along, waiting for him to decide, was an elderly man, Jimmy, the cashier and owner. He was a pleasant and patient man. "How can I help you, young man?" he said, giving Jesse his undivided attention.

"I would like three of those. No, four," Jesse stuttered with excitement.

"These?" Jimmy asked.

"No, not those, the other ones next to it."

"You want these?"

"No! The ones to the right," he said with even more excitement.

"These?" Jimmy said, now placing his hand on the box of penny candy.

"Yeah, that's it! And…can I have eight?" Jesse said with hesitation, hoping he had enough money.

"Sure. That it?"

Jesse held his head up high, took a few steps backward, and looked up. To him, the cashier looked like a giant. He dug into his pocket for what little change he had. As he stood on his toes and placed the pennies on the counter, he asked, "Can I have three red gumballs…please?"

Jimmy smiled. "Of course."

"Have…have I got enough money?" Jesse asked nervously.

"You just made it," Jimmy said while throwing a few extra pieces in the bag.

"Thank you!" Jesse said with a beaming smile.

After receiving his candy, he stuffed one in his mouth and the rest in his pockets. He then strutted through the crowded store toward the door with his pockets bulging and weighing him down. Mission accomplished.

As Jesse pulled open the damaged screen door to leave, from the corner of his eye he noticed something. The dark shadow cast against the wall had moved. As Jesse made his way through the door, the shadow slithered its way through the cracks, like a dark vapor. It camouflaged itself well even though it was daytime.

Then Jesse heard a voice, like a distant whisper.

"Hey."

He heard it again.

"Hey, little man."

Jesse slowly looked over his shoulder as his mouth went slack from chewing his candy.

From the dark mist appeared a young man with deep, darting eyes. Jesse didn't know who he was. He had never seen him around the neighborhood before.

"Yo, I got some candy," the voice said. "Come on."

Jesse felt a shove from behind, and he was ushered across the street.

The man continued talking fast as his head spun around, looking in all directions. "What kind of candy do you want? I got all kinds. Hurry up. My little brother will eat it all if you don't walk faster. Move!" His voice became more demanding as he seemed to sense he was losing Jesse.

Jesse's heart began pounding. His mind couldn't catch up with the words he wanted to say.

Jesse found himself hurried up the front steps of an age-old house that looked dark and spooky. His mind told him to get away from the situation, but his body wouldn't respond. Jesse was scared.

At the porch, standing before the entrance of the doorway, Jesse saw the gloomy interior. His body stiffened, and he came to a halt.

"The candy is upstairs," the voice boomed from the shadow. "Go on!" it demanded when Jesse didn't move.

The man shoved him roughly up the stairs. Jesse became terrified. He wanted to run, but the voice in the shadow was right behind him. Each broken wooden stair he climbed made a loud creak.

Climbing the stairs seemed to take forever. As the journey continued, Jesse lost all sense of time, place, and direction. His environment was now unfamiliar to him.

When he reached the top, the man shoved him into a room just beyond the stairs. Jesse stood there breathing heavily. He felt an awful feeling in his stomach, and he swallowed hard. The room was stale and pitch black except for one window, with thin, stained, flowered curtains.

The slightly open window let a summer breeze come through, allowing the curtain to flap in the air. A very thin line of light came through the small opening of the window.

"Get on the floor!" the voice thundered as Jesse was shoved onto a torn, mildewed rug. "Don't worry. This won't take long."

Jesse felt his shorts being removed and his candy falling out of his pockets. He lay there frozen, frightened, and in shock. He felt weight and pressure on top of him and heard several grunts. He felt as if he would drown as he was engulfed by darkness. He felt as though he would suffocate as his fingers gripped the rug. He wanted to holler but couldn't.

In a moment, it was over. Immediately afterwards, for a brief moment, Jesse heard children outside the window laughing and playing. He lay still, confused and paralyzed by fear. Finally, the six-foot figure stood and pulled up his pants.

"Get up."

Jesse lay there with his face pressed downward on the floor, afraid to move. Finally, he stood, trembling, as he quickly pulled up his shorts. He now stood facing the shadow.

The perpetrator lay back, resting in a large, cushioned chair. "What the hell are you looking at?" it snarled, its head darting and rolling, while making loud hissing sounds. "Move! Get out!"

Jesse didn't move. He didn't know what he should be thinking or doing. His chestnut eyes froze open and swelled with tears. The candy he had been chewing now lay on the rug, soaked in a pool of saliva. Drool slowly fell from the corner of his lips onto his now dirty white shirt, which was his new favorite. His mother had given it to him the day before for his birthday, along with green toy soldiers, one of which now dangled from his pocket.

The shadow of darkness leaned its head back, struck a match, and took a long, calm drag from the cigarette. The white smoke from the burning red tip spiraled its way toward the ceiling. A smile with stained, jagged teeth glistened in the darkness. The creature held the cigarette while flicking the ashes onto the rug.

"Get out of here!" the voice rumbled again, shooting through Jesse's frail frame like a bolt of lightning.

Blindly, Jesse stumbled out of the room in a daze and down the stairs, almost losing his balance. He clung tightly to the railing and made careful, deliberate steps down each stair. He could not fully comprehend what unspeakable act of violence had been committed against him. His legs trembled. He was in a living nightmare.

Once he reached the last of what seemed like a thousand stairs, he heard the booming sound of laughter, which surely shook the very foundation of the house. The sound was sinister and inhuman.

Jesse was still trembling when he walked outside onto the porch. He looked around, seeing blue, purple, and green, which turned to blue again. He continued to look around, panting. He attempted to make a dash from the porch, but tripped and fell on an untied shoestring, hitting the floor hard.

Looking up, he noticed someone there he hadn't seen before. In a rocking chair sat an elderly woman with thinning gray hair. Their eyes met. Hers were distant, and her mouth wore a frown as she turned her head away. Jesse quickly made it back to his feet and ran home as fast as his skinny legs could carry him.

Once back home, Jesse sat on his steps behind the closed gate and tried to catch his breath and calm himself down. It seemed as though he had never left. Everything had happened so quickly. He was sure no one had noticed he was gone. They were all in the backyard.

He sat there void of emotion. He felt numb. The more he sat, the more he thought. Rage boiled in his mind. He wanted to tell someone. Who? If he did tell someone, he could not suffer the humiliation of the truth of how he had been tricked, bullied, and violated.

He wanted to strike something. He was mad. His face kept frowning, and his lips trembled to hold back the tears he felt inside. Then he felt embarrassed that he hadn't run sooner and that he had been enticed for a moment by the offer of some candy. He knew he would be teased, or maybe no one would believe him. Maybe they would think he went willingly. Maybe they would think he wanted that person to do it. Maybe they would call him a faggot. That's what they called men who liked each other. They would dress up like women and parade the neighborhood, and people would shake their heads and laugh.

Bile rose up in his throat and he thought he was going to vomit, but he forced it back down.

"I'm gonna find him," he muttered. "I'm gonna find him and beat him up!"

Jesse tensed up his shoulders and then dropped them with a sigh. His attacker was ten times bigger than Jesse. There was no way he was going to be able to beat him up. The best he could do was block it from his mind and try his hardest not to think about it.

Jesse remained sullen and quiet the rest of the day, telling no one what had happened. The only joy he had was looking forward to his dad's coming. He waited and waited, and still nothing. The sunlight turned to the dusk of evening, and still the white convertible with red interior never turned the corner. His father never came.

Tears burned his eyes. He wiped them away angrily. He vowed that would be the last time he would ever wait for him or anyone. That evening, the sky was dark with crows.

"I tell you the truth, unless you change and become like little children, you will never enter the kingdom of heaven. Therefore, whoever humbles himself like this child is the greatest in the kingdom of heaven. And whoever welcomes a little child like this in my name welcomes me. But if anyone causes one of these little ones who believe in me to sin, it would be better for him to have a larges millstone hung around his neck and to be drowned in the depth of the sea."

—Matthew 18:2-6

CHAPTER 8

LIKENESS OF RED

JESSE SLOWLY GAVE up playing with his green plastic military fig-ures, and they were gradually replaced by comic books. He had all sorts: Sgt. Rock, Fantastic Four, Captain America, Batman, Silver Surfer, Green Lantern, and Conan the Barbarian. He collected them all, but his favorite was Spiderman. He would cut some of the figures from the comic books and play for hours at the kitchen table using his imagination to create new and dangerous missions for his superheroes.

His mother would observe from a distance while preparing supper. When the food was ready for everyone to eat, she would ask him to clear the table. Jesse immediately obeyed, even when some adventures were reaching their peak.

These table adventure sessions were short-lived. He soon realized that by cutting out the figures, his comic books were no longer a collection, but scraps. Slowly he began drawing the Marvel heroes more and more. To draw one character sometimes took an entire day, but Jesse wouldn't give up until he felt satisfied with the completed work. He hung them on the walls around his room. At bedtime he stared at them until he fell asleep.

In the fall of 1968, Jesse once again found himself in the familiar surroundings of his third-grade classroom. Everything was the same, except the students, of course. Jesse felt discomfort and embarrassment being the old among the new. He also knew that if any of the students discovered he had failed the previous year, he would be ridiculed to shame. So, every morning when they dutifully placed their hands over their hearts, heads held high, and recited "The Pledge of Allegiance," Jesse leaned forward to look at those around him. He then placed his right hand over his heart with his fingers crossed and squeezed tightly on both hands. For double security, he closed his eyes and prayed, hoping that Ms. Lipani would not reveal his identity. It seemed to work, because she never did.

Although students were encouraged to raise their hands and participate, Jesse dreaded this. He never felt part of the class. In fact, he alienated himself. He was quiet, shy, aloof, and felt he had nothing in common with his classmates. Many students proudly raised their hands and participated. Jesse admired and respected them for their enthusiasm and effort.

Periodically, Ms. Lipani would circle the room, having children read from their textbooks. At first, children would volunteer. When there were none left, she would call out names. Jesse was seldom selected, which suited him just fine. When he was chosen, his heart would begin racing, palms sweating, hoping to get through the paragraphs he was given to read without a mistake. To be unable to pronounce a word led to silence, then stumbling over the pronunciation until someone whispered the correct word to him, hopefully before he heard whispers and chuckles from the other students.

One day of every month was selected as "Dress Down Day." The students were encouraged to wear whatever they chose in place of their uniforms. During the class period, there was always a fifteen-minute recess. The children were served an assortment of milk and cookies. During recess, the students were allowed play freely.

Most of the students wore dashikis, loose-fitting, brightly colored tunics. Many were conscious of their black culture. The dominant colors were red, black, and green. The color red related to the blood of the people, black related to race, and green symbolized the land of Africa. The children were constantly reminded of the struggles for equality and the difficulties they would face growing up in America. They also heard stories of Frederick Douglass, Harriet Tubman, George Washington Carver, and slavery. They were surrounded by constant reminders of where they had come from.

Throughout the neighborhood, there were continuous whispers of Malcolm X. Muhammad Ali captivated the children; whenever he stepped into the ring, it was always seen as black versus white. There was also the standby Tommie Smith and John Carlos in the 1968 Mexico City Olympics. Upon receiving their medals, they stood and raised their fists toward the sky while wearing black leather gloves. To many blacks in America, this Black Power sign represented their struggle in America. James Brown music blared through the neighborhood: "Say It Loud, I'm Black and I'm Proud." Children used Afro combs and picks with the clenched fist representing the Black Power sign.

During recess, kids slapped each other five, but if one displayed his open palm side, which was lighter, the other kid would say, "Naw man, the black hand side." The kid would slide the back of his hand along the back side of the other kid's hand. They both would then break out in loud laughter, hugging each other.

Congregating in the corner of the classroom were children beating the bottoms of cardboard boxes with their hands or pencils, creating a rhythm. The children proudly danced, their clenched fists displaying the black power sign, punching the air. Ms. Lipani always looked on in amusement.

While those activities went on just about every break period, Jesse attempted to fight off several of the tough boys who often jumped him in the closet in the back of the classroom. They wrestled and slapped him on the back of his head because of his bald haircut. Jesse would fight to defend himself, but usually there were just too many. So, when Ms. Lipani rang her bell and recess was over, he almost always found himself lying on the closet's wooden floor. He was one of the last trying to get up and get to his desk with his clothes disheveled, wrinkled, and dirty. Jesse sat quietly with his dark blue clip tie barely attached, dangling from his collar. His head throbbed from the hits he had received. Class continued while Jesse stared forward, never saying a word.

One day the students were instructed that they would be going to art class for a period, which was an hour long. Jesse had never gone to an art class before and had no idea what to expect.

Once the class arrived, they met with the instructor, Sister Theresa Martin. She was a short, elderly nun, heavyset, quiet, and very stern. She seemed always preoccupied in thought and seldom smiled. Maybe her disposition resulted from not being able to find dedicated students. She was always disciplining students and struggling to keep them focused on their assignments. It seemed to make her frustrated.

Art classes continued for several weeks, and Jesse always eagerly looked forward to them.

During one class, Sister Martin gave them a homework assignment. The students were to complete a project of their choice using charcoal pencils. This assignment had to be completed by the next class session. Jesse was very excited, because other class assignments had always been simple. Jesse found a picture of a hawk and began his drawing. He chose this bird because he felt it represented a warrior, with its short-hooked bill, strong claws, and penetrating eyes.

The following week, Jesse handed in his art assignment, along with everyone else. He attempted to make a quick survey of what the other students had done. He had discovered that art class was one of the few classes that held his interest, and where he felt most comfortable.

One evening after supper, Jesse found himself in another heated confrontation with his brother. The children were given kitchen chores, which were to be alternated daily. Whenever Eric's turn came to wash the dishes, he always developed amnesia, which triggered a major argument between the two boys. Somehow Eric always seemed to get his way.

"You think you're bad enough to whup me?" Eric challenged as he stood face to face with Jesse.

Jesse held his ground. "It's your turn, and you know it!"

At this, Eric tightened his jaw and clenched his fists, while Leah stood by and watched with frightful anticipation.

"So what you gonna do?" Eric barked.

At that moment, their mother walked into the kitchen area.

"What's going on in here?" she asked.

Both boys fell quiet, surprised to see their mother standing before them. The tension between them left as quickly as it had come.

"What's going on here?" she asked again, demanding an answer.

Jesse and Eric replied at the same time, one trying to shout over the other.

"He started it!"

"No, I didn't!"

"But you—"

"He always—"

"All right, hold it!" she interrupted. "One at a time. Jesse, you'll speak first."

"W-well," Jesse stammered, "Eric is trying to make me wash the dishes when it's his turn."

"Is that true?"

"No! It's his turn," Eric argued while staring at Jesse, which ignited an argument between them again.

Their mother quickly quieted them down.

Then Leah said, "What's the big deal? I'll wash the dishes."

"Are you sure?" their mother asked.

Leah shrugged and began preparing to wash them.

Their mother turned toward the two boys and said, "Both of you should thank your sister. Jesse, you'll dry the dishes, and Eric, your job is to sweep the floor when they're finished."

As Jesse completed drying the last few dishes, their mother returned. "Jesse, I received a phone call from your art teacher, Sister Theresa Martin. She said your charcoal rendering of the hawk was an exceptional drawing. She chose your drawing with a few other students' to display in the class."

Standing on a chair near the sink, Jesse looked at her with surprise. He himself was also very satisfied with the outcome of the drawing.

"You possess a special, unique gift from God," his mother said. "Sister Martin said that you are very talented, and that you should never allow your gift to be wasted." She leaned toward Jesse and told him that she was proud of him.

Jesse met with Sister Martin the next day. She asked Jesse if he had other drawings at home. Jesse did, and later he brought them to class, displaying his drawings of his comic book heroes. Sister Martin carefully looked them over and gave Jesse brief instructions. In time, she began giving Jesse prominent black historical figures and current leaders to illustrate.

Whenever Jesse finished a group of black portraits, Sister Martin hung them along the corridor wall, directly outside the classroom. The corridor was filled with the likes of Mahalia Jackson, Ralph Johnson Bunche, Mary McLeod Bethune, and Dr. Martin Luther King, Jr. Over a period of time, with Jesse's permission, she distributed the drawings among the students and parents. As time went on, Jesse received recognition as an artist by his classmates and teachers. During all this, however, Jesse shied away from the attention.

Jesse sat on a hard wooden bench, watching the activity. He could hear a few words mumbled, but barely above a whisper. It was Ash Wednesday, and the students were required to attend the afternoon mass. Jesse sat alone in the third row inside the massive church with its high ceilings, observing as students passed by with markings on their foreheads.

He watched with great curiosity as the students stood in line, waiting their turn to drink from the silver chalice and receive wafers that were placed on their tongues. The entire ceremony was carried out in silence. The only voice heard was the priest's, and it was in a low monotone.

Everything was quite different from the Sunday church meetings he attended with his mother. Jesse had been informed earlier that he would not be able to participate due to not being Catholic. So there he sat, wondering if they would ever run out of wafers and whatever they were drinking from the chalice. Once all the children had gone through the line, the priest spoke for a brief moment, and everyone was dismissed.

Once home, Jesse finished his homework and began his drawings. Nearly every day of the week, Jesse's stepfather, Caesar, sat in his brown leather reclining chair, reading the newspaper and watching the evening news. On this evening, Jesse witnessed his green soldiers and G.I. Joe toy coming to life. It was the first televised war that reached every American's living room: Vietnam.

Jesse stood and watched for several minutes. The bombings, fires, air strikes, and blazing villages haunted him. Soldiers constantly fired their weapons and braced themselves under cover for return fire. In the midst of all the chaos, a newsman always stood, giving his report while ducking his head and looking behind himself as the battle raged on.

On his left wrist, Jesse wore a black braided band that his uncle had sent him while in the war. He hoped that his uncle would return home alive.

"Jesse, you're blocking my view of the television," Caesar said in a demanding tone, while leaning forward in his reclining chair and staring intently at Jesse with newspaper still in hand.

Jesse looked over his left shoulder at Caesar.

Caesar leaned in closer, and with the voice of a Navy captain said, "I need you to go down into the basement and remove the dead rat that's lying on the ground."

Jesse's brown eyes widened. "OK."

"Use the shovel that's down there."

By now, his stepfather's voice was like a distant echo. Jesse's knees weakened. The thought of handling a rat terrified him. He also remembered how he dreaded taking out the garbage when it was his turn. Usually, a rat jumped from the garbage can as he took the lid off, or he heard them squirming inside the trash can. And in the house late in the night, while half-asleep, he could hear them crawling through the wall next to his bed. Now, Caesar was forcing him to have direct contact with a rat.

He had witnessed his upstairs neighbor, Pedro Rodriguez, at a distance, torturing them. It amazed him how brave Pedro was; maybe it had to do with being a grownup, he thought. Pedro sometimes found two rats that had fallen into an empty garbage can and were unable to get out. A smile would spread across his face as he tossed a newspaper soaked with lighter fluid into the garbage can, closing the lid partially as he set the inside ablaze. He seemed to get satisfaction from hearing the rats bounce around in the can in frenzy. Other days, he just filled the garbage cans halfway with water and watched them drown. Another time, Pedro slammed the garbage lid shut, capturing one rat in an empty can, and vigorously shook it, listening to the thuds as the rat was pounded against the walls. Eventually, he opened the lid and released the rat on the pavement. The rat appeared paralyzed due to the pounding it had received and could only attempt to move, which sent Pedro roaring with laughter.

"Jesse, don't just stand there in dreamland!" Caesar now thundered. "Head downstairs and get rid of the rat."

Jesse blinked and found himself heading toward the dreaded basement.

The basement was always dark, even at midday. As Jesse slowly made his way down the creaking wooden steps, he felt the chill of the cold and dampness upon his skin from the basement. Once there, he felt an urge to run, but continued creeping slowly forward in search of the dead rat. He felt the uneven dirt and rock of the basement floor beneath his sneakers, as if it had been carved from a cave.

Above his head hung spider webs, metal pipes, and old wiring, tangled together in all directions. The walls were rock and cement. He slowly made his way around the old stone columns, carefully planting one foot in front of the other.

To him, the basement always had an eerie presence. The shadows kept him from venturing into that part of the house. Most items stored in the basement were covered by a thick film of dust. Farther back in the corner of the basement was a small room with an old wooden door barely hanging on its hinges. Jesse was terrified of going near that haunted room, scared of what he would find inside.

Now, peeking around the furnace, he noticed the shovel that he was supposed to use to lift the rat. He grabbed the shovel, but it was so heavy he could barely lift it with two hands, so he dragged it behind him. The metal from the shovel made screeching sounds as it scraped across the floor.

In the distance, he saw the rat lying there unmoving, as the sunlight from the basement window penetrated the darkness, casting a radiant glow. The only electrical light was a light bulb directly above it, with a hanging string. Jesse knew he wouldn't be brave enough to stand on a crate and pull the switch, so he just stood staring. Maybe the rat wasn't dead, he thought as he held the heavy shovel in hand just six feet away.

He stood there for what seemed to him like hours, contemplating. The rat was far larger than he had imagined, at least, a lot larger than the rats he had seen Mr. Rodriguez torturing. He even thought he saw it breathe.

What would he do if it jumped up and attacked him? What then?

As he stepped forward and pushed the shovel in the direction of the rat, he wondered how the weight would feel once the rat was on the shovel. Very slowly and carefully, he nudged the rat with the edge of the shovel as he gripped it with his quivering hands, his heart going into overdrive. Then, suddenly, the rat moved—or at least, he thought it did.

Just then, from the corner of his eye, he saw a dark figure flash by. Instantly, the shovel fell from his hands, causing a loud clanking sound that echoed through the darkness. Jesse's legs became like noodles. Frantically, he ran backwards, which caused him to trip and fall. He then became disoriented in the darkness while scrambling back to his feet. Terrified, he spun around and crashed into a pile of boxes. He found himself covered with dirt and spider webs. He lay face down on the cold ground, frozen for a moment, almost too afraid to move. Then he was dashing up the stairs, taking two steps at a time, leaving behind the shovel and the poisoned rat.

CHAPTER 9

BATMAN

BACK IN SCHOOL, during a recess period, the students seemed more active than usual. They chased each other around the desks. Paper airplanes flew through the air, some traveling quite far, out the second floor window and into the faculty parking lot. Tiny paper spitballs found their targets when blown through straws. Several girls gathered around desks, whispering and giggling, with their fingers pointing and hands on their hips. Others sat alone, not having been accepted into any of the circles.

Ms. Lipani was quite busy and unaware of what was going on in the closet. Somehow, Jesse found himself back there again, surrounded by boys ready to attack him.

As four boys moved in closer like scavengers, two stood at a distance and one served as the lookout in case the teacher approached. Jesse hesitated, uncertain how to react. But then a certain feeling came over him that even the boys detected, which made them move in more slowly.

Jesse felt a bit more confidence in himself. He was no longer looking for a way out. He was willing to stand his ground. What made the difference? Jesse had spent several evenings watching the television show *Batman*, and after viewing the fighting scenes, especially when the Green Hornet and Kato fought Batman and Robin, he felt well equipped to defend himself. His energy was still highly charged after watching Bruce Lee as Kato, performing martial arts. He felt this was the moment to put what he had learned into action. Although he was still nervous, he tried not to show it.

As the boys closed in, Jesse heard the *Batman* theme song playing in his mind. Suddenly, one boy surprised him from behind by swatting him on the back of his head. *Pop!* The boys laughed aloud and taunted him. Jesse felt more hurt from the insults and laughter than the actual attack, but he remained standing, ready for the next attack, holding back the tears of embarrassment.

Just then, another figure walked into the closet. Wayne was the biggest of the other students. His size made all the other third-graders wonder about his age. Rumor had it that he had failed several times, which accounted for him being much larger than everyone else. Wayne was the bully of the class, and everyone feared him. Now he was pushing himself through the other boys approaching Jesse.

Standing directly in front of Jesse, Wayne cast a shadow over him. As Jesse looked up at him, he heard the *Batman* theme song again, and his confidence grew.

Just then, Wayne reached with both hands to grab Jesse by his collar. Jesse responded by performing a fighting technique that he had watched Batman perform numerous times on television. He gripped both of Wayne's extended arms, leaned back, and used Wayne's momentum to pull the bigger boy toward him. As Wayne began to fall forward, Jesse placed his right foot on Wayne's torso, leaning further backward. Jesse continued falling backwards, while also placing his left foot on Wayne's torso.

Wayne attempted to catch his balance, but before he could react, Jesse pushed off with both feet on Wayne's chest, propelling the boy upward and over his head as he let go of Wayne's arms. For a brief moment, he saw a look of shock in Wayne's eyes as he fell backwards onto a pile of boxes with a loud crash.

The throwing technique hadn't gone the way Jesse had watched on television, but it was good enough. All the other boys watched in awe as Jesse lay sprawled on his back, with Wayne struggling to get up behind him.

Then everyone heard Ms. Lipani's voice as she approached the closet. The boys scrambled to exit the other door at the far end of the closet. A few of the boys became jammed in the doorway briefly while trying to rush out at the same time.

With everyone now in their seats, Ms. Lipani approached the front of the class and spun angrily on her heels to face them. She gave an extensive lecture on the students' behavior during recess, stating that it would no longer be tolerated. The students sat in silence, some with bowed heads. Jesse sat at his desk with a slight grin and feeling of satisfaction. He marveled at how he had been able to defend himself, especially after throwing Wayne. As his mind wandered, he could barely hear Ms. Lipani scolding them.

By day's end, the final school bell rang. After donning their coats, gloves, hats, and boots, the children stood in line, holding their colorful lunch boxes. They marched out of the classroom in a single file down the stairs, surprisingly quietly. The only sound was the patter of footsteps.

Jesse was walking near the back of the line when he suddenly stopped. As before, he sensed *her* staring at him. He looked down the stairs, and there she was just like before. She never moved, with her penetrating eyes directly on him.

Jesse walked down the stairs toward her, while convincing himself he was not going to be afraid. He was going to be brave and not allow her to scare him anymore. He stood directly in front of her, glaring up into her eyes, trying not to blink. He stood silently, his black winter cap with flaps covering his ears, boots unbuckled, holding his lunch pail in one hand and books in the other.

"You don't scare me anymore," he said.

She didn't say a word. Jesse felt she was ignoring him. Leaning forward on his toes, he attempted to make closer eye contact, even though there was a significant height difference.

"I'm not afraid of you, and I'm not running anymore!" he said loudly and with confidence. He continued the eye contact to see who would give in and blink first. She seemed to lower her chin, and the intensity of their eye contact grew. Jesse saw her lips part as she spoke, or at least he thought he did.

"Jesse, who are you speaking to?" asked Ms. Lipani as she stepped around to view him from the top of the stairs. Jesse dropped his head suddenly and looked at the floor as he hurried down the stairs, past the statue of the Virgin Mary.

With all his weight, Jesse leaned against the door and pushed it open, entering the outside world, where rain had started to fall. There in the large, open parking lot, the children had scattered in all directions. Some chased each other endlessly in circles, laughing. Children reaching to tag one another yelled out, "You got the cooties!" if the other students hadn't crossed their arms, legs, or fingers before being touched.

One little girl, in a hurry to unwrap her candy, dropped it on the ground. She seemed deeply disappointed as a few others looked on. Then, after a brief moment of thought, she blurted out, "God made dirt, and dirt don't hurt!" She picked it up off the ground and popped it in her mouth.

A few students watched with puzzled looks on their faces and accepted her reasoning for picking up the candy from the ground and eating it. Another student yelled back, "Yeah, but it's got germs on it!"

The little girl shot back with more determination on her face and defiance in her voice, "So what? God made dirt, and dirt don't hurt!"

With that, the bickering began.

As a yellow bus full of students drove away, in the back of the bus, a hand reached out the partially opened window, holding a clear plastic cup to catch raindrops.

In the far corner of the parking lot, Jesse noticed a little girl dancing around a fire hydrant. Startled, he stood and observed her. Her name was Ellen. She had round, rosy cheeks, a slight smile, and big, brown, gleaming eyes. She was happy singing and dancing by herself while playing in her make-believe world. With flowing ribbons tied around her wrist, she circled the multi-colored fire hydrant. Oblivious to everything else around her, she spoke in whispers to no one in particular.

Surprised, Jesse stood nearby and wondered if he would receive an invitation. Noticing him, she invited him in. The two held a brief conversation. Jesse was given a ticket to enter. They smiled and giggled. It was a world where there were only a few invitations. Their joy and happiness were untainted for a moment, until the shout rang out.

"Jesse likes the white girl! Jesse likes the white girl!" several children shouted louder and louder, before being joined by others.

Ellen was one of the few whites who attended the school. She did not associate very often with other students. She tended to stay to herself, but now she had an audience.

They both stood still, interrupted. Ellen's head dropped, and tears swelled up in her eyes from the taunting of the other children. Jesse was shocked by all the attention he had received for playing with someone who was different. He had just wanted a friend.

He looked at Ellen. Her rainbow had vanished, and tears streamed down her cheeks.

He made his way through the circle that had formed around him and began a slow, disheartening walk home.

That evening after supper, the dishes were cleared from the table. Leah, Eric, and Jesse completed their kitchen chores. Afterwards, they took their baths and were allowed to watch *Batman* before going to bed for the night. Jesse was last to take his bath. He rushed inside the bathroom and sat in the bathtub. Through the closed door, he heard the *Batman* theme song as the show came on television, which made him more anxious to hurry with his bath. He was especially excited about the upcoming episode, to see how Batman would escape the fiery furnace.

As he sat in the tub, hurriedly scrubbing his face and washing his head, the door opened and Caesar walked in. He had frequently checked on Jesse while taking baths because he tended to sing songs and play in the bathtub for a long time. Caesar towered over him, his muscular form intimidating. Jesse stood in the bathtub, exposed and dripping wet.

"Now, wash your penis!" Caesar commanded with the voice of a drill sergeant.

Jesse was puzzled as Caesar repeated his command. Then, suddenly, Caesar struck Jesse with a towel he had twisted, causing the tip of the towel to make popping sounds as it stung him upon impact. Jesse stood frozen as the hits continued. After several strikes, the towel dropped to the floor and the door slammed shut. Jesse began to tremble uncontrollably. His face tightened, and tears formed. The tears rolled down his cheeks and over his lips, leaving a salty taste in his mouth.

Confused, Jesse closed his eyes. He wished that what had happened hadn't. Past traumatic experiences had nearly crushed him, but now his spirit felt broken. His thin legs buckled as he withdrew deeper into his thoughts. He envisioned himself plunging into dark waters. He flailed his arms and kicked his legs, fighting vigorously to stay afloat, but the current was too strong. It seemed too much for him to overcome.

Overpowered and underwater, he continued to fight, refusing to allow his last breath to be taken away. In time, his head burst through the surface of the waters. Gasping for air and desperately clinging to survival, he saw in the dark, thundering skies a beautiful kite with radiant colors. The kite struggled between the powerful, raging winds. It often disappeared into the storm, only to resurface defiantly. The colorful kite would not allow itself to be overcome by darkness.

Jesse slowly opened his eyes. The images inside his mind faded. The attack upon him had been emotionally overwhelming.

"Why?" he wondered. He constantly searched his mind for answers, and found none.

After removing the stopper from the drain, Jesse stared at the circular current of water flowing downward into the drain. He cleaned the tub with a sponge and Ajax until it looked spotless. After putting on his pajamas, he faced the closed door, waiting to exit. Tears flooded his eyes again as he wiped them away.

On the other side of the door, in the family room, Jesse heard the ending of the *Batman* episode: "Same bat time, same bat station."

He sat down on the edge of the bathtub, shipwrecked, and sobbed in silence.

CHAPTER 10

CHANGE

"COME ON, HURRY up! I ain't got all day," the tall, lean, dark man yelled in anger. "That's why I can't take you no place. Always taking your time. Let's go! Hurry up!"

Standing in the street, he looked back over his shoulder and around the corner, his eyes wide with exasperation. He wore a bright green, yellow, and orange shirt with elaborate designs, with the sleeves rolled above the elbow. His forearms were like oaks, with protruding veins that looked as though they had been carved from wood. His cuffed orange bell-bottoms matched his shirt. His shoes were green, along with the wide-brim straw hat. Everyone in the neighborhood knew him as "Fast Eddie."

It was early Saturday morning, and the streets were empty and quiet except for Jesse across the street, sitting on his new green Sting Ray bike. The bike had a slick back tire, banana seat, and V-shaped handlebars tilted slightly forward. Jesse was parked with one foot planted on the curb and the other on the pedal, with both hands on the handlebar grips. He had stopped to watch after hearing all the commotion to see what was going on.

"Come on, I said!" Eddie shouted again as he continued to stare around the corner impatiently.

Just then, a tiny white poodle squirted around the corner, wearing bells. Eddie was taking her for a daily morning walk. Jesse watched him scoop her up from the sidewalk and continue scolding her as he made his way down the street. Jesse dropped his head with a slight smile and a chuckle.

On the weekends, he made a practice of rising early in the morning to work on his drawings, and by seven A.M. he was riding his bike through the neighborhood. He enjoyed the quiet, empty streets at that time. It was an overcast spring morning, but the sun was attempting to break through.

Jesse pushed off on his left front pedal and casually rode his bicycle down the avenue. Jesse was now eleven years old, soon to be twelve. His unbuttoned blue shirt flapped behind him as it caught the breeze. He wore a white T-shirt underneath and blue jeans rolled at the bottoms, displaying his impeccably clean white canvas Converse All-Stars. As he continued riding, he did zig-zags in the middle of the street, since no cars were around. His eyes darted back and forth, observing his surroundings but looking at no place in particular. He looked at the old worn storefronts, fish markets, and dilapidated homes.

After a short ride, he pulled over to the side, applied his brakes, and came to a stop. The neighborhood had changed. It was the ghetto, or at least that was what they called it.

Under all the joy, happiness, brotherhood, pride, respect, and love, flowed a current of evil. You couldn't see it, smell it, taste it, or touch it, but you knew it was there. If you weren't careful, you could easily become its next victim.

The number one form of substance abuse was alcohol, which contributed to many people's problems, along with low income and a high unemployment rate. Other destructive courses resulted from oppression, denial, and people simply wanting to use others for their own benefit, no matter what the cost. The streets were filled with hustlers, dealers, pimps, and gangs.

In the midst of all the madness stood the religious zealots. The Jehovah's Witnesses arrived in pairs early in the morning, knocking on neighborhood doors. The Muslims stood on corners and on streets between traffic, with polished appearances, selling newspapers and pies. There was always a lone person on the corner, yelling loudly to anyone who would listen. The message was simply stated: "You're all going to Hell!"

Jesse pedaled his bike along the street, heading toward home. There, he completed his weekend chores and ventured back outdoors with his basketball under his arm. He made his way through a few neighbors' backyards and vacant lots until he reached an old, dilapidated garage. At the entrance of the garage was a rusted, bent basketball rim hanging from a decaying sheet of wood used as a backboard. The backboard itself was attached to the edge of the roof with several braces of rotten wood and rusted nails.

Jesse stood below, looking up at the rim, which seemed to reach the sky. Below the rim, a pool of water had formed during the previous night's rain, which had filled most of the playing area. A sewage drain in the uneven concrete was clogged, as usual. On days like this, Jesse had the unhappy task of trying to solve his dilemma. After several minutes of thought, he removed an old, worn broom from the pile of junk in the dark garage and tried to sweep the water from the concrete onto the grass. As soon as he swept the water up the slight incline, the water quickly returned. Time passed, and his arms began to ache. He realized his efforts were in vain.

After searching around, he noticed a wooden platform lying in the grass at a distance. Jesse struggled with the large wooden platform, dragging it into the water within a few feet of the rim. Now, standing on the unsteady platform with soaking wet sneakers and untied laces, he sighed with relief, having a sense of accomplishment.

Looking around, he saw the basketball in the grass. He jumped off the platform and landed in the water with a splash. The basketball had been worn smooth and desperately needed air. He made his way back to the platform and lifted the ball with both hands above his head. To him, the ball seemed like a boulder. His arms strained as he thrust the ball toward the rim.

Plop! He missed the entire rim. In fact, it never even came close, but landed in a thick patch of mud. Jesse grinned sheepishly, disappointed, but that didn't stop him from trying. He immediately retrieved the ball, cleaned the mud off with his shirt, and tried the shot again, but this time underhanded. He heaved the ball upward. Again it missed terribly, splashing in the water.

Jesse leaned forward, using the broom to bring the ball closer to the edge, where he would retrieve it, return to the platform, and try another attempt. This lasted most of the day, into late afternoon.

As Jesse continued shooting, a tall, lanky boy approached. His name was Dean Armstrong. Dean was very tall for sixteen, with long legs, long arms, and enormous hands that easily palmed a basketball. He was known as one of the best basketball players in the neighborhood and high school. He displayed a grace in his movements that resembled a gazelle on the court as well as off. He never seemed to be in any hurry, but when needed, he had the quickness and speed of a cheetah. Dean also kept a watchful eye over Jesse, and would contribute words of encouragement whenever possible.

He apparently stood quietly at a distance for some time, watching Jesse, until finally he yelled out, "Li'l Jesse, what are you doin'?"

Jesse spun around, startled by the disruption of his concentration. After collecting his thoughts, he stuttered, "I'm—I'm shooting the basketball."

"I can see that, but why are you standing on the platform in the middle of the water?"

Jesse stood with his shoulders slumped, trying to figure out how to explain himself.

"Well," Jesse said hesitantly, "I couldn't get all the water out."

"I'll tell you what," Dean said, clearly seeing Jesse's look of discouragement. "There's a push broom in the garage. Grab it, and I'll help you get rid of the water."

Jesse was delighted. He jumped from the platform, landing in the water, and headed inside the garage to the push broom. He wondered why he hadn't seen it earlier. The two of them worked rigorously to remove the flood of water and unclog the sewage trap. Within twenty minutes, the task was completed. Jesse continued shooting the ball, with Dean instructing him.

Eventually, older players arrived and began shooting with their basketballs, taking over the area Jesse had just cleaned. Jesse made his way quietly to the grass sidelines as the other boys took shots to choose teams.

Dejected, and cradling his worn, almost deflated ball, Jesse turned around with his head down and started his walk home.

Then someone shouted, "Hey, Jesse, where ya goin'?"

Jesse turned in surprise. Dean was jogging toward him. "Home. My mother's going to take me shopping." He knew it was still early for him to arrive home to meet his mother.

Dean then asked, "Can I hold your basketball?"

Jesse reached out with both hands, handing him the ball, and Dean gave Jesse his. "Here, you can have this one. It has better grip and bounce. It will help out when you practice."

Jesse was excited. To him, the ball looked practically new.

"Are you sure?" he blurted out.

Before Jesse realized it, Dean had turned and was jogging back to the basketball court. Jesse stood holding the ball in amazement. A huge smile stretched across his face as he sprinted through the tall grass and weeds toward home.

Once home, Jesse quickly washed and changed his clothes and was on his way to shopping with his mother.

When he and his mother reached the neighborhood shopping center, the parking lot was abuzz with activity. Conversations were constant. Two people leaning on a car with bottles of liquor in brown paper bags chided each other playfully. A woman was yelling from her porch to no one in particular that her man was no good. Cars and truck horns honked, trying to get the attention of anyone to say hello. Every vehicle played its driver's favorite tune on eight-track tapes: Sly Stone, Earth Wind and Fire, B. B. King, War, Kool and the Gang, Ohio Players, Mandrill, Bobby Blue Bland, and Wilson Pickett. The list was endless. Some stood around arguing and defending their favorite band as the best.

In other sanctioned corners of the parking lot, there also were the usual illegal activities. Several guys were in a huddle throwing dice, drinking with money in hand and some bills in a pile on the concrete. There were also those who hung around for sheer entertainment, waiting for something to happen. Kids darted in and out of cars while riding their bikes.

To a stranger, this environment would seem chaotic and out of order. This was the culture of these people, with an energy and rhythm that involved everyone. It helped them get away from their problems, stress, and the tiring, low-paying jobs they held during the week.

Beneath all the activity and laughter, there was a deep sense of hopelessness. Congregating in the shopping center parking lot every Friday and Saturday helped to heal the pain, if only temporarily, as most of their situations worsened.

Jesse strolled behind his mother with both hands tucked in the pockets of his jeans. Growing older, he had developed an independent sense of cool about himself. They entered a clothing store, and his mother immediately began looking through the children's suit rack. Grace had spent the last two weeks after work trying to find a suit for him to wear on Easter Sunday. Every suit she had shown him he disliked. Jesse's mind was set on having a double-breasted black pin-stripe suit, and nothing else would do. As her patience wore thin, she attempted a compromise.

"Jesse, here is a brown pin-stripe, and it's just your size," she said with enthusiasm. Jesse looked at it with disapproval but did not say anything. She quickly placed the suit back on the rack and then presented another one.

"Here's the one!" she said, looking on with excitement.

Jesse looked eagerly. The suit was black with pin-stripes, but then he noticed it wasn't double-breasted, and again a look of dissatisfaction crossed his face.

Seeing he wasn't satisfied, she placed it back and continued looking. "Well, with all the suits in the place, your suit must be here somewhere," she said, pushing one suit aside from another on the rack. As she continued searching, Jesse wandered about the store.

As he browsed through the shoe section, he heard the song "Jesus Christ Superstar" play over the store's speaker system. The song drew his attention as he stood by the counter and cash register. As he looked over the glass counter, an image of Jesus Christ seemed to gaze back at him. Jesse stood still, mesmerized by the music and image.

"Jesse…Jesse! Don't you hear me calling you?"

Jesse quickly turned to see his mother holding the suit he had been looking for. He smiled and said, "That's it, that's the one! Do you think it will fit?"

His mother smiled. "It's your size." As she ushered him to the changing room to try the suit on, she said, "One of these days, you're going to come off that high horse of yours."

After seeing that the suit fit perfectly, his mother purchased a pair of black buckled shoes, a tie, and a shirt of Jesse's choosing. They departed the store, Jesse holding his suit, and his mother clearly relieved that the search for the infamous suit was over.

On Easter Sunday morning, Grace sat in church in the front pew with her children, all in their Sunday best. As usual, the church was filled on this Sunday with standing room only. Jesse looked around eagerly at everyone, proud to have his suit on.

The choir sang several songs, including "Oh, Happy Day," and soon afterward, the pastor began his sermon. On this day, there was quietness in the church that seemed out of the ordinary. Time went by quickly, and before Jesse realized it, the sermon was over, and everyone was filing out of the aisles to exit at the rear of the church.

The following weekend, when it was nearing dark, Jesse walked home along Plymouth Avenue after playing football with several neighborhood boys. A white Eldorado sped around the corner and slammed on the brakes, coming to a screeching halt in front of him as he stood on the sidewalk. The back door swung open, and a middle-aged woman's hand reached out as she attempted to step out of the vehicle. Laughter came from the driver and front passenger, who both held a can of beer. As the woman struggled to leave the vehicle, Jesse noticed her battered face and torn dress. She seemed to be desperately trying to fight off the man who also occupied the back seat. As the man reached for her and yanked her back into the car, Jesse caught a glimpse of his face. He looked familiar.

Suddenly, Jesse recognized him as the man called Brother Benson who had been baptized years ago in the church. Briefly, their eyes met as the door slammed shut, and the car spun off, screeching down the avenue. In the back window of the car sat a small brown dog toy with a head bobbing up and down. Jesse stood watching until the vehicle disappeared from sight, feeling helpless to do anything.

Monday evening, news had spread around the neighborhood that there had been a horrible accident on the Plymouth Avenue bridge. People said the car had been speeding along Plymouth Avenue just after midnight and spun out of control. It struck the bridge and caught ablaze. Fortunately, the fire department had arrived, saving three people, who were now in critical condition. There had also been a fourth person trapped in the vehicle. Paramedics and firemen had been unable to save him in time. The person was later identified as Chad Benson.

Say to them, "'As surely as I live,' declares the Sovereign Lord, 'I take no pleasure in the death of the wicked, but rather that they turn from their ways and live.'"
—Ezekiel 33:11

The following day, around mid-afternoon, Jesse and his little sister, Crystal, arrived home early from school. He stood in the backyard for a short period, tossing the football to Crystal, who was now five years old. He was getting her acquainted with the game and building her confidence.

"You're supposed to catch the ball!" he yelled, teasing her. They stood only ten feet apart.

"You're throwing it too hard!" Crystal snapped back.

"All right, here, catch this one."

He made the next toss.

"UMMPHH!" The sound escaped Crystal's mouth as the football bounced off her tummy and landed in her cradled arms.

"I caught it! I caught it!" she screamed with excitement. Jesse joined in the celebration. This continued until they were called inside for lunch.

They sat at the kitchen table, eating their lunch that Caesar had prepared. Lunch consisted of tomato soup, crackers, peanut butter and jelly sandwiches, and a cold glass of milk. Shortly after finishing their lunch, Jesse and Crystal danced to the music over the radio, while strumming on broomsticks as make-believe guitars and microphones. The singing and laughter continued for some time until that became tiresome. They sat at the kitchen table, where Jesse continued being a playful nuisance.

During their bickering back and forth, one of the toys fell on the floor. Crystal wanted Jesse to pick up the toy, but he refused, while laughing and teasing her. Crystal protested even louder, but Jesse would not budge. Instead, he sat there smiling.

Swiveling in his chair, he looked up, and there stood Caesar.

"Didn't you hear me tell you to leave her alone?" Caesar barked.

Before Jesse had a chance to respond, he felt several thundering blows to his face and head. The attack ended as quickly as it had started. Jesse found himself sprawled on the floor next to an upturned chair. He struggled to get to his feet as the room spun. His legs buckled beneath him as he stumbled to his bedroom. There he sat with eyes puffy and his vision blurred with tears. The humiliation hurt more than the pain itself.

Pain replaced with hurt
Hurt replaced with grief
Grief replaced with anger
Anger replaced with hate
Hate replaced with distance

In class the next day, the teacher held up an album cover and expressed how remarkable it was. After a brief description of the artists Simon and Garfunkel, he played the song "Bridge Over Troubled Waters."

In another class, Jesse and his classmates were introduced to a film titled *The Red Balloon* by Albert Lamorisse. The story was about a lonely boy whose only friend was a red balloon. The boy and the balloon were inseparable. Eventually, neighborhood boys became envious, trapped the balloon, and crushed it, destroying the boy's joy and hope. Suddenly, balloons came from everywhere to the little boy. As the balloons gathered together and surrounded him, he held on to the strings as they lifted him into the sky.

When the film had finished and the lights were turned on, Jesse noticed a poster on the classroom door with a positive poetic statement. Next to the poem was a black and white photograph that resembled him. After class was dismissed, Jesse walked to the door and read the poem. The poem spoke about being yourself and remaining positive. The author of the poem, called "Motto," was Langston Hughes.

Before going home, Jesse decided to go to the public library. Once there, he leafed through several art books and gradually made his way to the music aisles. He sat in a plastic green chair next to a round table. An album sat on the record player's turntable.

Jesse just sat for a moment and flipped the "on" switch. He then slowly picked up the needle, placing it carefully onto the album to avoid scratching it. He skipped over several of the songs, not allowing them to fully play, until he reached one song that caught his attention. He tried to adjust the huge headphones to fit his head. After a while of struggling, he gave in and just decided to tilt them to prevent the headphones from slipping off. When the song finished, he picked up the needle and played the same song over and over again.

As time passed, he looked toward the receptionist, who was busy writing at her desk and didn't seem to notice him. There was no one else in the area, and Jesse felt at peace. He thought about leaving, but quickly decided to stay. He placed the needle over his now favorite song and listened as though it was his very first time hearing it. There he sat the entire evening playing the same song, "Hey Jude," by the Beatles, until closing.

To Jesse, home wasn't home anymore.

CHAPTER 11

TRANSCEND

IN 1973, JESSE suffered from a severe asthma attack. During the attack, his mother rushed him to the emergency unit at the hospital and practically carried him inside. He was barely able to breathe. Wheezing, he desperately gasped for air. His eyelids were too heavy to keep open as he fought to remain conscious. Jesse's arms and legs went limp. He was too weak to muster the energy to move them.

Once inside, he was immediately attended to by doctors and nurses. They laid him on a gurney on top of a white sheet. He felt someone unlace his sneakers and pull them off. Forcing his eyes open, he squinted against the glaring bright lights. People dressed in white moved about urgently, with concerned expressions on their faces. Their muttered conversations were short and abrupt. Shifting his glance, Jesse saw his mother in the background, hands folded almost as if in prayer, with a look of worry on her face.

He lay motionless as the doctor placed a mask over his mouth and nose to make it easier for him to breathe. At that moment, Jesse began to contemplate death.

Well, you could just fade away, and this would be it—gone, Jesse thought. He envisioned the funeral at the church. He could see himself lying perfectly still in the casket while everyone walked by, mourning, just like in the movies. He saw himself floating about the church near the ceiling like a ghost, observing everyone. Then he had second thoughts. Thinking in more depth, he figured in time he would be forgotten. Sure, they would be sad for a moment. Then what? The more he pondered the idea of death, the more he felt it wasn't a good choice.

Just imagine all the girls and friends I would never have a chance to meet, and all the fun I would miss out on, he thought.

Jesse was convinced that it would be best not to die, but to live.

With his mind made up not to fade away, he slowly opened his eyes. He felt relaxation come over his body as he breathed more easily. When his eyes fully opened, he saw his mother standing there with his sneakers in her hand.

After the hospital experience, Jesse's views on life began to form, although he had just as many unanswered questions. He believed in one God, and that was unwavering. He also had faith in Jesus Christ, even though he didn't know exactly who Jesus was or his purpose. He wondered why there were so many religions with their own separate rules. He felt religions were used to control masses of people. He believed people were making God into what they wanted him to be.

He had stopped attending church years earlier. He had always believed there was only one truth. The question remained, *What is the truth?* Jesse knew he had been placed on the earth for a reason, which he was driven to find out. *Who am I?* he wondered. That question haunted him day and night, month after month, and year after year.

Tall for his age and skinny, Jesse joined the football team in his freshman year. His head was so large that they couldn't find a helmet to fit; he had to settle for the older model. With his square helmet, oversized shoulder pads, and sagging uniform, Jesse didn't look like much, but what they couldn't measure was his heart and determination.

Jesse didn't win a starting position, since there were far better quarterbacks, but that didn't deter him from putting forth effort. In practice, he would yell out the signals in his high-pitched, squeaky voice, for which he was teased constantly. In the second year, he switched his position to defensive and offensive end, with the results being the same. He sat on the bench.

One Saturday morning, Jesse rose earlier than normal, jubilant and with anticipation. His football team had a game scheduled for that afternoon. At six A.M., Jesse looked outside his bedroom window. It was still dark. After making his bed and attempting to be extremely quiet and not wake Eric, he laid out his uniform across his bed in a meticulous fashion. His socks seemed as though they had been pressed, along with his white T-shirt. Next were the pants, knee pads, shoulder pads, cleats, helmet, and finally his jersey. He wore number ninety. He felt it was an unusual number and was proud to wear it. He laid his jersey across the bed carefully, not allowing it to be wrinkled in any way.

By eight A.M., the sun was up, and daylight had arrived. He thought about breakfast, but he was too excited to eat. So, he sat on the bed going over in his mind the plays and his football assignments. He stared into blank space, allowing his imagination to run wild. He saw himself perform spectacularly on the field as the crowd roared.

"Maybe I'll get a chance to play this time," he whispered as he closed his eyes, folded his hands, and prayed.

Nine o'clock arrived. *Still too early to leave*, he thought. He needed something to do to calm his nervousness. He picked up an album by one of his favorite bands, Sly and the Family Stone. He quietly placed the album on the record player and placed the needle over the song, "I Want To Take You Higher." The nervousness left him, and he immediately found himself dancing to the funky music while pretending to play the bass. While sitting on the edge of his bed, he continued listening to Sly Stone with his head down, eyes closed, and feet tapping to the rhythms, seemingly lost in his own world.

After a few moments, he felt tension in the air and a presence above him. Looking up, he saw Eric towering above him.

"I told you to turn that noise down," Eric growled.

Jesse stood up to face his brother. At seventeen, Eric was now taller and bigger than Jesse, with an intimidating presence.

"The music isn't loud," Jesse said.

"I didn't ask you that." Eric punched Jesse in his eye and stomach and shoved him back onto the bed. Jesse hadn't anticipated the attack. He lay sprawled across the bed, wincing in pain and gasping for air. Eric slammed his fist on the record player, causing the needle to streak across the vinyl. He then calmly walked back to his bed, lay down, and fell back to sleep.

Jesse maneuvered his way to the edge of his bed, bent over in a cramped position, waiting for the pain to subside. As the pain faded, he felt his eye swelling shut. He thought about retaliating, but what chance did he have? Now tears of embarrassment formed in his eyes. He gathered his equipment, which had been scattered on the bed and floor, and left the room for his game.

To his surprise, while preparing for the game in the locker room, no one asked anything about his swollen eye. He appreciated that his high school teammates seemed not to notice.

During the home game, Jesse stood on the sideline as usual, watching his teammates play. The coach approached him to send in a play in the fourth quarter with minutes left. They were on the twenty-yard line from the end zone in need of a touchdown. Jesse was surprised that the coach would send him in as an offensive end with a play. The coach looked at him with anticipation and excitement in his eyes, so in he ran toward the huddle.

"Slot right, I right, twenty-four dive, pitch eighteen on one," Jesse yelled to the quarterback nervously, while fastening his chin strap and placing his mouthpiece in his mouth. It was a play they had practiced throughout the week especially for this situation. The quarterback repeated the play twice in the huddle, and everyone yelled, "Break!" and clapped their hands once in unison. Then everyone sprinted toward the line of scrimmage.

Jesse was lined as the offensive end in the slot right position, and the play was a wide pitch to the running back coming his way. His job was to block the defensive back as the running back would attempt to run around the corner and into the end zone to score. When the offense was set on the line of scrimmage, the quarterback began barking the signals. Jesse remained in his three point stance, knees bent, back straight, and staring straight ahead, not wanting to give away the play.

"Reeeady!... Down!... Hut one!"

With the ball snapped, everyone went into motion to complete their assignments. Pads clashed and footsteps pounded the ground. Jesse came up from his stance, running a wide, circular angle toward his right as the pitch was made to the running back. Jesse could hear and feel the running back coming around his end; at the same time, a defensive back was running toward him to make the tackle. The only thing between the defensive back and the running back was Jesse. If his teammate was going to score, he would have to make the only block to spring him.

Jesse and the defensive back sprinted toward each other at full speed, both determined. Heads down, shoulders squared, feet pumping underneath them, they ran head-on into each other like two battering rams.

BLAM!

Upon contact, Jesse saw black as he fell backwards onto the grass. Everything became still and quiet for a brief moment. Then screams and yells of jubilation erupted from the fans and players. Jesse's final block had cleared the path for the running back to dash down the sideline for the winning touchdown. Meanwhile, Jesse and the defensive back lay sprawled and dazed on the field.

Throughout his high school years playing football, he never sat the bench again, and he adopted the nickname "Pain" as a defensive end.

Jesse began lifting weights, determined to turn his skinny frame into muscle. Eventually he made a significant change in his build. While strengthening his body, he also discovered he was less prone to asthma attacks, which encouraged him to lift weights even more.

In 1976, dramatic changes developed within Jesse's family. He was now a junior in high school. Leah had begun her career in accounting and was raising a family, while Eric had purchased a home and begun work as a machinist. Jesse also had taken more of the big brother role to Crystal, who was now twelve years old. He took pride in introducing her to music and sports, while maintaining a watchful eye over her.

During the month of January 1977, Jesse stood in the family's living room, anticipating the long-awaited twelve-hour miniseries *Roots*. He wanted to view what blacks had endured through slavery, which he felt the school systems had ignored.

"Why are you blocking the television?" Jesse heard behind him.

He turned to see Eric's angry eyes. They now stood facing each other.

"I was—"

POW! Eric unleashed a slap across Jesse's face. Jesse stood stunned as the sound echoed through his head. Eric returned to his seat at the kitchen table to finish his home-cooked meal that their mother had prepared. The anger boiled inside Jesse as he watched Eric calmly eating his food and reading the newspaper as though nothing had transpired between them.

Moments later, Jesse tapped Eric on his left shoulder. As he looked up, Jesse returned the favor with a slap across his face. *POW!*

Eric's eyes widened with shock, and before he could respond, *CRACK!* Jesse had struck him across the forehead with a broom handle. After overcoming his shock, Eric lunged forward from his chair toward Jesse like a ferocious lion attacking its prey. Jesse backpedaled while throwing a combination of hooks, jabs, and uppercuts, as Eric desperately tried to grab hold of him. They stumbled back into the living room, knocking over pictures, lamps, and furniture. Eric barreled into Jesse, slamming into him and pinning him against the wall. Jesse placed him in a one-arm headlock and continued throwing blows with the other fist.

"Stop!" Crystal screamed. "Stop! Stop!"

Their mother stepped into the room to see what was happening, and everyone froze.

"What is going on here?" she yelled. Before anyone could respond, she continued, "Both of you are brothers. Why are you fighting?"

Neither Eric nor Jesse said a word, out of respect for their mother.

Then Crystal spoke. "Mommy, when I walked in, they were beating up on each other. I tried to stop them, but they wouldn't."

Grace thanked Crystal and told her to go back to her room. Crystal was happy that order had been restored and hesitantly retreated to her bedroom. Then Grace continued, "Why don't the two of you start acting like brothers? It saddens me to continuously see strife between you. Straighten this room up, and once and for all, please stop arguing and fighting with each other."

She led Eric into the kitchen area to place an ice pack on the knot that protruded from his forehead. Jesse had turned off the television and began putting everything back in order. After the fight, he had lost interest in watching the movie series. He was proud that he had stood up against his brother. It was the last time they ever fought, even though constant tension remained between them.

Jesse had been given a homework assignment by his eleventh grade art instructor to draw his portrait. He thought the assignment would be a simple one to accomplish. As he sat in front of a large mirror attempting to draw himself, he found it an intriguing and difficult challenge. He sat there for at least fifteen minutes with a large sheet of paper on a desk in front of him with pencil in hand, staring. The more he stared, the more his mind wandered. The more his mind wandered, the more questions he had. Leaning forward, he gazed into his own eyes. For that moment, Jesse attempted to press beyond the visual; he wanted to go to the core. By penetrating his pupils, he tried to discover the essence of his being.

Then he stopped. For a brief moment, it became too frightening. He placed the pencil down and walked away.

While attending high school, Jesse drew whenever possible. It was common for him to be drawing at the kitchen table after school from five P.M. until three A.M. while listening to the music on the radio. From three A.M. until six A.M., he would nap, and then walk one hour to school. He avoided the bus when possible. Jesse didn't like crowds, and walking allowed him time alone, when he could think.

One night while drawing and listening to the radio, he heard a song that demanded his attention. The song was "Cat's in the Cradle" by Harry Chapin. It was about a father who had ignored his son's request to spend time with him. The father was too busy, and would promise his son there would be time later, but later never came. As the years passed, his son married and raised a family of his own. The father had grown old and looked to spend time with his son, but now his son didn't have any time for him. At the end of the song, the father regretted that his son had grown up to be just like him.

After the song finished playing, Jesse changed the radio station and came across another song by the Commodores, titled, "This Is Your Life." The song spoke of following one's dreams. Jesse listened intently as it spoke about life's struggles. The message was to be strong and follow your destiny.

He sat quietly pondering the songs. At three A.M., he lay his head down for a nap, then arose at six A.M. and began his long walk to school.

In the spring, Jesse was stunned when his mother told him that Dean Armstrong, the tall boy who had given Jesse his basketball, had been killed. As Jesse roamed the neighborhood in search for answers, witnesses recalled that Dean had been playing basketball across town. An argument had ensued after he was constantly fouled throughout the game. One of the players from the opposite team left and returned moments later with a pistol. The player shot Dean several times and drove away, leaving him dying on the asphalt while others tried desperately to revive him. Eventually, the person was apprehended, but nothing could replace the life of someone so dearly loved throughout the community.

On Sunday, Jesse sat in the last row of pews at Dean's funeral. Hundreds had arrived, leaving many outside. The inside of the church was filled with insurmountable sadness. He watched Dean's mother scream in anguish as the pallbearers removed the casket from the church. Because of his shock and numbness, Jesse hadn't heard the pastor's eulogy. He departed early because Dean's death was just too unbearable for him. Jesse hadn't viewed the body in the casket, because he wanted to remember Dean the way he was and not in death.

Later in the afternoon, as Jesse walked through the neighborhood, he noticed statements sprayed on storefronts, sidewalks, and abandoned buildings throughout the neighborhood. The words read, *Long live Dean Armstrong.*

In 1978, his last year in high school, Jesse felt alone and distant. Although he had gained popularity through his art, and playing football, he never felt like he belonged. Jesse watched as girls with eyes of promise, hopes, and dreams fell prey to adult men waiting in their cars for them after school. He saw fellow students succumb to peer pressure, drugs, and alcohol. He also saw teachers with no concern about educating; they were there merely to collect a paycheck. Other teachers involved themselves with inappropriate relationships with students.

When graduation arrived, he was glad it was over; he had no regrets. He had never attended a Junior Prom or a Senior Ball, never purchased a senior ring, and hadn't attended a school assembly where he was to be honored with a National Graphic Design Achievement Award. When it came time for senior pictures for the yearbook, he simply drew his picture rather than taking and submitting a photograph.

He was once told by a teacher that he would be best skilled for a job in housekeeping, and another that he would be a total failure. The comments reminded him of how his brother mocked him and told him he would never accomplish anything. Jesse's stepfather often remarked that he was "lazy and good for nothing." Jesse ignored all the comments and statements, because he knew there was a purpose for his life.

Maybe the comments came because he was different, an artist. They say people fear what they can't control or understand. Jesse was a dreamer and he had visions, and in his mind it was a matter of moving on and not looking back.

CHAPTER 12

BEYOND
THE UNKNOWN

HEY, BOY! COME here, boy!" Jesse heard behind him as he walked between cars in a large parking lot. The shouts became louder as the footsteps drew closer. Jesse ignored the demands on his attention, maintaining his direction and keeping his eyes forward.

"Hey, you! Stop!"

Jesse stood still with a disturbed feeling. Turning, he saw two police officers running toward him, out of breath.

"Where are you coming from, and where are you going?" the older one demanded.

"Why?" Jesse replied.

The police officer looked startled by his response, as the younger police officer eagerly looked on.

"Well, what's in the bag?" the officer snapped.

Jesse had a leather bag strapped over his shoulder, which he always carried with him. He faced the older officer directly in front of him, while the younger officer stood behind with his hand gripping the brown, worn leather bag. Jesse now turned slightly, positioning himself to make eye contact with the younger officer. He stared at both officers without a response.

"Would you mind if we take a look inside your bag, boy?" the older officer growled.

"Why?" Jesse repeated. Still, he received no answer from the officers. Jesse's face tightened as he tried to maintain his composure. At that moment, the younger officer unzipped his bag. His face displayed a look of disappointment as he discovered only books.

"Why did you give us such a hard time?" the angered older officer demanded.

"Why did you call me 'boy'?" Jesse replied.

"How old are you?"

"Nineteen."

"Well, well…You just made it," the officer replied with a smirk, while the younger officer displayed a gallant smile. Jesse clenched his teeth as he stared into the officer's eyes. He hesitated a moment, zipped his bag, and walked away.

In September of 1978, Jesse was now in his first year of college. He had grown to be six feet and two inches tall and weighed approximately 175 pounds. He wore a mild Afro, while his clothing consisted of jeans, sneakers, collared shirts, and thin, colorful ties, usually psychedelic. It wasn't out of the ordinary for him to wear a tie with a T-shirt. He simply dressed as he felt, which at the time didn't go along with the norm.

Jesse was a rebel, a radical, and defiant in his own quiet way. He would not allow himself to be defined by society or the system. It seemed whatever direction others were going, he went the opposite. At times he even questioned himself, but he was driven from within. The word "compromise" was not in his dictionary. He was a renegade gone wild, but in control of himself. He wanted to choose the path no one else dared. To him, there was no safety net; life was meant to be lived to the extreme. He valued life and everything it had to offer. To him no day was guaranteed, and he would not allow anyone to place chains on him. To be told he couldn't accomplish something only made him try harder. The production line life was not for him; there had to be something else out there. His mind was set on its wild, unwavering path to freedom.

Oddly, in contradiction, he was also shy, introverted, and lacked confidence at times. With all that said, anyone who knew or met him found that he never lacked vision or dreams. He was an unbridled soul who refused to be broken by the hardness of the world.

Jesse was enrolled in a community college that did not offer an Associate Degree in art, which left him at odds. He was like a fish taken from a pond and cast out at sea. The environment was unfamiliar to him, and he was not prepared. No matter how hard he tried, he felt like he was destined for failure. In this college, art was not recognized as a career choice. Students enrolled in majors such as engineering, criminal justice, business, and dentistry. Art was taken as an elective and considered by some to be a waste of time. To put it simply, art was seen as a hobby and surely not a way to make a living.

Jesse's high school art instructor had suggested to his parents that he enroll in this college and register in the audio-visual technology program, in which he had no interest. Jesse had been accepted into a four-year school, which had been his dream, only to learn he didn't have the finances. While in high school, scholarships were given to students with the best portfolios. Jesse had worked extremely hard throughout the year preparing his portfolio in hopes of winning a scholarship. When word arrived that he had not won one of the scholarships, but a nationwide award for design, he was sadly disappointed. The door had closed shut. It disturbed him for a great period of time that he had not won a scholarship, while one of his classmates had. It was later brought to his attention by one of the judges that he had missed receiving a scholarship, as they say, "by a hair." After further discussion, Jesse learned a few art pieces had not been submitted with his portfolio, and if they had been, he would have won a scholarship. Upon hearing this, he was devastated.

Jesse sat in the back row of his first day in psychology class in an attempt to make the best of his situation. The professor had each student announce his or her name and major around the class. After each statement, the professor would make a positive comment.

"Next," the professor said while looking at Jesse from the head of the class.

"Jesse Battle, liberal arts," he answered. The professor hesitated and then continued with the next student. Jesse was embarrassed because he felt other students saw him as someone who did not know what he wanted to do with his life. But for the moment, it was the only program he could be placed in. He had chosen a psychology class because he wanted to understand how the mind worked and what motivated people to do what they did. Philosophy also seemed to hold his attention. He had more interest in the abstract than in science. He wanted to understand the basis of human thinking, which was undefined and immeasurable.

Jesse eventually transferred to the four-year college that he had initially wanted to enroll in at the beginning of his college years. The school seemed cold and distant. He didn't have any friends among his classmates. Jesse did connect with one student in his art design class. She had a vibrancy about her and greeted him with a cheerful "hello." Jesse also connected with his art design professor, Anne Clarke. She often made lighthearted, humorous statements during class. The statements seemed to come across as hilarious only to Jesse. He would find himself laughing hysterically at a brief comment the professor had made, while everyone else remained silent, not quite getting the joke. Professor Clarke would give a hint of a smile and then continue the lecture.

During this class, Professor Clarke showed slides of historic artists and their contributions to society. Many of the works depicted religious themes as though the artists themselves had received revelations from God. Jesse sat and wondered what he could possibly contribute. These artists were obviously masters at their work. He knew he didn't compare and never would. He was only attempting to be the best that he could. Other artists, professors, and students inspired him to achieve excellence in his art. Jesse felt overwhelmed by these works and their themes; he began to question himself as an artist.

Late one evening, Jesse sat in the artists' painter's studio section of the building, admiring one artist's work propped against the wall, which was a work in progress. The piece depicted a band performing in a club in front of an audience. The painting had a strong sense of energy and seemed to come alive. It stood seven feet tall and six feet wide. Jesse stood staring at the painting for a period of time, awestruck. The paintbrush strokes themselves mesmerized him.

"Hello, Jesse!"

Surprised, Jesse turned and saw Professor Clarke. She was a petite woman with short brown hair, whose dark eyes exhibited joy and excitement. She seemed to possess boundless energy.

"Hello, Ms. Clarke."

"It's a delight to have you in my class," she said with a smile.

"Thank you!"

"How are your other classes coming?"

"I'm doing fairly well, even though it's frustrating following a system set up for freshman students and not being able to select the art classes of my choosing."

"Are you alone? I mean, is there anyone giving you support?"

Jesse hesitated for a moment, thinking of the assignments he would hand in late because he didn't have the money for supplies. "Nope."

She leaned back and, clearly seeing the discouragement on his face, said, "You make sure you hang in there."

Jesse was pleased at hearing the words of encouragement; it had been such a long and difficult journey. "It doesn't seem as though they're teaching fine arts here. Everything is pushed toward graphics and the computer."

"What you're saying is true. A great deal of the art department is geared toward graphics and corporate designs. You must continue drawing and painting or you'll lose your true calling in life, and become like everyone else, geared toward money."

Jesse stood without making a comment. He was glad she had spoken the truth.

"Hang in there! I'll see you after the holiday break," Professor Clarke said while heading on her way.

After a two-week recess, classes resumed. As Jesse sat in class, he noticed that someone was missing: the girl with the bright smile and cheerful hello. After the second week of class, she still was not present. Immediately after class, Jesse spoke with Professor Clarke and gave a brief description of the girl because he didn't know her name. He expressed concern for her whereabouts.

Professor Clarke paused for moment as she looked at Jesse. "Catherine Kline was her name," she explained solemnly. "She was badly beaten and raped by a group of male students while jogging early one morning. The school wanted to keep it quiet. That's why it wasn't publicized."

Jesse continued sitting at his desk, now in a solemn mood.

Weeks later, Jesse attended his Creative Art class. Professor Harman drew a circle on the chalkboard, and within the wide circle, he placed a dot. He said that most of society was in the center, where that dot was, meaning they played it safe. He then placed a second dot closer to the circle's inside edge and said that very few people in society would dare walk closer to the edge and take chances. After expounding on that a great deal, he placed a dot on the circle's edge and said that true artists walk the line of challenge and chance. Immediately, without hesitation, he marked a dot far outside the circle, stating that even fewer had the courage to step out into the beyond and unknown.

He gave a class assignment that was due the following week. The assignment was to complete an illustration that would depict the type of work they would be doing twenty years into the future. After that, class was dismissed.

Jesse thought a great deal about the project to be completed by the next class. This assignment he could complete on time, knowing his supplies would be limited. Ideas flowed through his mind for several days of what he wanted to say and how to say it. After several thumbnail sketches and rough renderings, he finally decided on how to complete the work. One day before the class assignment was due, he worked into the wee hours of the morning until he was satisfied with the work. The only step left was a written statement to represent the drawing and deliver its best impact. A thought came to him, and he scribbled it down on a scrap piece of paper before it was lost. After reading over it several times and adjusting it, he considered it a profound statement for his drawing.

The only thing left was to mount the statement to the illustration and prepare for class.

Jesse sat near the back in the last row and watched nervously as other students presented their projects. A buzz of curiosity and excitement passed through the room after each project was presented. The professor and fellow students critiqued the work after the students gave their presentations. Everyone was impressed by each student's presentation. Then came Jesse's turn. When the professor called his name, he stood, feeling a bit uneasy. He removed a sheet of overlay from his work, displaying his illustration. In the foreground stood a half-man, half-machine, with an unplugged cord extending from him. The man himself looked robotic. In the background stood a scientist with oval glasses, hands folded, and sadness on his face, eyeing his invention. As Jesse began reading his statement, the room fell silent.

Professor of Science

He knew all the answers
Logic he invented the word
Reason, of course, reason for everything –
JUSTIFICATION

Man and technology
One and the same, they say
Until the moment of Truth
Man on the road to destruction

The System
He thought he was doing for the good
Of the people, Information Super Highway
Until his time arrived
Total replacement
Machine; XL 2179

After he read his statement, no one made a sound.

Hours later, Jesse left the library and was walking along the campus grounds when he saw Professor Harman approaching in his direction. Jesse froze.

"Did you mean what you wrote and read in class?" Professor Harman asked.

Jesse nodded. "Yes."

"Well, that's why we need persons in higher positions of authority to make a difference." After giving a brief nod of approval, Professor Harman continued on his way.

When Jesse arrived home that evening, he overheard a discussion between his mother and Caesar. The negative comments continued about him, but fell in favor of Eric. Rushing inside past them, he said tearfully, "I'll be moving out in a few days."

His mother attempted to stop him, laying a hand on his arm. "Jesse, you know how much I love you."

But Jesse felt so much pain, rejection, and scorn that he knew there was no other choice but to leave.

CHAPTER 13

SOLITUDE

BROKEN. THAT WAS where Jesse was at this stage in his life. Like a defeated fighter, he couldn't respond to the bell from his corner. It was a technical knockout, TKO.

Jesse moved into a small, institutional green room, which turned into an icebox at night because of the lack of heat. The old, rusted radiator was missing its knob, the paint on the walls was peeling, and the large, dirty windows, which previously had been painted shut, were now covered with dark blankets to prevent sunlight from entering. He lay on the cold linoleum floor, bare light bulb overhead, with thoughts of the past continuously racing through his mind. The place in which he now lived was like an insane asylum, missing only the padded walls and straitjacket.

He had rented this room from the manager of the office building. The six-story building in the downtown area was not residential, but he lived there. At night, no one else was around. The corridors were dark. The only sounds he heard were in his head. It was just the way he liked it, quiet, with everyone shut out. He had never imagined being in this position, but in the back of his mind he had always known it was possible.

Jesse had been suspended from college. He had known it would only be a matter of time, because he had given up. The negative remarks, especially from those closest to him, had begun to take effect. The detachment from friends, community, and his personal life had taken its toll on him. Merely trying to survive in life was enough for one person. He was dealing with many difficulties coming from all directions.

He had been told enough times that the art field was a difficult road to travel. He had been labeled and doomed even before he tried. He hadn't chosen art; art had chosen him. He was driven by visions, inspired messages, and statements to be relayed through his art. He had a choice: follow what he was compelled to do in life, or go mad. It was a combination of sorts that had sent everything crashing down on him, leaving him lying on the floor in a frigid room, dismantled.

Jesse sat up as cold air shot through the cracks of the window frame. He glanced around the room. It did look depressing, but that was how he felt—depressed, angry, and frustrated.

It was April of 1983. Outside his windows, the gray, overcast skies added to the dreariness of the day.

Jesse finally stood in this empty room. His mind roamed, mercifully lost in a dense fog. He wore badly wrinkled clothing due to often sleeping in them in order to keep warm. Hungry, he noticed a can of Campbell's chicken noodle soup on the floor in the corner. He had one small metal pot and hot plate, which he turned on. In eager anticipation of something to eat despite his lack of money, he realized he did not have a can opener or utensils. He searched frantically around the room and through boxes until he came across a screwdriver. He pounded the metal edge into the tin until it gave way. Laughing to himself, he wondered how everyone would view him now, knowing he had failed and been reduced to nothing. That thought crossed his mind for a moment before he slowly drank down the warm soup and went back to sleep.

Several months passed, while Jesse's state remained the same. He awakened one evening after a long nap in his room of despair, eyes blinking as they searched the high ceiling. He later found himself staring at a lonely wall clock and the hands that didn't seem to move. It was as if time had ceased, and silence entered when there was nothing with which to occupy oneself. Jesse fully understood then why one of man's greatest fears was to be alone. The silence itself could drive a person mad, being tortured by one's own recurring thoughts.

He sat still for hours in the corner of the dimly lit room. As the night grew still, the room began to darken, and the building became hauntingly quiet. As time passed, voices inside his mind began to taunt him as they often did.

"You'll never be anything."

"You're not good enough."

"You're slow."

The numerous wrenching comments from the past overtook his mind, repeating over and over like a broken record. Jesse moved further and deeper into despair, now trapped by the darkness that surrounded him. His body became rigid as he brought his knees to his chest, placing his hands on the floor. His jaw tightened as tension grew on his face. Flashbacks of abuse began to accompany the words of torment, causing him even more sorrow.

The scars were deep, and now, in yet another night of agony, they came to the surface. He felt like screaming, but for what? Who would care? No one. He was slowly becoming a prisoner within his own mind, and anger began taking over. His body tensed, and tears flooded his eyes as his mouth quivered uncontrollably. Glancing around, he focused on the wooden door across the room, as though he were expecting someone to enter and relieve him of his unbearable loneliness. Contemplating his past life experiences brought on even more resentment. Deeper and deeper his thoughts spiraled down.

By midnight, the room had become black, but Jesse's soul-searching continued. He was now slumped in the corner, withdrawn from the world. Everything seemed to be crashing down around him. He had lost all sense of direction and vision. He was a failure, falling through the dense, dark clouds of despondency. He felt as though his heart had been ripped from his chest, leaving him an empty shell, emotionally detached and lost in obscurity. Out of hopelessness, three words escaped his lips and penetrated the darkness of the room.

"Leave me alone."

After collapsing into a deep sleep, he awoke at two A.M. To Jesse, the nights always seemed longer, even though there was no relief from the pain in the daytime. *If only I had a father for guidance*, he thought. Instead, he found himself suffocating in a neighborhood and community of negativity, manipulation, and destruction. He had been told that if he worked hard enough, he could achieve anything; the sky was the limit. But after an avalanche of events had come tumbling down on him, he finally realized that was not true. *Lies*, he thought *all lies.*

Now more tears began to fall as his eyes searched desperately around the nearly vacant room. Jesse's drawing table sat against the wall. Maybe he had placed it there to instill hope, but he had no desire or ambition to draw anything. Also against the wall near the door was a record player. He stared intently at it for a moment before crawling toward it.

While sorting through his small collection of albums, he removed one from its sleeve: *Hello I Must Be Going*, by Phil Collins. He held it and looked closely at the black vinyl as though it were a newfound friend. He needed something, anything, to escape his tormenting inner thoughts.

Jesse placed the album on the record player. The song "I Don't Care Anymore" began to play with a dramatic drum roll, which matched his anger as he listened carefully to the words. Standing in the middle of the room facing the window, Jesse imitated the voice and sang along. After removing the blanket from the large windows, Jesse stared without blinking into the night as his singing transformed into screams of anguish.

Once the song finished, he hesitantly placed the needle back at the beginning of the song, still deep in thought. He played the song over and over. The heavy drum beats and Jesse's screaming voice likely echoed along the empty corridors and down the stairwells.

As the night continued, his words became louder and louder.

"I don't care anymore!"

"I don't care anymore!"

This continued night after night, week after week, month after month. He played various artists with similar songs, and the message was always the same.

Early one morning, after lying still for hours, Jesse eventually crawled toward the window. He was tired of his state of despair and wanted out. He decided not to allow darkness to engulf him any further. Slowly, he lifted the blanket from the window, allowing the blinding sunlight to rush through as he squinted his eyes.

It's a beautiful day, he thought as his face gave way to a brief smile. For some odd reason, he felt that from that day forward he would have better days. In his mind, he decided to erase the past and start from zero. He would focus on moving forward, not allowing negativity, regret, or doubt to enter his thoughts. He had come to realize the battlefield within his mind would destroy him only if he chose to engage in mental warfare. So he stepped away from the train wreck and continued on with his journey. Jesse knew there was something that had to be accomplished, and that time was essential. Exactly what had to be done was still a mystery.

Late that night, Jesse walked along the back alleys downtown in search of a pizza parlor. He quickly found himself among the homeless, the derelict, and the lost. Heavy drops of rain began to fall, and by the time he reached his destination, he was drenched. But he didn't care.

The place was empty except for the cashier, which was exactly the way he preferred it. He approached the counter, ordered a slice of pizza, and sat down, staring at his reflection in the window as cars drove by. Moments later, the cashier walked around the counter and deposited a coin in the jukebox. Jesse quickly turned his head toward the jukebox as the music demanded his attention.

The song was "Baker Street" by Gerry Rafferty. Jesse focused totally on the jukebox while listening closely to the lyrics. He remembered the song from his past.

When the song stopped playing, he sat for a moment. The cashier had disappeared into a back room. Standing, Jesse began slow, calculated steps toward the jukebox. He placed a coin in the slot, pressed the buttons for his selection, and listened to the song play again. Turning, he glanced around the parlor, walked over to the window, and sat back down. He remained there until closing, dreaming.

CHAPTER 14

BLUE SKY

AT AGE TWENTY-SIX, Jesse had an athletic, muscular build at 6'3" and 215 pounds. His hair was cut to a low Afro, and he wore no facial hair. He looked remarkably younger than his actual age. When he walked, his body movements were slow and measured. His face was usually the same, expressionless. He was a quiet, subdued person who never spoke or acknowledged others. He often stared into space while preoccupied with his own thoughts. But once in a while, he let go with booming laughter and a flashing smile. When others witnessed it, they commented that he should smile and laugh more often. He knew many saw him as aloof, enigmatic, and eccentric, a man of few words. He was, as one would say, straightforward.

There was one other peculiar thing about him. He would sing at any given time. The songs were sung out of key with no effort to duplicate the songs correctly. He never came close; in fact, some of the words he sang were not part of the actual lyrics, and whatever he didn't make up, he hummed or mumbled. Strangely, most of the songs he chose to sing had never been heard by anyone else in his company. He could see others staring with quizzical expressions on their faces, yet he continued as though totally oblivious to his surroundings. Although Jesse appeared aloof, he was very aware of how others perceived him. He simply was not concerned about it.

From 1982 to 1984, Jesse stopped drawing. He wanted nothing to do with art, even though ideas and visions weighed heavy on his mind, clamoring for attention. Times were difficult for him, and he struggled to remain positive. There were days he survived by eating candy bars or potato chips as a full course meal. Eventually, he was able to gain higher income than he had at his previous job, working security at a hotel in the downtown area where he lived. He later occupied a larger space in the same building and was able to afford the rent by working another part-time job and several overtime hours at his full-time position.

On a typical day at work in the security office, a unique person stopped by. He was an employee of an outside electronics company, attempting to repair the security monitors. That particular morning, Jesse had been looking through the yellow pages of the phone book in search of a kung fu school to join.

Earlier in his life, he had been inspired by the television series *Kung Fu*, starring David Carradine. What really intrigued Jesse was the philosophy, wisdom, and life lessons the program presented to the viewer. Another influence in Jesse's life was the 1978 movie *Enter the Dragon* starring Bruce Lee. He had seen the movie with a close friend and was captivated by the fighting scenes. But more amazing to him was Bruce Lee's presence. His energy and spirit left Jesse awestruck.

From a young age, he had always wanted to enroll in kung fu classes. His mother had visited several schools with him, but the classes were too expensive. So now, at this later stage of his life, Jesse felt it was time to fulfill his aspiration to study martial arts. He felt that practicing kung fu would help him remain focused and disciplined, because more often than not, he had a short attention span. At other times, he had found himself short on patience and easily aggravated.

Jesse sat at a desk with his head buried in the telephone book, flipping through the pages. He was completely involved in his search for a school until he heard someone say, "What are you up to?"

Jesse looked up and saw the technician who was adjusting the monitor. Jesse was surprised that the man had spoken to him, due to his apparent preoccupation with the security monitor. Hesitantly, Jesse said, "Well…I'm trying to locate a martial arts school to join."

"Yeah?" the technician continued without turning to face him.

"Yeah."

Finally turning, he studied Jesse. "Well, I'm trained in kung fu, and I do have some experience."

"Yeah?" Jesse replied with a hint of curiosity and excitement in his voice. "Would you be willing to teach me?"

"Well, first you'll be required to go through a testing period for a year. If you survive, I might teach you."

"Are you kidding? Don't worry, I'll survive!" he said with confidence.

The unusual fellow now stood over Jesse, who remained seated. He was of average height, with a lean build and unusually wide shoulders. His dark brown hair was cut short, except for the back, which fell just above his collar. He had a sharp jaw line and intense eyes.

"I never kid about the martial arts, and we'll see if you survive," he said, this time in a flat, monotone voice. "I'll meet you at my place next week." He gave Jesse his address and a time to meet with him, and then departed.

Jesse sat contemplating what had just transpired. He thought he should have said more about accepting his challenge. But for some reason, he had remained quiet. Something made him wonder about this guy. There was definitely something different about him, lurking just under the surface. Nervously, he leaned forward with his elbows on the desk and chin resting on his hands, wondering. He said to himself just above a whisper, "Now what have I gotten myself into?"

The following week, Jesse arrived at the technician's home at the appointed time. As he made his way around the house, he saw the instructor sitting there on the side porch in a meditating position. Jesse waited patiently, not wanting to disturb his newfound instructor.

After a short waiting period, the man invited him to sit down. He sat in front of his instructor and tried to duplicate the position he held, with his legs crossed, back straight, head held as though extended to the sky, and arms resting across each leg. Jesse looked around, not knowing what to think. He did notice a shift from the busy and active city streets to this area he now occupied. It seemed everything had come to a screeching halt.

His instructor introduced himself as Stephan. He looked directly into Jesse's eyes.

Jesse hesitantly introduced himself, and then the questions began.

"So, why is it that you wish to practice kung fu?" Stephan asked.

"I know the martial arts are the study of the mind, body, and spirit," Jesse replied, sounding sure of himself. "But I'm more interested in the spiritual and mental aspects than the physical, even though I know they all are one."

"Well, I've never heard anyone give that response before. Have you ever practiced in the martial arts?"

"No."

"Do you believe in God?"

"Yeah!" Jesse answered emphatically. *But I don't know who God really is.* These words passed through his mind but were never uttered. He sensed Stephan wasn't looking for a discussion or explanation, so he kept his answers concise.

"I'll begin teaching you breathing techniques and meditation. You must follow my exact instructions, because if someone is practicing witchcraft in the area, you may leave yourself open, and demons could possess your body."

Surprised, Jesse stared at Stephan and answered nonchalantly, "OK."

Stephan immediately seemed disturbed. "There are numerous stories of people who were found dead of unnatural causes due to unexplainable reasons."

"OK, I'll follow your instructions," Jesse said quickly after realizing the seriousness of Stephan's statement and hearing the urgency in his voice.

"Good. Well, let's begin with a breathing exercise and body posture."

Stephan demonstrated as Jesse attempted to pay close attention and follow along. Jesse sensed not to ask many questions, and to absorb what was being taught in silence. After fifteen minutes of concentration and focused breathing, he opened his eyes.

This is different, he thought, looking forward at Stephan, whose eyes remained closed. He waited awkwardly and slightly impatiently until Stephan's eyes opened.

"We will meet twice a week at this time," Stephan said. "Every session will begin and end with a formal salute." He paused as though waiting for a response.

Jesse continued sitting still, remaining attentive and quiet even though a thousand thoughts were racing through his mind.

"Well, then, I'll expect you next week," Stephan concluded.

"OK," Jesse muttered, and class was dismissed. As he walked from the side porch toward the city streets, he became more conscious of all the noise and confusion surrounding the house.

Jesse went through unbearable pain the following months as Stephen took him through conditioning exercises. Some of the exercises involved basic techniques, which taught balance, movement, focus, and patience.

Jesse practiced constantly, trying to achieve precision and perfection of the techniques. During most training sessions, Jesse felt excruciating pain in his arms and legs. The burning sensation in his thighs was often so unbearable that his legs quivered uncontrollably. It was during these times he questioned himself. However, once class was over, and his clothes were dripping with sweat, he was elated that he had survived. There were plenty of days he didn't think he would make it through the difficult training sessions. Almost a year of training passed.

One thing Stephan was persistent about was running, which Jesse hated. He hated running with a passion. He never expressed his view toward running, but just decided to take it on as a challenge. Together, he and Stephan ran for miles.

On one of the most hot and humid days in August, Jesse had to complete a run. He was instructed to maintain a faster pace than usual, and Stephan said he would be running ahead of him. He also was told he was being tested.

When the run began, Jesse set a fast pace, with Stephan half a block ahead of him. Jesse couldn't allow himself to fail. In the beginning of the run, the pace seemed extremely fast. His lower back muscles had tightened, and he couldn't seem to control his breathing. After the first mile, he forced himself to concentrate harder.

At the halfway point of the run, Jesse began to have more difficulties. His heart raced out of control, his breathing was erratic, and the muscles in his legs ached as they pounded against the simmering hot pavement. He could see Stephan running ahead at a distance through his half-closed eyes, which stung with perspiration. With each step, his legs felt heavier, as though he were running through quicksand. His head gradually lowered, until he was looking at the sidewalk. His mental strength had collapsed. There had been days when he would make this run, but on this day, he was having difficulty. The one word he didn't want to hear began echoing through his mind: *Quit.*

Sadness formed in his eyes as he saw one of his dreams begin to slip away. He had now slipped from a jog to nearly a walk. The next step would finish him.

Jesse heard a yell. "Hey!"

As he lifted his head, through blurred vision, he saw Stephan running toward him. At this time, he could feel his body barely moving forward, one step from stopping.

"Don't quit now," Stephan said as he began jogging at his side. "You've come too far. Whatever you do, keep putting one foot in front of the other," he added with a tone of encouragement. "Running will help with your breathing technique. Proper breathing is the utmost in any martial art."

Jesse listened, while continually moving with his head still down. As Stephan continued jogging beside him, he spoke of ancient Samurai warriors, Shaolin monks, and the tests they had to endure. He also began speaking about his experiences. It was the first time he spoke a great deal about himself.

While moving slightly faster, Jesse slowly lifted his head, looking forward. Focusing, he gradually recaptured his breathing as he listened to Stephan speak. The energy from Stephan seemed to transfer to him as his pace quickened and his legs found life again.

"You have one gift that stands out among the rest, and that's determination," Stephan said as they both increased the pace. "Your quest is to find out who you are. I can guide you, but that search is for you alone to accomplish." He sprinted forward and yelled back, "I'll see you at the finish line!"

After their run, Stephan escorted Jesse into his backyard, which he had turned into a training ground. Jesse was given a foam vest to put on and was told to fight and defend himself as well as possible. Stephan explained that he would spar on his level.

After several minutes of sparring at a slow pace, Jesse felt Stephan had left an opening in his defense that he could exploit. He quickly took a lunge toward Stephan, and for a split second, Stephan wasn't there—vanished.

Before Jesse could recover his balance... *Wham!* Stephan planted his foot in Jesse's chest, which stopped him cold. With his eyes bulging and arms extended, Jesse heard Stephan's wife scream from the back porch window, where she had been observing them.

"Your problem is your pride," Stephen said flatly to Jesse. "You're also off-balance and overextended."

He began demonstrating how to apply the techniques he had been training. Stephan demonstrated how to use upper and lower blocks, along with the forward punch, and Jesse was told to train on the new basic techniques.

Soon, Jesse was invited into Stephan's home. While inside, Stephan sat rocking back and forth in his chair, exhibiting limitless energy. He held conversations with his wife and playfully tickled his two small daughters, ages seven and five. While they occupied his attention, he also played computer chess and read a book while watching the evening news. Jesse sat quietly, amused by all the activity.

While making a move with one of the chess pieces, Stephan turned to Jesse and said, "You must pay careful attention to your every movement, as well as technique. While practicing, the techniques should be performed over and over correctly. Begin each technique slowly, without tension. Whatever you can do slowly but correctly will be accomplished correctly when done fast. You must reach the point when applying your technique does not involve a thought process. It just is. You must develop your skills so your body responds without thought. This will take time and diligent practice. While training and sparring, understand that the only competition is yourself. If you have no knowledge of self, you definitely have no sense of who your opponent is."

Stephan hesitated a moment while tossing a toy toward his daughter. "Your eyes and facial expression telegraph everything, along with your body. You must drop any expression or feeling from your face. Your eyes must mirror your opponent so he can sense nothing. And your mind must remain in a relaxed state as though you're not being challenged. You should be thinking of nothing in particular."

He briefly stopped to observe Jesse as if to see if he understood. Jesse had been sitting quietly, trying to take everything in.

"Your training begins now," Stephan finished. He then turned around and continued with his activities.

Jesse sat for a moment, realizing that even though it had not been spoken, his session was over.

For months, every morning Jesse would arise at five A.M., sometimes earlier, and train. The only light that illuminated the room was a small candle that had been placed on a saucer that sat on the floor. Usually, a sheet of paper taped above the lit candle offered a philosophical statement. Sometimes, the statement was given by Stephan, and other times, Jesse found them. Dutifully, he performed warm-up exercises, then sat in front of the candle in a meditative position for several minutes. He began his breathing technique and meditated, subtracting one thought from the next until his mind was clear. Upon standing to begin training, his mind was focused and concentrated. Slowly he moved across the floor, as though in a trance.

When he had first begun training, he had found his movements to be awkward and mechanical. Over time, Jesse had learned numerous techniques. Some movements seemed quite odd to him, but he trained nonetheless. With his consistent training, he could feel and see the improved results. Friends and associates even commented that they saw a difference in him. He wasn't as impatient and seemed less aggravated. He had a calmness about him, a controlled, quiet presence.

On this particular morning, Jesse trained in front of a large wall mirror, practicing his forward punches. To his right were two windows. Outside, the city streets were still quiet, absent of activity in the early morning. While standing in front of the mirror for hours on end, Jesse had learned a great deal about himself. Now he stood performing one punch after another, staring into his own eyes.

Who am I? Jesse wondered. That answer had evaded him for years. Maybe he was searching for answers to questions that couldn't be answered. But he knew he was someone. There was a task or challenge of importance to be faced. *But what?*

Life had not been easy on him. Many failures and extended periods of loneliness had left him with no sense of direction. But despite these obstacles, he felt an inner drive to continue moving forward, and sensed that someone was watching over him.

Who am I? What am I to do in this lifetime? What is my purpose here? he thought as he continued throwing punches, with little effort on his part. His muscles tightened and regained control. Faster and faster, his arms moved forward and back, alternating. After twenty minutes, the tension in his arms and fists had gone.

Eventually, training ceased, and Jesse sat in front of the dimly lit candle. He pondered for a moment what he had learned from his instructor in the past few months. At the same time, in the back of his mind, he wondered where all this was taking him.

It was a cold night in the late fall of 1987. Jesse and Stephan stood on a three-foot-wide ledge just below a bridge. The river raged over the rocks. If someone fell, death would surely follow. Jesse clung to the rock wall, while Stephan stood nearby, nonchalantly facing the river below.

"What are you afraid of?" Stephan asked. "You only need to walk from this point to that one."

Jesse remained still, frozen in fear. His mind would not allow him to cross.

"Well, you can quickly get this done, or it is going to be a long night," Stephan added.

All Jesse could hear was the roaring river below. As he risked a glance down into the night, the river seemed dark and mysterious. This was a test he needed to pass. He could either back down or cross the stone ledge.

Jesse slowly moved forward, and once on the other side, he was relieved. Stephan was sitting on the ledge with his legs dangling over, seemingly enjoying the fresh air. He continued staring forward as he held a one-way conversation with Jesse.

"Fear comes from within," he said. "The only way to conquer those fears is to face them. And the only thing you have to fear is fear itself."

The year was ending, and Jesse had been training in his studio and was expecting Stephan's arrival. Shortly, Stephan arrived with his wife, Carolyn, whom Jesse politely greeted as she sat on the floor against the wall. Stephan had changed clothing and now wore only a white T-shirt and sweatpants. His facial expression and body language were more amplified than usual. He approached Jesse, and they both bowed, facing each other.

"From this point on, you are to remain on guard at all times," Stephen stated.

Jesse's eyes searched his face with curiosity as he nodded.

"We will begin sparring. Are you ready?" Stephan asked.

Not knowing what to expect, Jesse nodded again.

In a grim tone, Stephan announced, "Let us begin."

Abruptly and without warning, Stephan began jumping up and down in a chaotic fashion, flailing his arms in the air while at times holding a boxer's position, screaming, "Come on, white boy! Come on, white boy!"

Jesse readied his position, not knowing what to think. He was amused, since Stephan was white.

Now smiling and laughing aloud, seemingly out of his mind, Stephan continued, "Come on, white boy! Come on, white boy!" He continued this while bouncing up and down on the balls of his feet.

Suddenly, Jesse found he had been struck in the chest by a blow. Stephan immediately followed with a strike to Jesse's face.

Stephan stopped and began instructing Jesse on what he should have done to prevent the attack. As Jesse listened carefully, he was struck in the chest again by another blow. Surprised to have landed the blow, Stephan said, "Didn't I tell you to remain on defense at all times?"

Jesse was surprised and disappointed that he had allowed the strike to land by not anticipating and remaining on guard.

Stephan continued with his frantic and frenzied actions while screaming and yelling, "I'm gonna knock your block off!"

He bobbed and weaved, while shuffling his feet. He moved as though anticipating to land a hook, jab, or upper cut. Before Jesse realized it, he was bent forward with his hands on his knees in pain. Stephan had kicked him in the groin. Stephen leaned over and looked Jesse in the eye, obviously making sure he was OK, and said, "Always expect the unexpected."

Jesse slowly stood, nervous and anticipating anything. Stephan had his undivided attention.

Stephan now waved Jesse over to sit on the floor. As they faced each other with their legs crossed and arms resting on their knees, Stephan spoke and shared his abundant wisdom. These were the moments Jesse treasured.

"Your training has come along well. At this moment, I have nothing more to teach you. I only hope you have found what you were looking for. If not, I hope you continue your search. I will contact you for our next training. Until then, I hope you diligently continue to train. Your journey will—"

Pow! In one motion, Stephan had leaned back and unleashed a front snap kick to Jesse's face, striking his nose with the ball of his foot. His wife, sitting against the wall nearby, let out a scream as blood flowed from Jesse's nose onto his T-shirt.

"You had plenty of time to react," Stephan admonished him. "I placed my hands behind me. I then brought up my knee and extended my foot."

He motioned for Jesse to stand. They both bowed, not taking their eyes off each other. At this point, Jesse was a nervous wreck and ready for anything.

Observing his disposition, Stephan calmly said, "Now that we have bowed, there is no need for you to anticipate an attack. This session is over."

Dumbfounded, Jesse didn't know whether to believe Stephan or not. One thing he did know was that it wouldn't hurt to remain on guard. After briefly speaking with Jesse, Stephan dressed and departed with his wife.

The following morning, Jesse woke up early to train. He slowly and quietly stepped into the dark room, looking both ways, left then right. He even looked behind the door and over his shoulder, expecting Stephan to jump out from anywhere at any moment. His senses were now sharp. He was astonished by his keen sense of awareness. What had fallen asleep was now awakened. He now understood the only way to learn from the previous day's lesson was to go through the experience. Verbalized instructions would have meant nothing to him.

Jesse chuckled to himself and thought about his relationship with Stephan. With time, they had gained respect and trust for one another. Jesse felt the search for his destiny was just beginning. He didn't realize it was just around the corner.

CHAPTER 15

DECEMBER

The key had turned, but the door had not yet opened.

JESSE HAD BEGUN working in his art studio again in 1985. But it wasn't until late fall of 1988 that he decided to work on a major drawing. He spent time in deep thought, deciding on a subject matter. During this time, he also spent hours reflecting on his life.

Those who knew him described him as different. He had a mystique about him. He was a recluse locked within his own mind. Others were uncomfortable in his presence because of his long periods of silence. Most said he was allowing his mind to wander too far and ask too many questions. Jesse was an outsider looking in, even at himself. His mind never seemed to rest, even while asleep. He had very limited social contact with others. Many would say it was his choice. So, Jesse kept to himself, haunted by his own thoughts and unanswered questions.

Finally, after weeks of contemplation, Jesse decided on a subject for his drawing: himself. He felt the time had arrived to face himself in the mirror. This drawing would summarize him and life as he saw it.

The cold chill of early December had arrived. Darkness arrived just as the workday was ending. Jesse sat at his drawing table, having just finished a day's work of overtime. He was tired, but he always allowed time for his artwork. He carefully thought of the objects to be used in the drawing and what they would symbolize. In time, he decided on a chess game, staircase, hourglass, and ghostly figure.

The next step was even more difficult. What would be the best way to design and illustrate his story for the viewer? With pencil in hand, he began quick rough sketches. Dissatisfied with many of his results, he would crumble up the papers, toss them to the floor, and immediately start over. This continued into the early morning. After many attempts, he became frustrated but finally developed a composition with which he felt satisfied. Exhausted, he clicked off his drawing lamp.

The moonlight reflected through the windows, and the downtown streets were still and quiet. After several moments of sitting and examining his work, he stood slowly, walked over to a lounge chair, and quickly collapsed into a deep sleep.

He stood inside an enormous cathedral with a towering ceiling. Sunlight shone through beautiful stained-glass windows, and elaborately carved designs decorated the mahogany pews. Numerous small, white candles glowed in clear glass holders throughout this dark, somber place, even though most of the wicks were at their end and the wax had melted into liquid. In the distance stood an altar and the infallible Pope's throne. Yet something didn't seem right. The place had an eerie and uncanny feeling about it.

Jesse stood frozen with his teeth clenched shut. As his eyes searched about, he noticed a few huge, white, humanlike marble statues that dominated the church. Throughout his life, Jesse had developed an insurmountable fear of statues. It wasn't what was on the surface that frightened him; the fright came from what he saw within. There were times he had even felt too terrified to go near them.

He became overcome with panic as his heart repeatedly slammed against his chest. He quickly spun around, searching for a way out. As he glanced over his shoulder, he saw the floor near the altar rip open. As the slabs of concrete, rock, and gravel gave way, hundreds of the wooden benches fell into a fiery pit and were engulfed in flames. The benches added to this fiery furnace, causing the flames to reach to new heights as the heat became scorching. Once the floor fully collapsed, Jesse realized it was a mouth, with sharp, jagged teeth and flaring nostrils. The fiery flame from the mouth reflected in its hideous eyes. The entire cathedral represented this devouring, haunting, evil face.

The stone ceiling began to collapse around him with thundering sounds. A powerful wind blew in, causing the stained-glass windows to implode, sending fragments of glass flying. Huge banners were ripped from the walls one at a time, and the candlelight was extinguished immediately. Lamps flung across the room and smashed into walls, while the loud tower bell rang from above: *CLANG-CLANG! CLANG-CLANG!*

Suddenly, the gigantic bell came crashing down. *WHOOSH... BOOM!*

Horror had come to visit this place.

While destruction continued and chaos surrounded him, Jesse stood still, too terrified to take a step in either direction. At that moment, he saw the statues begin to move. Suddenly, before he could react, a statue stood, casting a shadow over him as it placed itself directly in front of him, blocking his path. Its eyes were hollow, cold, and empty, with no facial expression. Jesse spun around and made a frantic run in search of escape. He arrived at a door that he was unable to open. The door was over twenty feet high, made of dense, thick wood and heavy iron. The knob was a large, heavy metal ring he gripped with both hands. With palms sweating, he braced himself and began pulling. His heart pounded as he frantically strained to open the door along this dark chamber. Nothing.

Worn and exhausted, he allowed the metal ring to fall from his grip, a thud bellowing through the church as it slammed against the door. A deeper darkness descended on this place. Jesse shook uncontrollably as the thundering steps of the monstrous statues drew closer. From the corner of his eye, he saw a figure clothed in a white robe run by in frenzy, ablaze in flames. Judgment Day.

"Noooooo!" Jesse screamed. Exhausted, he slowly slid down to the floor as the church became engulfed with fire. He closed his eyes and covered his face as the statues began closing in on him.

Riiiiing!

The alarm clock abruptly awakened Jesse from his sleep. Now sitting up stiffly in his chair, he was physically shaken. His T-shirt was damp with sweat as his fingers gripped the armrest of the chair. He quickly looked around, searching for something familiar in his surroundings. After a few seconds passed, he realized that he had just awakened from a terrifying nightmare.

He fell back into his chair, collecting his thoughts. He tried to understand and interpret the nightmare, but couldn't. It was 5:20 A.M., and he needed to prepare himself for work at his part-time job. As he became preoccupied with his morning routine, the thoughts about his nightmare gradually faded away, until they were replaced by the activities of the day.

Several days passed before Jesse returned to his drawing board to continue developing his composition. Before starting to work, he sat for several minutes, studying his rough drawing. The message, design, and perspective all seemed to work. Every object in the drawing symbolized different aspects of his life. For the next several weeks, Jesse spent endless hours developing his final drawing. In mid-December, he completed the drawing.

The drawing was rendered in graphite and white charcoal on a 30" by 26" gray illustration board. In this illustration, Jesse attempted to capture the emotions within himself. He wanted the intensity of his work to make an impact on the viewer. Jesse had drawn himself sitting with arms folded at an old, discarded wooden table. He was in a cold basement with ancient stone walls and dirt floors. The place was consumed by despair and gloom.

In front of him on the table sat a chess game. The chess game represented the game of life. He had drawn the chess pieces strategically on the board. Across from Jesse, hovering slightly above the table, was his opponent. The ghostly figure wore a dark robe and hood, which concealed his identity. Jesse's mysterious opponent had haunted him all his life, ever since childhood.

Who exactly was he? Was he playing against himself, as his worst enemy? Or was this his nemesis? Maybe it was someone he would eventually face. These lingering questions he couldn't answer. But he had always sensed and felt this adversary's presence. Now, at this point in Jesse's life, he was unavoidable.

The white pieces on the board were Jesse's, and the black ones belonged to the ghostly specter. By looking closely at the few white pieces, the viewer would notice they were cracked. Those pieces indicated that Jesse was on the edge of losing the battle.

On the table just below the figure in darkness were most of Jesse's collected white chess pieces, crushed. Jesse imagined a thunderous smashing and grinding sound as his opponent destroyed each piece one at a time. Anger at its highest state manifested itself. There were no second chances or hope in this game of life.

Now, his adversary was methodically moving his dark rook across the board with vengeance. He was extremely patient and had tolerated waiting years in the shadows in an attempt to conquer Jesse in this final moment. It was as though he was reaching for Jesse's very soul. Destruction was near.

Jesse's remaining chess pieces, the pawn, bishop, queen, and king, stood firmly on the board. But as pressure mounted, the cracks in each piece became more pronounced. The one exceptional chess piece that stood brightly off-center of the board was the knight. It symbolized the warrior's bold, unwavering spirit and courage to fight under any circumstances and against all odds.

Hearing the pounding of his heart, Jesse sat in a rigid position, trying hard to conceal his feelings of fright and panic.

In the drawing, Jesse wore a black tunic, torn and frayed, representing his state of poverty. Also drawn around his neck, outside his robe, dangled a small, simple, shining cross. The cross symbolized his faith in Jesus Christ.

Time seemed to crawl as his fingernails dug deeper into his sleeve, tearing at the material. Jesse's mind was as a storm at sea. His eyes and expression held an abundance of emotions, but only displayed defiance and relentless determination. His eye ducts became filled with tears, but not yet overflowing, due to the thought of possible defeat. His throat was parched dry as his tongue remained pasted to the roof of his mouth. The only moisture was the salty taste of perspiration flowing from his forehead onto his lips as he remained speechless.

A lamp hung just above Jesse's head. Its light pierced the darkness and cast a glimmering glow over center stage. To his right he had drawn an hourglass. The sand was quickly vanishing from the top and filling the bottom. The hourglass represented a person's lifespan. Jesse was desperately running out of time.

Across the floor rose a set of seven dilapidated wooden stairs. The first step represented people who merely existed through life. The second step reflected complacency. The third stair had collapsed, which symbolized those discouraged and broken by life's trials and struggles; many fell through at this level. The few who remained faithfully strong would face the last four stairs to climb, which seemed too weak to stand upon. Only those with a strong mind, faith, will, and focus made it to the top landing. Once there, they would face the ancient stone wall. Some would venture back down the stairs, never to return. Seldom did anyone go beyond the wall into the unknown.

The only piece missing from the drawing was the hangman's noose. Jesse had planned to sketch it in the far background of the drawing. But, for some reason, he decided not to.

Jesse sat flipping through the pages of one of his art magazines. He came across an ink pen rendering on one of the pages that demanded his attention. It was an illustration of a ferocious wolf disguised as a shepherd in sheep's clothing, leading a flock of sheep into a path of doom.

He found himself wondering why someone would illustrate the innocent being led to slaughter with no sign of hope. The drawing seemed hideous to him. He discovered he had become emotionally upset and wondered why. It was as though he wanted to warn and save the lambs, which to him represented lost people deceived by the wicked one. He eventually began turning to other pages. But moments later, he found himself staring back at the same page again. He finally placed the magazine down and began flipping through another.

Then he saw something that made him gasp and exclaim, "JEEEEZUS!" He jumped up and slammed the pages of the magazine shut, throwing it onto the desk. The combination of what he saw and felt had become unbearable. The portrait was a black and white photograph of a male covered in dense black muck. The image did not seem human. The only light was in the eyes, which were evil and unrelenting. The stare had drawn Jesse in for a moment. It seemed he had an engagement with death that brought fear that penetrated his very soul.

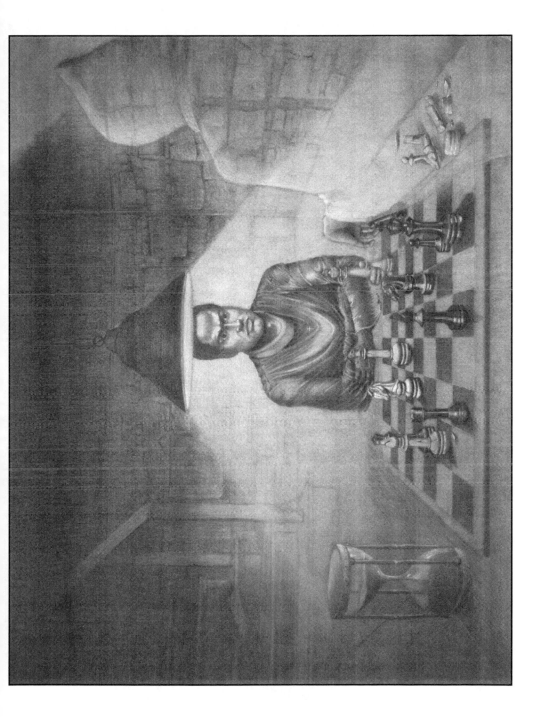

PART II
VISION. LIFE. HOPE.

CHAPTER 16

THE STORY

IN APRIL OF 1989, Jesse began renting another large space to practice martial arts. During that time, he met a karate instructor named Gerald Holdman. They both agreed to open a karate school in hopes of enrolling enough students to cover the rent. Gerald offered very little financial support. He only volunteered his services as an instructor. So, the financial burden weighed heavily on Jesse.

In the late fall, a friend named Dale Parker enrolled. Eventually, Dale introduced an associate from his job to the karate class. Her name was Lisa Kastner. Lisa was a charismatic, middle-aged woman with dark hair and hazel eyes. She always seemed jubilant and eager to talk, give advice, share information, and help others whenever possible. It seemed she went to unusual extremes to satisfy and please others.

Lisa had sixteen-year-old twins, Laura and John, who had shown interest in karate. Lisa enrolled them both during the month of February 1990.

Gerald was an excellent instructor. At 5'6" and 146 pounds, he performed and demonstrated techniques with lightning speed, power, precision, and accuracy. The dynamics of his performances left viewers in awe, but he also was mischievous, unpredictable, and unreliable. He sometimes arrived late or not at all for the scheduled classes. Jesse wanted desperately for the school to succeed, so on those days, he took it upon himself to instruct the students with basic techniques. By this time, six students participated in the class.

One day, after a strenuous private training session, Jesse and Dale sat conversing while drinking glasses of orange juice. The chair Dale sat in seemed made for a toddler, due to his massive frame. He was an intimidating figure, with broad shoulders and massive arms. His legs were like tree trunks, and whenever Jesse shook his hand, he felt the power in his grip. His dark, somber presence was also intimidating. But Dale was a gentle soul with the manners of a gentleman. He enjoyed intellectual conversations with Jesse over a wide range of subjects. He was a highly educated and articulate man who conversed with logic. Life to him was cause and effect, based on facts and science. He seemed to find conversations with Jesse intriguing, since he was more of an idealist. They were opposites, with a great deal of respect for each other's philosophies about life and society.

On this day, Dale opened the conversation on a more personal level. "Jesse, I've been speaking to Lisa about her children participating in class, and she's very impressed."

"Yeah?" Jesse replied.

"Yeah. She thinks Gerald is a great instructor for the kids and really appreciates your helping out with the class instruction."

"Well, I'm glad."

"Jesse, she's continuously asking me questions about you."

"Like what?"

"About other aspects of your life. She's wondering if you're in a relationship with anyone."

Dale paused and waited for a response. Jesse stared at the floor, lost for words. His mind flashed back briefly upon past relationships that had never seemed to work out.

"Jesse, have you ever thought about marriage and raising a family?"

"Nope."

"Why?"

"Well, God has placed me on this planet for a reason, and I know there's something I need to accomplish. Until I complete whatever it is and find those answers, everything else is irrelevant. Marriage would complicate things and cloud my vision. Yes, marriage is important to me, but it's not my priority."

"Our company is having a party at the Hong Kong restaurant, and Lisa wants me to invite you."

Jesse shook his head. "I'm not going."

"Why?"

"I've got too much to do."

"Well, Lisa would be terribly disappointed if you can't make it. You could just show up briefly and leave early."

After seeing how important it was to Dale, Jesse said, "All right, I'll go." He also hoped that by attending, he might meet someone with an interest in joining the school, which would help relieve some burden of the monthly rent.

The following Saturday, around eleven P.M., Jesse appeared at the party. He wore a long trench coat, a white shirt buttoned at the collar, casual black slacks, and white tennis shoes. Upon his arrival, he felt awkward and out of place. The restaurant was busy, with loud music and people drinking, laughing, eating, and having a joyous time.

Lisa asked Jesse to dance. Strobe lights flashed from above while colored lights flashed through the clear dance floor. Songs from Kool and the Gang, the Commodores, and K.C. and the Sunshine Band played through the night.

After dancing with Lisa, Jesse made his way to the bar, ordered a Coca-Cola, and found himself wandering through a darkened area of the club when he heard a voice.

"Are you Jesse?"

After looking around in search of the voice, he looked down and saw a woman sitting alone on a sofa. She caught him by surprise.

"Yes," he said hesitantly.

"We've heard a great deal about you. We're like family here, and Lisa is a very dear friend of mine. So don't you dare hurt her."

Jesse stood looking at her, not knowing how to respond. By her remark, he assumed Lisa had been speaking about him at her job as though they were intimate. He hesitated briefly, gave a quick nod, smiled, and walked away.

Late that night, Jesse and Lisa returned to his studio. Lisa stayed until early morning.

The following week, they were in his loft space, and as she was dressing and preparing to leave, she removed her earrings and gave them to him. This immediately caused Jesse to wonder.

"Lisa, I shouldn't be involved with you," he said. "I don't want this to affect your kids. I also don't want to get involved in a relationship."

She paused and looked at him, then smiled. "I understand how you feel. I'm not looking for a commitment. I don't wish to invade your space, and whenever you want to get together is fine with me." Then came the question. "Jesse, do you have anything that you would wish to share with me?"

"Nope," he simply replied.

"Are you telling me you don't have anything of any sentimental value you wish to share? It could be anything, large or small," she persisted.

"No," Jesse answered.

After his second response, Lisa stopped inquiring and changed the subject. Soon afterward, she departed, clearly trying not to show her disappointment.

On Wednesday, after Jesse had instructed Lisa's children in a two-hour class, Lisa gave him a book titled *The Peaceful Journey*. Days later, Jesse began reading the book, which was about a young man in search of answers about life. The man met a mysterious gentleman who provided him with guidance.

As weeks passed, Jesse and Lisa began spending a great deal of time together. One evening in April, Jesse was working out in the martial arts studio while Lisa sat talking. "Jesse, it's amazing how similar our lives are," she said.

Jesse didn't respond.

After a few moments of silence, she continued, "We have the same outlook, views, and philosophy in life."

Jesse glanced over at her after the last statement, which drew his attention. It seemed Lisa had tried to fit herself into his life, attempting to make it seem there were similarities between them, while he felt they had very little in common. Jesse was trying to figure out where this was leading.

When Lisa presented her next question, it was delivered more like a statement. "Jesse, you and I…you and I don't believe in God, do we?"

Jesse stopped striking the punching bag and turned to face her, giving her his full attention. She was trying to persuade him. But why? At that moment, he felt the best response was none. He stood facing her silently, with a blank expression. Lisa continued, but this time with a more convinced tone in her voice.

"You and I believe in reincarnation."

"I don't know anything about reincarnation," Jesse replied immediately.

"Yes, you do! You read it in the book, *The Peaceful Journey*," Lisa said, now seeming sure of herself.

"Yeah, I read it in the book you gave me, but that doesn't mean I know anything about reincarnation or believe in it." He was now ready to take on Lisa in a debate, which led Lisa to begin pleading.

"But, Jesse, you read…"

Interrupting her in mid-sentence, he said, "Look, I don't know anything about reincarnation." The tone of his voice and the expression on his face conveyed that the conversation was over. Lisa apparently decided not to press the issue and fell quiet.

As days passed, Jesse began spending more of his time in his art studio. One late Tuesday night, he received a phone call that interrupted his work.

"Hi, Jesse! It's me, Lisa."

"Yeah, what's up?"

"I just wanted to know if I could stop over tonight."

"No, not tonight. I'm busy working on an illustration."

"I figured you were busy, but it's a full moon out tonight."

"Yeah, so what?"

"Well, I always get strange vibes when there's a full moon."

"I'm sorry, but I have a deadline to meet. How about next week?"

"All right…I'll give you a call next Wednesday," she said with disappointment in her voice. "Maybe we'll get together then?"

"Sounds cool. I'll talk to you then. Well…bye. Don't work too hard."

"Bye."

On Wednesday, Lisa stopped by Jesse's place after work. She brought food over to eat while they sat and talked.

"Jesse, when do you usually practice your martial arts?"

"Every morning at five o'clock A.M., and sometimes three o'clock A.M. when I'm unable to sleep."

"That's a good time, because the spirits are at their highest during those hours."

Jesse looked at her with suspicion. There was something very strange about her. He studied her more closely as the conversation continued.

"By the way," she said, "I have a meeting with a psychic reader in a few weeks."

"Well, why don't you see what you can find out about me?" Jesse said jokingly.

"What's your birth date, and what time were you born?"

Hesitantly, Jesse said, "June fifth, 1959, and I have no idea what time I was born."

"It should be on your birth certificate. If you could get that information, the reader can be more specific in her information about you."

"I don't have it," Jesse said sternly. "Just see what you can find."

"But, Jesse—"

Cutting her short, Jesse said, "Look, what's the big deal? Either she'll give you information, or she won't. It really doesn't matter to me. I'm not concerned about going to see a reader, and I'm not going out of my way to find out the time I was born."

"Jesse, why are you so difficult?"

"Difficult?" Jesse asked, surprised by her question.

"Yes, difficult." She was obviously frustrated and disappointed by Jesse's lack of cooperation. She removed a paperback book from her carrying bag and said, "Jesse, I brought by another book I think you might enjoy reading."

Jesse glanced at the title, *Living in Joy*. "Sure, I'll read it."

Lisa sighed with relief. Their conversation went into the night. Hours passed before they realized it was half past midnight.

Jesse escorted Lisa from his loft space. When they approached her car, Lisa abruptly said, "Jesse, the next time we meet, hopefully I'll have news for you from the psychic reader."

Now silent, Jesse stood next to the vehicle, eyeing Lisa awkwardly while waiting for her to continue.

Lisa took advantage of the silence. "My grandmother charted people's lives through the use of astrology, horoscopes, tarot cards, and readings. She was able to chart my uncle's death. Her prediction was that he would die in flames."

"And?" Jesse said, prompting her to continue.

"Well, my uncle did anything he could do to avoid flames at any cost. But as a hobby, he flew airplanes. He crashed and died in the flames. After that tragic incident, my grandmother discontinued charting lives."

The next day, he began reading the book she had given him. He found it to be an unusual book. In the strange introduction, the author spoke of being in contact with a spiritual being that communicated to him about the afterlife. This had supposedly compelled him to write the book to share and offer this information to others. Jesse became skeptical of the book as days passed.

A week later, Dale stopped by for casual conversation. After a few minutes of discussion about martial arts, he brought up Lisa.

"Jesse, Lisa's crazy about you."

"Yeah?"

"Yeah! She's constantly talking about you at work." With hesitation, Dale added, "If you asked her, she would marry you now."

Jesse gave Dale a concerned look. "She thinks there's a price tag on me, and she wants to know how much I cost."

At that moment, he had no idea how close he was to the truth.

CHAPTER 17

ROMANTIC REBEL

IN EARLY JUNE, Jesse sat in a small restaurant with Lisa. This was his favorite place. It was originally a family house that had been converted into a restaurant without losing its homey atmosphere. The wood-paneled walls were decorated with the artwork of local artists. There were also framed photographs of pictures from the 1940s and 1950s. Antiques were displayed throughout the restaurant, as well as items hanging overhead from the high ceiling. An old Steinway piano stood in one corner, and a chalkboard on the wall above it announced the specials of the day. The small wooden tables were positioned close together, but the room didn't seem cramped. Soft music played over the speakers, giving the dimly lit room an old-fashioned and intimate mood. Lisa seemed impressed with having been invited to his secret place.

On this Friday evening, the restaurant was full to capacity. Once inside, customers found relief and escape from the pressures of everyday life. People chattered constantly after a day's work, looking forward to the weekend; others gazed romantically at each other in the candlelight. Here, laughter was often heard. Waiters and waitresses, each with a personality of their own, casually made their way from one table to another. Most knew their customers because many were regulars.

Several minutes had passed since Lisa and Jesse had spoken. Their meals had just been served. During a moment of silence while they ate, Jesse decided to ask the question that had been circling his mind and invading his thoughts. "Have you gone to see the reader?"

Lisa, preoccupied by their surroundings, seemed taken by surprise by Jesse's question, since he seldom spoke.

"Oh…why, yes!" The mere fact that he had brought it up clearly excited her.

"Well, what did the voodoo child tell you?" Jesse asked sarcastically.

Lisa chuckled. Leaning forward, she folded her arms and placed them on the table. "The reader spoke to me about turmoil in your past since childhood. She spoke in detail about your struggles through life, and your search for your destiny."

As she described what the reader had told her in more detail, a whirlwind of thoughts raced through Jesse's mind. He focused his eyes on her, while he still tried to show lack of interest. To him, it wasn't possible for her to have this information, but she did. Jesse had never had an interest in psychic readers or astrology. He considered it all "hocus pocus," but this time she had piqued his interest. Temptation.

After several minutes, Lisa fell quiet and continued eating. Stunned and now in a perturbed state, Jesse blurted out, "And…is that all? What else did she say?"

He was curious about further knowledge that she might possess. He wanted information that he could analyze, interpret, and check for correctness. They were now engaging in a preliminary game of chess in the battlefields of their minds.

Smiling confidently, Lisa leaned closer and said barely above a whisper, "Jesse, I'll be quite honest with you. I met two readers before meeting you, and both of them spoke of you."

"Well, what did they say?" he asked, now even more anxious for an answer, but attempting not to show his impatience.

"They said you were unusual and different. An enigma. It was said that I would not meet you as I would the average person. Both readers said I would meet you through the back door. They also said you had insight and information to share with me. Once I received this information, it would be like fresh air rushing through an open window. When I first met you, I went back to see one of the readers. Before I could say a word, she looked at me and said that she knew I had already met you. She wanted me to share information with her, but I didn't know how to begin or what to say."

She paused briefly before continuing in a more urgent tone. "Jesse, I would like to offer you another book to read, but I know you won't read it."

"What's the name of the book?"

"The title is *Opening Your Channels*."

"Open my channels to what?" Jesse asked in a loud, defensive tone.

"Jesse! The readers said you shut yourself off from the world. You need to open up more. You're too independent and stubborn. The psychic reader also said that you and I could have a relationship that would be like one in a million, if only you would open up and allow it to work." She sounded desperate. When he didn't respond, she fell quiet and continued eating.

Jesse stared at her as he took a drink of water and leaned back in his chair. To him, they had very little in common. He studied her eyes and facial expression as he contemplated all she had mentioned. He began to wonder if she had lost her mind. Even more, he wondered why she was attempting to persuade him to read this particular book. Finally, with a tone of defiance, he said, "You're right. I'm not reading that book."

Disappointed, Lisa replied, "Well, Jesse, I will be attending a psychic seminar in two weeks. Would you like to join me?"

"Nope," he said flatly.

"Why not?"

"Why should I?"

"It'll be fun."

"Yeah, right. I ain't goin'."

"Jesse, you're so difficult."

Jesse shook his head and chuckled to himself.

Lisa, now agitated, blurted out, "The readers also said the last four girls you went out with, you could not have saved them!"

This statement forced more questions to spin in his mind as Lisa continued speaking. Jesse wondered why she had used the word "saved." Most people would have said the relationships would not have worked. *Save them from what, from whom? And who are these readers to tell me what I could or could not do?*

Jesse slouched back in his chair as his mind drifted further from her conversation. Lisa's voice faded as her lips continued to move. The more she spoke, the less he heard.

As Jesse became more aware of his surroundings, he noticed the restaurant had fallen quiet. The only sound was the ticking of an antique clock above his head. As his eyes searched the room, he was surprised to see the place empty. Everyone had gone. He continued looking, searching for someone, anyone. It was then he noticed a lonely waiter sitting in the corner of the room.

"Earth to Jesse! Are you listening?"

Jesse quickly turned his attention back to Lisa.

"It seems as though your mind drifted off someplace."

Gathering his thoughts, he looked at her blankly.

"I didn't realize how late it was," she said, clearly alarmed at the time.

"Yeah," he replied absently, as his thoughts remained adrift.

While leaving the restaurant, Jesse refused a ride and decided to walk to his art studio. They said their goodbyes. He needed time to think.

CHAPTER 18

GARDEN OF DENIAL

JESSE ENTERED THE martial arts studio at three A.M. on Monday morning. He had decided to train early because he was unable to sleep. Wearing a black Tai-Chi uniform with a white collar and sleeves, he stepped across the polished wooden floor and began breathing exercises. Candles sat aglow on four windowsills, casting shadows across the floor. After minutes of stretching, he felt strange. He couldn't concentrate. Finally, after staring into nothing, he sat down on the floor with his legs crossed, back straight, and arms at rest. In the quiet stillness of the room, he found himself unable to meditate. He had an uncanny feeling of being watched.

Nervously, he stood and walked over to the heavy bag that hung from the ceiling by a thick chain. He slowly began working his way around the bag, striking it with different combinations. Everything seemed to flow effortlessly. His focus was sharp, and he found himself amazed by his timing and precision. After several minutes, perspiration covered his skin. Suddenly, he stopped. Something was terribly wrong. His senses were screaming as he felt an intense, haunting stare. There was an eerie presence in the room. A trembling, nervous feeling came over him, sending a chill through his body. He hurriedly gathered his things and dashed to the door, locking it behind him.

While looking down the corridor, he noticed the hallway had become darker. The fluorescent lights hanging from the ceiling flickered dimly onto the speckled, pale green linoleum floor. The walls seemed to take on an eerie shade of gray. Now, an even greater sense of fear overcame him. As he continued looking down the corridor, he noticed a dark image approaching him in the distance, gliding along the ceiling. He continued staring until the oncoming mysterious shadow came into focus.

"A bat!" he yelled, unable to believe what he was seeing.

Scared stiff, he watched the creature move in his direction, until a voice inside his head yelled, *Run!*

Jesse immediately spun around and rushed to the door. In a frantic state, he fumbled the keys while attempting to find the correct one. He was so frightened, he didn't glance over his shoulder as he inserted the key into the lock. The key jammed and wouldn't turn. He felt the bat glaring at him as he attempted several more times to force the door open. Finally, the lock turned and he crashed through the door, falling to the floor. Jesse lay there with his belongings scattered. He found himself too afraid to look up at the bat drifting overhead. The creature's wings were like stretched leather. Its wide, pearly dark eyes were fixated upon him. Time seemed to slow as the bat drifted further inside. The creature continuously flapped its wings while aimlessly flying through the empty room.

Then, slowly, as though being drawn, the shadow found its way out of an open window and into the blackness.

A few days later, Jesse met with Lisa at his loft. Their conversation continued from their last meeting at the restaurant. As Lisa spoke, Jesse interrupted her and said, "You're watching me bounce off the walls, and you're laughing at me." It wasn't a thought; he just said it, to his own amazement.

She replied, "No, I'm not."

"How often do you visit these readers?"

"Only once a year. That's all I can afford," she answered, laughing.

"How many books do you have on astrology and horoscopes?"

"I have two or three," she said, smiling. "I only read them for fun."

Jesse knew Lisa was attempting to manipulate him. He constantly wondered why, and for what?

Before meeting her, his life had been simple. Now, it was becoming darker and more complex by the hour.

It disturbed him that he couldn't figure out what she was up to. This was one of the most difficult and unusual situations he had ever been involved in. He knew he could end it by just walking away, but his questions would go unanswered. He often found himself intrigued by her attempts to persuade him. It was obvious that she had the upper hand, because he was totally unfamiliar with her method of operation. *Mind games.* Up to that point, he had considered himself an observer. Now, it was clear he was a participant in this game. He had been all along, but hadn't realized it. His only option now was to make a drastic move across the board.

"I want the phone number of one of the readers," he said. "I want to call her and set up an appointment for myself."

He was bluffing. Jesse had no intention of going to see a reader. He just wanted to see if she would provide a phone number, and to his surprise, she did.

Lisa had called his bluff. Now what? He needed to find more information, and he definitely did not want to call that number. He guessed he'd have to wait.

A week later, during a phone conversation with Lisa, she asked, "How is the book *Living in Joy* coming along?"

"It's all right...but every other word is love, love, love. How much love is there in the world?" he asked with a tone of sarcasm.

Laughing, Lisa asked, "Jesse, do you get a warm sensation while reading the book?"

Hesitantly, he said, "Yes."

For some reason, as they continued their conversation, Lisa mistakenly thought Jesse mentioned that he had visited the reader.

"What? What did the reader tell you?" she asked, with a quivering tone in her voice.

"Lisa, you misunderstood what I said. I didn't say that I went to see the reader. In fact, I haven't even called her number yet."

"Oh! Well, huh...I sure wish I had more time to read those books. I usually read one or two books a day."

"One or two books a day? I usually read one or two pages and underline what's important to me and try to make it part of my life."

Their conversation continued another several minutes. Upon hanging up the phone, Jesse asked himself a question aloud: "Why did she become nervous after thinking that I went to visit the reader?"

After a moment's thought, he took mental notes and filed them in the back of his mind.

Two days later, Jesse had completed instructing a martial arts class with Lisa's children. He was leaving the studio when Lisa approached him and gave him a large bag of books. Back in his loft, he began unloading the bag and found martial arts books that he had allowed her son to borrow. The last book he removed from the bag was titled *Living in Joy*. He found this odd.

"Why would she purchase the same book again?" he said aloud. After a few moments of thought, he placed the book on the shelf and continued on with his evening.

The following week, Lisa met at his place. They held a casual conversation until she abruptly asked for her book. Startled, Jesse asked, "What book?"

"*Living in Joy.*"

He removed the book from the shelf and gave it to her. She quickly flipped through the pages, as though searching for something. Looking distraught, she said, "This isn't the book."

"What book are you talking about?"

"The first book I gave you, *Living in Joy*."

"Why the first book?"

"Well, I…I…I didn't mean for you to keep the first book. Th-that's why I gave you the second book. I only meant to loan you the first one. I always treasure the first book that I purchase. So, could I have the first book back?"

"Sure, but I'm sorry I don't have it here now. I mistakenly forgot it at my job, but I'll be sure to get it back to you."

"That's fine, Jesse, whenever you get around to it. I'm in no hurry."

Later that evening, they went out to see a movie. Throughout the night, Jesse had a terrible uneasy feeling brewing within him. He was never at rest, as thoughts of conversations with Lisa continuously raced through his mind in an attempt to put the pieces of the puzzle together.

Their night ended early, and Jesse sat in his loft space, pondering. His thoughts drifted well into the night, until he jumped up and pulled the book *The Peaceful Journey* from the shelf. He opened it to the inside jacket, where he was relieved to see that his suspicions were correct. On the page was written, *To Jesse, I hope you enjoy reading this book. Love, Lisa.*

He closed the book, remembering that he had read a similar statement Lisa had written in the initial book, *Living in Joy*, which meant she had given him the first book as a gift.

He realized the reason Lisa wanted the book back was due to their recent telephone conversation. He had told her that he had underlined what was important to him in the book. Lisa wanted to read what he had underlined. She wanted to know his thoughts. He had lied about leaving the book at work, when he had actually loaned it to Stephan for his opinion.

Midnight came and went as Jesse stood staring out the window into obscurity. His mind wandered in confusion. He now began to have more serious concerns about his relationship with Lisa. He decided to place more distance between them, but he also wanted to figure out her true intentions. Two nagging questions remained with him, which he spoke aloud as though speaking to someone in a distant realm.

"Why is she attempting to manipulate me, and what does she want?"

He had to find the answer.

It had been weeks since Jesse had last spoken with Lisa. Gerald had been regularly instructing the classes again, so Jesse's presence wasn't needed. He began spending more and more time in his art studio. As much as he wanted to conclude everything, he found himself slowly drifting away from the madness.

One Saturday evening, he began working on another drawing. He had spent hours working out his ideas on paper when the phone rang.

"Hello."

"Hi, Jesse, it's Lisa. What are you up to?"

"I'm working in my studio on a drawing."

"Well, I just wanted to know if I could stop by."

"Nope, I'm working."

"Jesse, I haven't seen or heard from you in three weeks."

"Yeah, so?"

"Well, I…"

"Look Lisa, I'm not in a relationship with you. I don't need to stay in contact."

"I know. I just wanted to see you for a minute."

Jesse hesitated. "OK, stop by." He regretted the words as soon as he said them.

After Lisa arrived, she stayed much longer than he had expected. Night arrived as they lay in his loft. The light from the full moon streamed through the arched gothic windows and pierced the darkness, giving the room an ominous glow. The mood in the room seemed set for a funeral rather than a romantic evening. The vacant streets outside his window over the city seemed melancholy and somber. Throughout the night, the shadows of stray dogs roamed the streets, like scavengers in search of something or someone. The sounds of barking and growling entered Jesse's place as time ticked on into the night.

Lisa rested her head on the pillow next to his, in wait. Her fingertips massaged his chest, as he lay still with his eyes closed from the tiresome day.

Feeling her hair falling lightly across his face, he opened his eyes and saw her leaning forward on her elbows toward his ear. Her lips parted, and whispered words drifted into his ear: "What do you think about the book *Living in Joy* so far? Some people would say the book is…satanic."

The question ricocheted off the walls of Jesse's mind as he lay there. Without movement or expression, he said, "Well, I don't know about that, but there's a lot of garbage in that book."

Lisa kissed him softly on the cheek, while her hand now caressed his face. Now, even more gently, she whispered the next question, as if pouring honey—slowly. "Jesse…you and I don't believe in God…do we?"

Without hesitation, Jesse answered, "Well, to be honest with you, I'm not here, anyway."

Lisa moved away from him slightly, looking baffled. "What?"

Jesse drifted to sleep. Some time later, the barking of dogs increased outside the window, then transformed into howling. Jesse opened his eyes. The neon hotel sign flickered outside. Suddenly, he saw Lisa over him, her eyes staring hypnotically as her face became contorted. Her mouth stretched wide, and she plunged her teeth into his neck and began gnawing under his jaw line.

Jesse quickly sprang up from his sleep, swinging his arms, as if waking from a nightmare. The force of his swings knocked Lisa away. But, due to exhaustion, he again collapsed back to sleep.

Later, he was awakened at 3:45 A.M. by Lisa running about the studio in a manic rush to get out. After dressing, she flung the heavy metal door open and ran down the hall toward the elevator.

After her departure, Jesse looked in the mirror and examined his neck for marks. There weren't any. He leaned against the sink, wondering to himself if the terrifying events had actually happened. Then he began to worry. In his mind, he changed her name from Lisa to "Psycho." He felt it was time to schedule an appointment with the psychic reader. Fear was now just around the corner, soon to be accompanied by terror.

CHAPTER 19

WHITE KNIGHT

IT WAS A sweltering, hot mid-July. Wearing a white T-shirt, sneakers, and jeans, Jesse pedaled his red twelve-speed mountain bike along the traffic of Exchange Street. He was on his way to keep his scheduled appointment with the psychic reader. He was enjoying his ride as he glanced at pedestrians walking in downtown Rochester. Jesse noticed a friend and waved. As he turned his attention back to the traffic, he became alarmed as he saw a car swerve across the lane against traffic. The car was speeding directly toward him in an inevitable head-on collision. Jesse's life flashed before him.

In the blink of an eye, the automobile swerved, just missing him, as his bicycle also made an adjustment turn. It wasn't a thought on his part; his body reacted to make the right choice to allow both parties to barely miss each other. *Thank God,* Jesse thought. A crowd of onlookers stood observing the near-accident. The expressions on their faces showed that they did not believe what they had just witnessed, and neither did Jesse.

Thirty minutes later, Jesse found himself standing on the porch of an old Victorian home at the entrance of the psychic reader's screen door.

What, am I losing my mind? he thought, but he felt it was the only move he could make in order to find out what was going on. He stood hesitantly on the porch, wavering between whether to ring the doorbell or not. He glanced nervously at his watch. It was now exactly four P.M. Just before he pressed the bell, the screen door opened. He jumped back slightly, surprised.

A tall, elderly woman appeared. "Hi. Please come right on in," she said with a southern accent.

Her red hair was streaked with silver. She seemed strong and stern, but gentle. She wore a long, colorful dress with floral patterns and brown, low-heeled shoes. This was different from what he had expected to see from a psychic reader.

The inside of her home was a drastic change from the bright colors of the summer day. The darkness of the place caused him to hesitate between steps, while observing the surroundings. The curtains were drawn closed, allowing only a few rays of light to enter. The house had a somber feel to it. A large wood and glass cabinet against the wall held her chinaware. Pictures of her and family members hung throughout the house. Jesse tried to walk quietly across the polished, creaking wooden floor as she escorted him into the dining room, where he sat down at an antique wooden table. He continued looking around, surprised at not seeing skulls, crystals, beads, tarot cards, diagrams, and strange pictures hanging on the walls. To his astonishment, the interior wasn't different from any other home.

She introduced herself while placing a tape recorder on the table. She explained that the session would be recorded and that he would be allowed to take the tape after the thirty-minute meeting ended. She sat in the chair across from him and, while smiling slightly, said, "Let us begin."

She pushed down the red record button. The only light in the room came from an old light fixture that hung above the table. Glancing over his shoulder, Jesse peered through the doorway entrance, where he saw a dark staircase leading upward. The psychic reader reached across the table, touched his hand, closed her eyes, and began speaking. She spoke about his art studio, and about several events in his life as though she was peering directly into his very existence.

Startled, Jesse snatched his hand away and nearly fell out of his chair. Her eyes opened, and when she saw that he was visibly shaken, she touched his hand again, while giving him a comforting smile. As she closed her eyes and tilted her head back, she continued speaking. Jesse's breathing became heavy as his nerves began to unravel.

"I see wheels turning; I keep seeing wheels turning. Is there anyone in your family who works a great deal on cars?"

"Yeah…that must be my stepfather," Jesse replied.

"No, it's not him. You're the thinker. This person takes things lightly."

"Oh...that's my brother."

"Yes, you give to your mother, while this person takes. You also tell the truth, and to put it lightly, this person bends the truth."

As she continued speaking about different aspects of Jesse's life, his thoughts wandered to God. Jesse realized that he had been watched throughout his life. He now had feelings of guilt about things he had done.

"I also see that you will be going on a vacation," she said with her eyes still closed. "I see you near water, but...you're not a swimmer, are you? No," she added, answering her own question. "You enjoy being near water. It gives you a sense of peace. During this time, you will feel as if a heavy burden has been lifted from your shoulders." She opened her eyes and now stared directly at Jesse. "Do you have any questions?"

Jesse studied her carefully. He felt she had made one false statement in forecasting the future for him.

Vacation? he thought. *I don't have money to go on a vacation.*

Nonetheless, he still sat quietly, surprised by what she did know. While trying hard not to allow any emotion to show, he wondered about her abilities.

"Nope, I don't have any questions," he said abruptly.

"Well, why did you come here?"

"A friend told me about you, and I just decided to visit."

He chose to play dumb. He felt it wasn't necessary to ask her any questions. Whatever she was communicating with had obviously been watching him closely throughout his life. Jesse decided to use his thoughts to communicate directly to her source, whatever "it" was. What he wanted was information about Lisa.

After giving Jesse a quizzical stare, the psychic reader closed her eyes and tilted her head back as if receiving another message. She slowly dropped her head, looked at Jesse, and said, "Romance! That's one subject we haven't covered yet. Well...you're not looking to get married at this time...But I do see you being challenged at this moment, and you're not meeting up to those challenges."

His suspicions about Lisa were accurate. Now, he had only one more question to be answered, one he'd had since childhood. The psychic reader's eyes remained closed, her head now tilted backwards. In his mind, he repeated the question over and over, pushing it to the forefront of his mind: *Who am I?*

Her head suddenly dropped below her shoulders as her face became distorted. Her glazed eyes rolled upward and transfixed on him. Suddenly, Jesse heard a growling, hideous voice that filled the room. "If you want to find the answer to that question, you'll need to speak to…" The monstrous voice then began grumbling.

Horrified, Jesse sat riveted to his chair, his mouth gaping open. His entire body became numb as evil seized his heart and seemed to stop its beating. An eerie silence now filled the room. Jesse hadn't heard the completion of the statement. He wanted to know, and at the same time, he didn't.

Click!

The tape player had stopped recording. His session was over.

CHAPTER 20

THE CONFRONTATION

A WEEK HAD passed since Jesse had spoken to the psychic reader. Events in his life had now become darker. He felt it was appropriate to change Psycho's name again.

During this time, he had purchased several astrology and horoscope books to further his investigation. He spent his days trying to come to grips with everything. He was walking down a dark tunnel, searching for answers. The further he ventured, the darker his life became. His head was constantly spinning in all directions. He was losing weight, and he couldn't sleep. He wanted out.

He had received a phone call from Lisa, saying she needed to talk. So, without hesitation, he invited her over. Now, with his new information, he was ready for his confrontation with "Madame Evil."

Jesse met Lisa at the entrance door. They exchanged greetings, and he invited her inside.

"Jesse, I haven't seen or heard from you in days," she said.

"And?"

"Well, what's going on?"

"Nothing. You called and said you wanted to speak to me about something."

She stood and looked at him in silence as he moved items around in his studio, pretending to be occupied. He finally broke the silence by saying, "Oh, yeah! By the way, I forgot to tell you I went to see the reader." He spoke with a cheerful voice and attempted to come across happy and excited. He also wanted her to believe the thought came to him unexpectedly.

"Wh-what did she tell you?" Lisa asked nervously.

"Oh, she just mentioned things in my life that I needed to improve on," he said nonchalantly. "She spoke about a few other topics in general."

Madame Evil stood dumbfounded as Jesse walked toward her. She clearly now realized that he had information that contradicted what she had told him in the restaurant.

"Is there anything the readers told you that you may have forgotten to tell me?" he asked.

"N-no…No, there's nothing I can think of," she answered, stuttering.

"OK, well, let me escort you to the door." As they left the building and headed to her car, Jesse said, "Lisa, from now on I want nothing to do with you. When you attend the martial arts class with your children, don't say 'Hi' or 'Bye' to me, just leave me alone."

Sitting in her car, she looked up at him with a cold, calloused expression. "Jesse, while driving over here today, I read a sign mounted on the back of a bus. It read, 'The battle is won, but the war is not over.'"

As they parted, he had no idea this was only the beginning.

CHAPTER 21

A BEAUTIFUL DAY

IT WAS AUGUST, and Jesse's life had turned in a new direction. Everything seemed brighter now that Madame Evil was out of his life. Earlier that day, he had awakened for a morning jog. While on his run near the river, he heard the sound of the wind singing among the golden fallen leaves as they rustled along the earth, and the daylight as it glistened through the trees. Jesse stopped jogging for a moment and stood in awe of his peaceful surroundings. The quietness and stillness captivated him, as seagulls drifted over his head against the azure morning sky. He was happy. It was a feeling he hadn't felt in a long time, and it felt great.

After his jog, he had breakfast and arrived early at his art studio. As he looked out over the city through his large windows, the clouds had cleared, leaving nothing but blue sky. He said, "Thank you," aloud with a sigh of relief. He walked toward his drawing desk and turned on his telephone recorder to retrieve his messages.

That was when everything drastically changed. A growling, threatening, demonic voice screeched through the machine and invaded his body, while wrenching his mind in all directions. His legs trembled and weakened. He felt dazed and short of breath. For a moment, he lost all sense of his surroundings as he searched desperately for somewhere to sit.

For several minutes, he sat motionless in a chair, gazing at the floor, unable to respond. Then it all came back to him. The psychic reader had said that he would be going on a vacation. He now realized that it wasn't an actual vacation; it was a state of mind. He had always taken mental vacations, but this time he had been jogging near water, which brought him peace of mind. The reader had been correct, and her other future predictions about his life swirled in his mind. Jesse felt he would now be forced to search for those events or situations that the reader had predicted, rather than allowing his life to naturally unfold. He felt cheated of his freedom of choice. Now, he would attempt to shape his life according to what the reader had said. Such thoughts would wrench at his mind and increase his madness.

He slowly looked up from the floor, attempting to get acquainted again with his surroundings. In time, shock was replaced with denial. He had heard the traumatizing voice before. This time, it seemed even more menacing and intense with anger. He heard it, but then he hadn't heard it. His mind wouldn't accept it. He began to rationalize it away. Perhaps someone was playing a game. *But the voice wasn't human. Maybe I should play it again and check it to be sure.*

He thought for a moment longer and admitted to himself that he was too terrified by the message to play it again. So he decided to shut it out of his mind and pretend it hadn't happened.

That Saturday morning, Jesse awoke at eleven A.M. He lay still for a moment, staring at the ceiling fan above his head. As sunlight filled the room, he felt he had succeeded in forcing the past haunting events from his mind. He convinced himself that his experiences with Lisa, the psychic readers, and strange voices were in his past and he was moving forward.

Sitting up, he leaned back against the pillow, which was propped against the wall. He glanced around the room as if noticing everything for the first time. A calm came over him as he observed two flies chasing each other around the room, while a spider waited patiently along its web.

Finally, climbing down from his loft, he wrapped a large towel around his waist and moved to the windows. Looking down from the fourth floor, he was taken by surprise when he saw Madame Evil entering a hotel across the street with another gentleman. He wondered if she was attempting to make him jealous. But he doubted that she would know that he would be looking out the window at that time.

"Whatever she is doing or trying to do is her business," Jesse said as he continued on with his day. "I definitely am not going to allow her to enter into my life, or even my thoughts, again."

Sunday morning, he awoke again at exactly eleven A.M. Glancing outside the window, he became petrified and speechless. For the first time, he had become afraid of Madame Evil. It wasn't a fear of her, but of not knowing what she was capable of doing. His body became numb and his brain shut down as he watched her enter a red vehicle with a sunroof, accompanied by the same gentleman from the other morning. What stunned Jesse this time was seeing another man in the back seat as they drove off.

When the vehicle disappeared from his sight, he glanced around the room, stricken with panic. He needed to know about her involvement with these men. His fear was elevated because of the new information he had collected while studying the astrology and horoscope books he had recently purchased.

Jesse recalled reading a particular book about spiritual astrology. It contained more precise and detailed information than the other books he had studied. Under Lisa's horoscope sign, the book stated that a person with a dark, somber, and dominating personality would cause havoc and destruction in other people's lives. Their need to control others would cause disruption in the lives of those associated with them, as well as their own. The book stated that these persons were selfish, manipulative, cunning, and deceitful. They used their craftiness to demolish others and reap their possessions. When Jesse had read the word *possessions*, he knew it meant *souls*. Further reading indicated that in their treachery, these individuals would lie about others' psychic readings.

Jesse found himself puzzled after reading his own sign. The book stated:

If you live in all joy, the spirits will have no use for you. It's like icing on top of a cake, where it's beautiful on the top, but ugly underneath. Also, once you understand the Trinity and your Heavenly Father from your earthly father, you will speak the word of God. There will be nothing to stop you from what you must do. You will wage war against Babylon.

He had no idea what the words *Trinity* or *Babylon* meant, and as far as speaking the word of God, he had never even read the Bible. He also had no idea who God truly was.

In his studio, he nervously paced the floor, trying to put the pieces of this nightmare together. Glancing over at the phone, he pondered whom to call and talk to about his dilemma. He hesitated a moment, unsure of himself, and then frantically reached for the phone, knocking the handle off the cradle and placing the receiver to his ear while dialing the numbers.

After several rings, Dale answered. "Hey, Jesse, what's up?"

"Well, I don't know how to explain this, so I'll come right out and say it."

"Say what?"

"Lisa is a witch, a vampire or something."

Dale laughed.

"You're laughing, huh? I know it sounds crazy, but I'm serious."

He went on to read from the books and explain what he had found in them. Dale immediately fell quiet. Jesse also shared his experiences and encounters with Lisa and everything he had gone through. After explaining everything, Jesse asked, "How often does she visit readers?"

"She goes all the time, and refers others to them, too."

"How many books does she have on astrology and horoscopes?"

"She has a shelf of books at work, and an entire library at home. She even studied in the Philippines for thirteen years."

They continued speaking for two hours. During their conversation, Jesse discovered more lies Lisa had spoken.

After another hour, he and Dale said their goodbyes. Within five minutes, the phone rang. Fearful, Jesse hesitated. He stood facing the phone with uncertainty as it rang. Whispering voices in his head began urging him to answer the phone as he held himself back.

Pick it up. No...No...No!

Now the whispering voices had become louder. The ringing continued. He waited, then slowly picked it up. He stared at the receiver for a moment before placing it to his ear, not knowing what to expect.

"Hello."

"Jesse?"

"Yeah."

"It's me, Gerald."

"Hey, how ya doin?"

"Good. The reason I'm calling is that I spoke earlier this week with Lisa."

"And?"

"She wanted a key to the front door to your building."

"For what?"

"She said the door is always locked when she brings the kids to class. So she wanted a key of her own to gain access."

"Gerald, she's lying. Do not give her a key!"

"Is there something going on?"

He thought about explaining everything to Gerald, but decided it was best not to. So he replied in a quieter tone, "No, just don't give her a key."

They continued speaking briefly before Jesse hung up the phone. Immediately, the phone rang again, and without thought, Jesse picked up the receiver.

"Hello."

"Hi, Jesse. It's Lisa."

"What do you want?"

"Well, I wanted to speak to you about us."

"And?"

"Jesse...I feel hurt and devastated because you—"

"Wait a minute, Lisa, stop the games. You had your fishing line out, and you thought you were reeling me in nice and slow. You put the net under the water to retrieve your catch and got upset because I wasn't in your fishing net."

"Fishing line?" Lisa screamed into the phone with rage. "Jesse, you were never on the fishing line in the first place! Who do you think you are? You were never—"

Click.

Jesse gently placed the receiver on the cradle, not allowing Lisa to complete her sentence. He unplugged the telephone.

Time passed quickly, and nightfall arrived. He checked the lock on his door as an afterthought. Alone, he now stood staring at his reflection in the glass window pane. He gazed through the window and into the darkness. The feeling of terror was now deep within him.

CHAPTER 22

THE VISITATION

With methodic precision, the Specter moves his black rook forward across the chessboard. More pieces are placed aside and crushed. Checkmate.

MIDNIGHT ARRIVED. JESSE was struggling desperately to stay awake, afraid of what might happen if he fell asleep. As minutes ticked away, his flushed red eyes became heavier. Time seemed to stand still, and even the quietness of the street below became haunting. His head nodded more frequently as fatigue set in. Jesse knew it was only a matter of time before he collapsed and surrendered to sleep. He was terrified with anticipation of what awaited him. So, kneeling and looking up, he made a desperate plea to God.

"God, please help me. Something is going to happen tonight."

He turned off the lights, further darkening the room. He hesitantly lay down and began drifting into sleep as his restless eyes closed. He awoke at 2:45 A.M. and glanced around the room, surprised that nothing had taken place. Half asleep, he climbed down from the loft and drank a glass of juice. Still feeling uneasy, he went back up to the loft and went back to sleep.

THE HOUR OF DARKNESS

Spiritually, he was suspended in an abyss of total darkness. The air around him was still, and a feeling of isolation surrounded him. He stood afloat with his arms outstretched, his fingers extended and reaching outward into nothingness. His eyes attempted to penetrate the heavy blackness that surrounded him, yet there was only an absence of sight and sound.

"Am I dreaming?" he asked himself, even though he certainly didn't feel he was.

Suddenly, in the far distance, he saw three ghostly demons gliding toward him. With each blink of his eyes, the demons drew closer. Their features were terrifying and violent. Their elongated, razor-like teeth glistened in the dark. Jesse stared as the creatures drew closer. As he continued watching in dismay, a still, calm, yet thunderous voice said, "This is not a dream. If you do not fight, you will not wake up."

Jesse found himself surrounded and overwhelmed by the demonic spirits as they pressed forward, circling around from all directions. He maintained a defiant stance of strong will and faith. The spiritual battle would be for his existence. His reward would be his life; theirs, his soul. Jesse had no time for thoughts of fear, for he knew evil fed on fear. He knew any hesitation would be his doom.

The spirits loomed overhead, observing their victim. Suddenly, they unleashed their ravaging attack upon him. Their teeth gnawed and ripped as their claws slashed through him. The demons were fervent and restless in their quest to conquer his soul. Despite their colossal size, Jesse's unyielding spirit continued fighting under the condition of these insurmountable odds. Jesse endured the onslaught, but as time passed, the savage attacks began to overpower him, and the darkness became suffocating. In his last cry, his mouth opened and released a passionate, unheard scream of agony in his refusal to die.

Finally, it was over. While forcing his eyes to open, he continued repeating the words, "You have no authority over me...You have no authority over me..."

Hearing his own voice, he let his words trail off. He stared at the blurred red digital numbers of the clock face; it was 3:55 A.M. His body felt stiff and immovable. His eyes searched around, attempting to focus on anything familiar. Gradually, he began moving one finger at a time.

He pinched his thigh to convince himself of his existence. Slowly, he sat upright, while placing his feet on the thin gray carpet. He touched his face, head, chest, and legs. He felt excited, as though overcome by life itself. He whispered, "I am still here…I'm still alive."

His mind accepted normality as he looked down over his studio space from his loft. His legs quivered as he climbed down, stepping back into reality. He fought within his mind to accept that it had only been a nightmare. Reaching the sink, he turned on the faucet and splashed cold water over his head. The water ran along the contours of his face and seeped into his mouth. He turned on the light above his head.

Jesse was barely able to stand as his body swayed. He braced himself against the sink. After several attempts, he was able to turn off the faucet and watched the swirling water disappear down the drain. Pausing for a moment, he lifted his head and was surprised by his own hypnotic stare. His eyes were wide and dilated. He stared intently at this unknown face. A warm, vibrating sensation flowed through his body to the palms of his hands. He glanced at his palms, stunned and baffled.

Time elapsed while Jesse frantically paced his studio, desperately trying to understand what had just taken place. He began preparing for work while saying to himself, "She's a witch, a vampire or something, but this can't be happening. This can't be real. Things like this only happen in movies."

At seven A.M., Jesse punched in at work and entered the security office. He noticed a psychology magazine on top of a file cabinet directly in front of him, with an article titled "Vampires." Reading the article, he was dumbfounded to realize that there were people who actually believed they were vampires. He opened the dictionary and read it throughout the morning and afternoon while at work. Some of the words he looked up were *horoscope, medium, astrology, God, spiritualism,* and *demons.* Consumed by his search, he flipped the pages to the word *Satan,* where he read, *The Devil, the chief great adversary seeking to destroy humanity. Enemy of God and human beings.* He flipped through the pages as one word led to another.

Around mid-day, the security director, Tom Callahan, called out to Jesse from behind his desk. "Jesse, why are you constantly looking through the dictionary?"

Callahan was a stout, older gentleman. He had been retired from the police force for several years, which may have been part of the reason he had an analytical approach to almost everything.

Jesse glanced over his shoulder and said, "As soon as I find out, I'll let you know." He turned back and continued through the pages.

"What?" Callahan asked with a note of surprise.

Jesse gave Callahan a perturbed look. "If you really wanna know, I'll tell you. I had to fight off spiritual demons last night while I slept. They were trying to take my soul."

"Jesse, that's not possible," Callahan thundered. "You probably had a terrible experience during the day and just had a bad dream."

Facing Callahan with a look of disdain, Jesse said, "You can say whatever you want. I was there, not you. I know what happened, and I'm sorry, but one plus one does not always equal two."

After work, Jesse arrived at his loft space and met with Dale. He explained to Dale how he had been attacked by demons, and described the voice he had heard. After listening quietly and intently, Dale said, "Jesse, I recently spoke with several friends about Lisa, and they advised me to stay away from her." He paused, then added, "Jesse…I think you're losing it."

Dale's comment caught Jesse off-guard. Shaking his head in disbelief, he replied, "Go to the newsstand and purchase the magazine *Psychology* and read the article on vampires. It states there have been reported stories throughout history of people believing themselves to be vampires. The article also said that there are modern-day vampires. There were incidents when, after murdering their victims, the killers drank their blood and bathed in it. They believed that they could gain vitality and magical powers from the blood."

Hearing the urgency in Jesse's voice, Dale watched him intently, apparently searching for signs of insanity. Jesse chose to remain quiet, in case others thought he had gone insane.

A few days later, Dale and Jesse met again. Jesse asked if he had purchased the magazine and read the article.

Dale shook his head. "I searched all over the newsstands for the magazine and couldn't find it anywhere."

"What do you mean you couldn't find it?" Jesse asked in disbelief.

"That's it. I couldn't find the magazine anywhere."

"Are you sure?"

"Yes," Dale said with certainty as he picked up the magazine from Jesse's desk. Then he said slowly in disbelief, "Jesse, this magazine is seventeen years old!"

The magazine was dated October 1973. It was now August 1990.

CHAPTER 23

SANITY

AFTER THAT DAY, Jesse was unable to sleep or eat. He was petrified day and night, but the night terrified him most of all. He did anything he could not to go back to his loft. He stayed with friends, family, girlfriends, anywhere, as long as he wasn't alone.

On his job, he met a woman named Elisha Williams and began spending a great deal of time with her. Elisha was quiet and a mystery to him. She was attractive, with short, braided hair, hazel eyes, and bronze-colored skin. They shared thoughts and laughed almost constantly. While together, they remained in a joyous state of mind and in a world of their own. Yet, there was a private side that Elisha kept to herself, and Jesse never asked during the moments she seemed withdrawn. She was allowed to be herself. Jesse had spoken to Elisha about his encounters, which she found intriguing and accepted in a casual manner.

Elisha began to mention strange events happening in her life. She said someone had broken into her car but hadn't stolen anything. She also told Jesse someone had attempted to break into her apartment. She had not been home at the time. Elisha's upstairs neighbors had contacted the police and told the authorities that they had not seen anyone come or go. They also said the banging noise was so loud at her door that their apartment upstairs shook, causing pictures on the walls to shake. When the police arrived, they found an old rifle bayonet at the entrance of her apartment door.

As she spoke of these incidents to him, Jesse just listened. He wondered if these events had anything to do with his past involvement with Lisa.

The following week, on a Friday night at eleven P.M., he met Elisha at a dance club. It wasn't long before two A.M. arrived, and they departed the club.

"I'm house-sitting for my uncle and his family," Elisha said. "They'll be out of town for a week. Would you like to stay overnight?"

"Yeah, sure."

As they approached her car, Jesse noticed Elisha's name had been scratched in large jagged letters onto her trunk with a sharp object.

"Who did this to your car?" Jesse asked.

Elisha stared at the markings in surprise. "I didn't notice that until you mentioned it," she said.

As they sat in the car driving to her relative's house, Jesse's thoughts raced. The incidents and everything up to that point boggled his mind.

When they arrived, Elisha fed the dog and took him for a walk. When she returned, they walked up the stairs to the parents' bedroom. Elisha took two paperback books from the shelf and gave them to him. Then she crawled onto the bed and fell asleep.

Jesse stood with the books in his hands. *Why did she give me these books?* he asked himself. He sat on the bed as his mind searched for answers. The time was now 3:15 A.M., but he was still nervous and unable to sleep. So, he opened one of the books, randomly selected a page, and read the first sentence aloud: "'You're a deserter, and we will seek and destroy you.'"

As the words penetrated his thoughts, he slammed the book shut. His nervousness became overwhelming. Now, sitting on the edge of the bed in the dim light, he tried to convince himself that what he had just read was a coincidence. Picking up the second book, he selected a page at random at the center of the book and read aloud as before: "'There's mutiny on the ship; you must walk the plank of death, and die in the deep dark, murky waters.'"

He dropped the book and frantically crawled backwards on the bed. Desperation set in. He glanced over at Elisha, who remained asleep. The thought of waking her crossed his mind, but what would he say to her? He couldn't even accept everything that was happening himself. Two words repeatedly echoed through his thoughts: *Why me? Why me? Why me?*

Jesse now lay stiffly on his back in the darkened bedroom. He hadn't remembered turning off the lamp, but the glow from under the shade had disappeared. His eyes were locked open as they gazed through the skylight above his head. Tree limbs swayed in the howling wind as heavy drops of rain pounded against the glass. The branches looked like skeletal hands clawing at him as they struck the glass windowpane. Jesse gasped as demon faces materialized among the dead branches.

Why me? Why me? Why me?

As Jesse continued looking through the skylight, he noticed a thin ray of moonlight that sliced through the darkness across the room. The light fell on an old wooden dresser. Jesse forced himself to sit up as he followed the light across the room with his eyes. He found himself staring at a large, circular pin-on button that was facing him. It glowed in the light of the room. He slowly read the words on the button, "'I Am Your Father.'"

The words sent a floodgate of emotions rushing through his body.

God? he thought in disbelief. He couldn't believe that God was communicating with him as his Father. He had been haunted throughout his childhood and adulthood by the absence of a father and his guidance. The thought of God was overwhelming, as he also remembered the "voice" that had warned him before the demonic spiritual attack. Stunned, he thought for a moment, attempting to place everything in perspective, which at that moment seemed impossible. His mind was in an extreme state of disarray. To escape this dream state he seemed to be in, Jesse fell back onto the bed and dropped his head onto the pillow, quickly falling asleep.

Jesse was awakened by the sunlight shining over his head on Saturday morning. He quickly got up and entered the downstairs dining room, where he continued searching through the spiritual astrology book. While flipping the pages, he began whistling the song, "Pop Goes the Weasel," for nearly thirty minutes.

Elisha awoke later that morning. Jesse didn't say anything to her about his overnight experience. They went to lunch, and she dropped him off at his studio.

Saturday evening, he was invited to the movies with friends. He sat nervously in the theater with soda and popcorn in hand as the lights dimmed to darkness. The first premiere of an upcoming film displayed a jack-in-the-box sitting in the middle of a wooden floor on the large screen. The handle slowly began to turn, while playing an eerie version of "Pop Goes the Weasel." Suddenly, an evil doll popped up with a haunting voice that said, "Child's Play…Part Two!"

Jesse sat aghast as his heart pounded uncontrollably and his popcorn spilled across his lap. He gripped his chair, stunned by how the events in his life had unfolded, bringing him to this point. He was beginning to understand that he had been thrown into the middle of a spiritual battle between good and evil.

He sat focusing on the movie, *Mo' Better Blues*, as he tried to block out the threatening onslaught of evil upon his mind. When the movie ended, he read the words, *A Love Supreme*. The words gave him a brief sensation of relief and calm, knowing that God was present. But then his thoughts began racing in all directions again, and he remained frightened, not knowing what to expect next.

CHAPTER 24

LABYRINTH

It is said that there is a thin line between the sane and insane.

THROUGHOUT HIS LIFE, Jesse had been on a quest for the truth. Evil was in a savage race to destroy him, and God to save him. He was now living in two worlds at once. The mental attacks were constant and persistent. He felt as though he were on a screeching roller coaster ride, heading down. The more he screamed, the faster the ride. There was no getting off or turning back. The signs he received were many. The mental attacks were used for one purpose: to drive him insane.

Monday, Jesse arrived at his mother's home. As always, a wide smile formed across her face whenever he visited. Crystal was on a visit from her home in Washington, D.C. She was now twenty-six. After her years in high school, Crystal had attended college, begun a successful career as an accountant, married, and had two beautiful children. As usual, her long, curly hair was carefully styled.

Crystal and Grace hadn't seen Jesse in several months. So, obviously, they all were elated and overjoyed to see each other as they exchanged hugs.

"It's great to see you," Crystal said. "How are you doing, and how's the art coming along?"

Jesse thought for a moment and figured a simple answer would be best. "Well, I'm doing OK, and the art's coming along fine."

Crystal and Jesse sat down to talk while Grace prepared something for them to eat. After a few hours, Crystal said her goodbyes, while Jesse and Grace remained talking at the kitchen table.

"Mom, when I was born, did anything strange occur?" Jesse asked.

"No, but I'm certain the doctor dropped you on your head."

Jesse chuckled. "Funny, Mom."

"Well, why do you ask?" she said with concern.

"Nothing, just a lot of strange things have been happening around me."

"Like what?"

"Well, it's something I can't explain now, but I'll talk about it later."

Grace watched him closely but said nothing. She knew he was a private person, but in time he would talk further when he was ready. They were just grateful for each other's company.

An hour had passed when Grace said, "Well, I'm getting tired. I'm going in to get some sleep. If you need more food to eat, there's plenty in the refrigerator, and be sure you take some with you."

They hugged as she departed to the bedroom.

After eating, Jesse sat in the family room. The house now had an unsettled quietness. The only light in the darkened room was the glow from the television as Jesse flipped through the channels with the remote control. While sitting in the large black leather recliner, Jesse felt a growing sense of danger. A chill overcame him as he stood and turned his head and glanced around the room. Leaving the family room, he began his search throughout the house. He looked behind doors, under tables, through windows, and even made certain all the entrance doors were secured. The only area he hadn't checked was the dreaded basement. He stood at the top of the worn stairs, which led down to the cold, dirty cement floor and jagged stone walls. He leaned forward, peering even further into the dampness as a chill came over him again. He then stepped backwards, heading up the stairs and returning to the family room.

Sitting down, he let out a sigh of relief. Then, suddenly, he stopped breathing as a demon's face surfaced on the television. Its dark, hideous eyes burned with fierce rage. It snarled and pointed its finger at him. The demon raged because it had not captured Jesse's soul on the night of his spiritual attack.

Stunned, Jesse watched as the demon faded back into the television. Jesse realized that the demon had been looking through the window of a plane at a passenger on a television show. The demon then began to destroy the wing of the plane. The male passenger was the only person able to see the demon. When he began warning everyone, many assumed he had gone insane. So, when the plane landed, he was admitted to the hospital. The episode was from the television series *The Twilight Zone*.

Jesse sat frozen with only his fingers moving frantically along the remote control, trying desperately to change the channel. He watched the Monday Night Football game. The New York Giants were playing against the San Francisco 49ers. There was a field goal attempt, and in the stands someone was flapping a gigantic banner. In huge letters it read, *GOD LOVES YOU.*

Jesse stared at the banner. He had never really felt loved by anyone, especially after experiencing the loneliness and difficulties in his life. "God loves me?" he murmured. He sat with his head lowered, pondering the statement.

He heard a voice above him. "Here, this is my Bible. Please read it. I think it will help you." Grace gave him her Bible and returned to her bedroom. Jesse sat staring at the cover. Moments later, he hurriedly placed the Bible in his carrying bag and rode his bike back to his loft space. It was several hours past midnight as he sat reading. He struggled to stay awake, but weariness soon took its toll on him, and he fell asleep at his desk.

He awoke an hour later. Looking at the Bible, he noticed that the pages had been turned. He read,

Astrology, Horoscopes, and Occult

Keep on, then, with your magic spells and with your many sorceries, which you labored at since childhood. Perhaps you will succeed, perhaps you will cause terror. All the counsel you have received has only worn you out! Let your astrologers come forward, those stargazers who make predictions month by month, let them save you from what is coming upon you. Surely they are like stubble; the fire will burn them up. They cannot even save themselves from the power of the flame. Here are no coals to warm anyone; here is no fire to sit by. That is all they can do for you—these you have labored with and trafficked with since childhood. Each of them goes on in his error; there is not one that can save you.

—Isaiah 47:12-15

Let no one be found among you who sacrifices his son or daughter in the fire, who practices divination or sorcery, interprets omens, engages in witchcraft, or cast spells, or who is a medium or spiritist or consults the dead.
—Deuteronomy 18:10-11

After reading, Jesse quickly began collecting the astrology, horoscope, and New Age books from the shelves and threw them into a plastic garbage bag. The information the books contained was powerful, but now he knew it was wrong.

He thought about Madame Evil and how she had attempted to deceive and manipulate him for the Devil's purpose. He realized the Devil had been using Madame Evil as an agent to recruit him. Satan's plan was to use the gifts and talents that God had given Jesse for his own purpose. If he had accepted the information Lisa had given him as truth, Lucifer would have succeeded. Jesse would have unknowingly aided Satan by leading masses of people to Hell, along with himself. Now, even though he understood, it was still difficult for him to see Madame Evil as a witch or vampire. The series of events was still too shocking for his mind to accept.

At 3:45 A.M., though fatigued, Jesse began climbing up the steps of his loft. He crawled across the futon and laid his head upon the pillow while closing his eyes.

Then a sinister voice spoke into his ear: "She's one of us, and we're going to take as many lives as we can."

The haughty words shot through his mind, forcing him into disarray. He leaped from his futon, and as his breathing increased and heart thundered, Jesse stumbled backward down the steps of his loft. While fumbling through the darkness, he heard growling voices in the next room, followed by shrieking sounds. Terrified, he tripped and crashed to the floor. In a frenzy, he scrambled back to his feet and pressed his back against the wall. For the first time, he felt trapped in a close encounter with his predator. Opening his eyes, he forced himself to look through the dark doorway. The horrific voices continued, followed by hammering outside his thick metal door: *Boom... Boom...Boom!*

Light from the hall began to creep around the edges of the doorway as the door vibrated with the onslaught of blows. Then the phone rang.

Suddenly, the outcry of voices and booming ceased. Jesse slowly slid down along the wall onto the floor, where he sat trembling in fright until morning. At sunrise, his eyes were tired, sunken, and bloodshot as he dressed for work. He was unshaven and his clothes were wrinkled and unkempt. At 6:30 A.M., he stood on the fourth floor in a delirious state, waiting for the arrival of the elevator. While rubbing his irritated eyes, he noticed a note next to the elevator. The note read, *In case of fire, take the stairs down, and go to Hell.*

As he exited the building, he noticed graffiti on the wall of a building across the street. It read, *Destiny.*

During his lunchtime break at work, Jesse stood outside in front of the hotel, staring across the street into space. He continued thinking about everything and why it all was happening to him. He now knew his purpose in life, but was refusing to pursue it. Silently, he stated his defiant position to God.

I'm not doing it. People will think I'm crazy. I'm going back to being normal. I'm going to live an average life like most people. Leave me alone. I'm not going to say or do anything.

An elderly man approached him and said, "What are you complaining about? There was a man who complained about not having any shoes, until he met a man who didn't have any feet." He stared intently into Jesse's eyes before walking away.

Jesse was startled by the elderly man's reply to him. He knew God had just answered him through this man, who had no idea what he had been saying in his thoughts. His mind was now in a state of bewilderment.

"Jesse, are you OK?"

Jesse turned to see the doorman looking at him strangely.

"Yeah," he said hesitantly.

"You were standing there as though you were in deep thought, lost in another world."

"Naw, I'm OK."

"Well, you sure look tired."

Jesse gave the doorman a blank stare. He began feeling overwhelmed. He walked directly to the human resources department and placed an immediate request for time off.

Later, after work, Jesse went to purchase an item from a local mall. As he left the store, he noticed a poster across the corridor on the floor against the wall. It was a black and white photograph of a woman who resembled Madame Evil. The closer he came to the poster, the more astonished he was by the resemblance. The picture looked like a black and white photograph from the 1950s. Above the woman's head were the bold letters, *WANTED.*

Beneath her portrait were the words, *For her loose talks have cost too many lives.*

CHAPTER 25

VISION

A desperate person will go on a manic pursuit for sanity.

WHILE ON VACATION in October, Jesse attempted to remain busy and keep his mind occupied. One early afternoon, he walked into a store and to a locksmith's booth to have a key duplicated. While handing the locksmith the key, he noticed a black sticker on the window with bold red letters that read, *I Want Your Body*.

The threatening statement forced him to take a step back as he tried to maintain his composure. Turning his head to his left, he noticed an elderly woman walking upstairs from the basement bargain store. She wore a long-sleeved white sweatshirt with an illustration of a tree. Above the tree was the words, *God's Family Tree*. By this time, Jesse was becoming more accepting of these occurrences, even though fear lingered inside him.

After departing the store, Jesse returned to his studio, where his mind became a battlefield unto itself. After hours of mumbling and conversing with himself, his thoughts began spinning out of control. The voices inside his head had reached a peak of agonizing torture. The Devil was now inside his head and seemed to be winning.

Trapped in the corner of his room, he felt overwhelmed by his thoughts as tears streamed down his face. The suffocating walls of depression began closing in. Thoughts of reason and logic became more and more unfamiliar. He needed to get out, and now, before turmoil changed into tragedy.

Jesse splashed his face with water to wash away the tears. Quickly gathering his things, he departed the building.

He began walking along Monroe Avenue, one of the many cultural areas of the city. A mixture of races, cultures, and nationalities filled the area. Restaurants lined both sides of the avenue with just about anything a person could want. Between the restaurants were a number of different stores, selling anything from health foods, skateboards, and records, to vintage clothing, antiques, books, and tattoos. As evening settled in and the sun faded, the bright signs and neon lights competed for attention.

During this time, the night crowd settled in. Many people congregated in this area: artists, punkers, bohemian types, college students, visitors, homeless, and those who were just different in their own way. Amongst the crowd were also the suburbanites and upper class who had arrived to join the excitement and activity. Even though everyone appeared to mingle, each group stayed among its own. Overall, the crowds seemed calm and relaxed, without a worry, enjoying themselves as the music escaped from the bars and onto the streets.

In the dark corners, some leaned against buildings and vomited from having too much to drink. There were youth who had dyed their hair black and wore dark clothing and heavy eye shadow. Women gazed into each other's eyes, while some men pretended to be women, as children looked on, confused.

Expensive cars idled on the corners, waiting for prostitutes and even attempting to entice young boys. Others sat negotiating inside their vehicles, while junkies stood hunched over, suspended in time by their stupor. The sounds of the street, voices, music, noises, vehicles, and footsteps blended and clashed at the same time. Everything was a blur, one continuous motion, as though the environment had a rhythm and energy of its own.

Jesse walked along the street, observing it all. Being in the middle of it relaxed and disturbed him at the same time. All the activity surrounding him distracted him and prevented the negative thoughts from pounding at the door to his mind, at least momentarily.

He approached the entrance of a poster store. Near the door was a homeless middle-aged woman slouched in a dark corner with her shoulders drawn. Dressed in black, she leaned against the brick wall with one hand, while holding large, torn plastic bags of clothing in the other. She seemed angry and agitated, mumbling obscenities to no one in particular. Jesse peered in her direction. The woman slowly rotated her head around and glared at him. Her face was twisted with malice as she shouted with a voice of outrage and disgust, "So, now you're all holy and everything, huh?"

Jesse chose to ignore the comment as he continued into the store, as shouting and harsh laughter continued outside the door.

Posters, postcards, and silk-screened drapery hung everywhere. The walls were covered and racks were filled with every kind of poster, featuring movies, art, music, and celebrities. It was difficult to move about the store. To Jesse's surprise, the store had only one patron: him.

After browsing for nearly an hour, he selected three posters and took them to the counter to purchase. The cashier was a youthful, energetic lady with freckles and a constant, gleaming smile. There was a narrow gap between her front teeth, which seemed to add to her personality. She wore a blue dress with numerous colorful, detailed abstract designs, along with a pair of funky, high-heeled platform shoes. Now, looking up at Jesse while swaying to the music from the speakers overhead, she asked excitedly, "Hi! Are you ready to purchase?"

"Yeah, I'll take these posters."

"Would you like to purchase any of these postcards? They're fifty percent off." She pointed to the postcards displayed on the counter.

"No, thanks." Jesse handed her the money as she rang up the purchase on the cash register. He was glad to converse with someone, even if only briefly. As the cashier began wrapping the posters in a roll of heavy brown paper, Jesse took another minute to glance about the store. While turning to his left, he came into direct eye contact with a horrifying image that had a hypnotic, menacing stare. It was Satan, the Devil himself.

The Devil's scorching, fiery red eyes were fixed on Jesse with hatred. His pupils looked like endless depths of darkness. His mouth was spread wide, with white, jagged fangs and a thick, elongated crimson tongue, stretching forward with the thirst for blood. The background color of the postcard was an intense dark green, the same as his dilated pupils. His nostrils were flared with hostility. The postcard represented Satan's dominating presence and essence of sheer rage.

Stunned, Jesse picked up the postcard from the rack, flipped it over, and read the back of the card aloud: "How the devil are you?"

Jesse quickly placed the postcard back in its place and turned to the cashier, shaken. Still dancing, the cashier remained preoccupied with wrapping the posters. Jesse began walking nervously around the store in search of an escape. He noticed a hologram card down the opposite aisle, which revealed two images. As he came closer, he saw an image of Jesus Christ and the Holy Shroud. The image of Christ was peaceful and humbling, and his eyes reflected depth.

Jesse rushed to the counter.

"Is everything OK?" the cashier asked, now noticing Jesse's nervousness.

"Yeah," Jesse said as he grabbed the wrapped posters and hurriedly made his way out of the store.

Late that night, Jesse returned to his loft and continued reading the Bible. As he read Genesis, he became extremely impatient. He felt the reading was going too slowly compared to the speed of events happening in his life. So, again, he called out to God.

"God, please help me. I'm reading, but this is moving too slowly. I need quick information on Jesus Christ and everything that's going on. The Devil is after me, and I'm running out of time!"

Jesse kept pleading throughout the night until he fell asleep near three A.M. It was then that he received a vision. It was a painted image of Christ on the cross, displayed on the cover of a book.

He awoke the next morning and went to work. The image remained in his mind throughout the day.

After work, he walked to the bookstore. He entered the mall area and went up the escalator with hesitation. While walking toward the entrance of the store, he spoke to God silently. *All right, I'm going inside. I just hope no one asks me what I'm looking for, because I'm going to sound awfully stupid trying to describe a cover and not knowing the title or author.*

As he stood in the aisle of the bookstore, a gentleman walked by. Jesse watched him as he continued down the aisle. As he turned and faced the bookshelf, he saw the book directly in front of him. There was the exact image of Christ on the cover that he had seen in his vision. The artist's name was Salvador Dali. The title read, *Life of Christ*, by Fulton J. Sheen. Surprised, Jesse gave a silent *Thank you* and purchased the book, along with *The Revell Bible Dictionary* by Fleming H. Revell Company.

As he read the Bible, book, and reference materials, everything began coming together. He began to understand the spiritual battle for souls, and the need for people to be saved. He was awakened to Satan's purpose and Christ's mission.

Also, during his reading of the Bible, Jesse came across the word *idolatry*. It was clear that God was totally against it. At this time, Jesse had three statues in the martial arts training studio. He had purchased them and placed them inside for decorating purposes. He never worshipped or prayed to them, but now he wondered if he was wrong for having them. He was unsure, so he asked God.

At about ten P.M., Jesse lay down to sleep. He placed his head on the pillow, and while closing his eyes, he had a vision. He saw the three sculptures falling through the air and exploding as they crashed to the ground. The next morning, he removed and destroyed the statues.

CHAPTER 26

SILENT LUCIDITY

B Y NOVEMBER, JESSE had become more accepting of his abilities to interact with the supernatural world. He had obtained balance in knowing that God was with him, and that evil was in a relentless pursuit to destroy him. Also during this time, after having placed himself in a position of overwhelming debt, he closed the martial arts training studio and began sharing his loft space with a roommate.

His roommate, Luca Fagen, was in his early twenties and had recently been hired by the security department. He had a wide nose and thick eyebrows, and wore his dark hair spiked on top. When Luca moved in, Jesse attempted to briefly explain his experiences and the need for Luca to save his own soul. But Luca wasn't receptive to what he had to say, so Jesse felt it was best to remain quiet.

On one chilly night, Jesse found himself unable to sleep. After lying still for an hour, he decided to rise and began reading the Bible at his desk. It was past midnight as he continued reading the book of Matthew, while Luca slept in the other room. Time passed slowly as he studied and labored over the scriptures. Both rooms were dark, with the shades drawn. The only light came from his desk lamp. In the quiet stillness of the room, Jesse whispered the text of Matthew 13:37-43.

"He answered, 'The one who sowed the good seed is the Son of Man. The field is the world, and the good seed stands for the sons of the kingdom. The weeds are the sons of the evil one, and the enemy who sows them is the devil. The harvest is the end of the age, and the harvesters are the angels. As the weeds are pulled up and burned in the fire, so it will be at the end of the age. The Son of Man will send out his angels, and they will weed out of his kingdom everything that causes sin and all who do evil. They will throw them into the fiery furnace, where there will be weeping and gnashing of teeth. Then the righteous will shine like the sun in the kingdom of their Father. He who has ears, let him hear.'"

At that moment, the silence in the other room was broken. Jesse heard the sharp, wrenching sounds of Luca gnashing and grinding his teeth. Jesse stood and peered through the doorway, but the horrendous sounds ceased. After wondering for a moment, Jesse returned to his desk and continued reading. Minutes later, he read Matthew 22:11-13.

"'But when the king came in to see the guests, he noticed a man there who was not wearing wedding clothes. "Friend," he asked, "how did you get in here without wedding clothes?" The man was speechless. Then the king told the attendants, "Tie him hand and foot, and throw him outside, into the darkness, where there will be weeping and gnashing of teeth."'"

Again, the sounds of gnashing teeth pierced the room. Jesse jumped up from the desk and stared at Luca, but he was still and appeared to be sleeping.

After Luca awoke at seven A.M., Jesse studied his every move. Hesitantly, he asked, "Luca, are you aware that you gnash your teeth while sleeping?"

"No," Luca answered as he continued dressing for work.

The following week, while asleep, Jesse found himself awakened by Luca sleepwalking in the late night hours. Jesse watched from the loft as Luca stood at the bottom of the stairs, blindly staring into space and mumbling. Finally he returned to bed and fell asleep. After having witnessed this numerous times, Jesse decided to bring it to Luca's attention.

"Luca, do you realize that you walk in your sleep at night?"

Luca shook his head, seeming unconcerned. "Nope."

"You may not realize it, but spiritual demons are going through you to get to me. You need to save your soul."

"And Jesse, how am I to do that?"

"Everyone is a sinner, because we're born into it. All you need to do is ask God for forgiveness for your sins and state that you accept Jesus Christ as your Lord and Savior."

"That's it?"

"Yeah, but it must come from your heart and soul. You must mean it. Then you will receive the Holy Spirit, and your soul will be saved from Hell. We are all sinners due to the disobedience of Adam and Eve eating from the Tree of Knowledge of Good and Evil."

"So, you're saying then my soul will be saved."

"From birth, we become creatures of God, the Creator of all things. Once we accept Christ as our Savior and receive the Holy Spirit, we become children of God. It's written that God wishes no one to perish. Christ is more concerned about those who are not saved. Jesus Christ also states that those who believe and are baptized shall be saved; those who don't shall be condemned."

Luca stared at him for a moment before responding. "Look, Jesse… you're into the Bible; I'm not. I believe in God, but I'm not ready to change yet. I love being with different women and having fun. You reached a point in your life where you were ready to change. I'm happy for you, but at this moment, I'm in the early stages of my life. Sorry, but I'll take my chances between Heaven and Hell."

Jesse wanted desperately for Luca to understand why he was warning him. But he realized it was useless to speak any further.

Several days later, Jesse returned late one night to his place after watching a movie with a friend. After unlocking his door, he entered his loft space. Upon entering, he noticed Luca asleep. Suddenly, he rolled to his right, facing the wall. He began grumbling, while lashing his tongue out toward the electrical socket directly in front of his face. His tongue continuously lashed from his mouth as he came within inches of inserting his tongue into the electrical socket.

The next morning, Jesse called him from work.

"Luca? It's Jesse. I need to tell you that you were attempting to insert your tongue into an electrical socket next to your head as you slept last night. The demons are going through you. You'd be dead now if it hadn't been for God preventing you from doing it. You need to save your soul."

There was a long pause. "Well, Jesse, I don't remember doing anything like that," Luca said. "I'll give it some thought, but right now I gotta get going."

Another late evening, Jesse was working in his art studio, attempting another project. His mind constantly returned to his illustration, *The Chess Game*. Throughout the evening, he found himself unable to focus. He wondered why he hadn't drawn the hangman's noose in the background of the drawing, which he had intended. Finally, after hours of being unable to concentrate, he went to a local bookstore in search of a particular book. While in the store for several minutes, he became discouraged, not being able to locate the book.

After a few more unsuccessful minutes, he approached the cashier for assistance. While looking down at the cashier's desk, Jesse noticed he was playing the game hangman with a co-worker.

Preoccupied with the game, the cashier looked up from the desk with surprise. "Can I help you?" he asked politely.

Jesse looked at him and his co-worker and then back to the drawing of the hangman's scaffold. Under the scaffold were five blank spaces.

"No," Jesse replied.

Leaving the bookstore, Jesse returned to his loft space, where Luca was asleep. Glancing toward Luca as he lay still, Jesse noticed gray duct tape over the electrical socket. As he entered the next room, he heard Luca mumbling loudly. From the other room, Jesse asked, "What?"

There was silence for a moment, and then the mumbling continued. When Jesse entered the room, he saw Luca sitting upright in bed, facing the window with a blank stare on his face, as if in a trance.

As Jesse walked closer, Luca remained still, staring ahead. The moonlight shone through the window upon his stiff body. Finally, he slowly walked around Luca and sat on the windowsill. Luca hadn't moved. Jesse found himself becoming more afraid.

"What?" Jesse asked again, trying to provoke a response from Luca.

"The rope is mine," Luca said in a flat, unfamiliar voice.

"What?" Jesse repeated, surprised.

"The rope is mine!" he said again, but with a voice of authority.

"Luca!"

Jesse shouted, hoping to awaken him from his trance. Luca rotated his body toward him. With intensity in his eyes, he stared directly at Jesse. Then he turned around and fell back to sleep. Jesse understood that God was letting him know that the hangman's noose was his. God had removed the noose, saving him from death.

The next morning, Jesse didn't mention the incident. At work in the security office, Luca approached him and said, "Jesse, I tore these two comic strips from the newspaper. I don't understand them. Here, maybe you can figure them out."

Jesse examined them closely. The first cartoon was a "Ziggy" strip. Ziggy sat at a table with a coffee mug on his right and a toaster on his left. The toast was burning as Ziggy stared at it. A voice coming out of the toaster said, "Stop! Please stop! I'll tell you everything. Please stop!" Ziggy represented Jesse. The voice from the toaster was Madame Evil begging for mercy while burning in Hell.

The second comic strip was from "The Far Side." The drawing displayed the corner of a building and a sidewalk. On the corner of the sidewalk was a sign. Footprints led toward the sign. When they came close, they turned in another direction toward the street. On the sign was a symbol of the hangman's scaffold. In this drawing, God was showing Jesse that he had been moving toward death, but now He was leading him toward life and freedom.

A week later, Jesse participated in a tackle football game in the park with co-workers. There were eight men on each team. On one play, Luca was running the ball when Jesse tackled him. Upon impact, Jesse thought he had broken his nose. As he got up from the tackle, he asked Luca, "Is my nose broken?"

"What?"

"Is my nose broken?"

"No, looks the same to me," Luca said, seemingly disturbed by the questioning. "You didn't hit me that hard."

Jesse continued feeling the bridge of his nose. It felt like his face had hit a brick wall. He sensed something strange and out of the ordinary was taking place against him in this game.

Thirty minutes later, Jesse was in the quarterback position, shouting the snap count: "Ready!...Down!...Hut One!...Hut Two!"

Jesse received the ball from the center, and while turning to his right, he attempted to hand the ball to the running back. In the corner of his eye, Jesse noticed Luca thundering in from his left, then...

BLAM!

The top of Luca's head slammed into the left side of Jesse's face. Upon impact, everything went black. Jesse's head spun to the right from the force of the blow, as his mouthpiece flew from his mouth. The jolt from the hit also forced him to fumble the ball as he fell to the ground. Now, dazed, Jesse stood covering the left side of his face with his hand.

"Luca! You need to chill out!" Jesse yelled as he walked away from the group. He could feel that his cheekbone had been crushed. Shaking his head in disbelief, he knew he needed to be rushed to the hospital. Walking back toward everyone, he continued holding his hand over his face in an attempt not to alarm anyone. He heard a calm voice say, "Pull your hand away from your face."

Hesitantly, he removed his hand, and could feel that his cheekbone had been restored. His vision remained blurred for fifteen minutes, but they continued playing football for another hour.

Upon returning to his loft with Luca, Jesse examined his face in the mirror. With his left eye now swollen shut, he asked Luca, "What did you try to do, take my head off?"

"Jesse, what are you talking about? I didn't hit you that hard."

"Didn't hit me that hard? Well, you knocked my mouthpiece out of my mouth!"

"Jesse, it wasn't a hard hit," was Luca's apologetic response.

Looking at Luca and hearing his response, Jesse realized that Luca truly didn't believe he had struck him hard at all. He was now convinced that something more was involved.

Later, at midnight during another sleepless night, Jesse went to his art studio to continue working on a previous drawing. The uncompleted drawing was of a nude woman bathing in a river, surrounded by trees. In the background were mountains and a clouded sky. He labored over the drawing for hours. Finally, at three A.M., while stepping back to study his work, he noticed an eye had formed in the clouds that he had not consciously drawn there. God was demonstrating to him that the spiritual demons used Luca as a vehicle to attack him. They had physically damaged his face, but God had healed it.

Jesse sat thinking of the spiritual, mental, and now physical attacks he had to endure. He wondered if the tests would end. At four A.M., he returned to his loft space. As he opened the door, Luca rose from his sleep and said, "Wait."

Jesse watched as Luca walked toward the window. He opened the window and leaned his upper body forward and out the window, while continuously saying, "Wait...Wait."

Jesse stood by the door, watching. After several minutes, Luca closed the window and lay back down.

Around nine that morning, Jesse asked Luca, "Did you realize you were leaning out the window early this morning?"

Luca looked at him without speaking.

"I know you don't want to hear this, but I'll say it one last time. The evil spirits are trying to go through you to get to me. If you would have fallen out the window, I would have had a hard time explaining it to the police. The only reason you're still here is because God is protecting you. You need to save your soul."

Time passed, and eventually, Luca saved his soul.

Weeks later, in December, Jesse entered his loft. He walked inside the room and flipped on the stereo. At that moment, a song came over the radio, titled "Silent Lucidity" by Queensryche. He had never heard the song before, and it captured his attention, so he sat and listened. After hearing the lyrics, Jesse realized the song was a message to him from God. The song was about his experiences and the tests he had endured. It spoke of being given a second chance in life. The song also spoke of living in two worlds at once, of being able to see the other dimension. God stated his soul was now free, and that He would see that his dreams were accomplished. He confirmed everything that had happened to Jesse through this song.

CHAPTER 27

UNVEILED

And no wonder, for Satan himself masquerades as an angel of light.
—2 Corinthians 11:14

JESSE MET NINA Sanchez in the hotel employees' cafeteria while reading the book *Life of Christ*. After hearing the song "Silent Lucidity," he had asked God to send someone who could provide him with more information. He knew he had a lot to catch up on in a short amount of time.

Nina was a twenty-one-year-old, petite, stubborn, determined young lady with an innocence about her. She wore her long, black hair curly and had a beauty mark just above her upper lip.

She appeared at his table and said, "Can I see what you're reading?"

Jesse looked up and shrugged. "Yeah, sure."

"Mmmm, *Life of Christ*. Mind if I browse through it?"

"Please do."

She took the book and sat down at his table. "This is an excellent book. What church do you attend?"

"I don't."

"Are you born again?"

"What?"

When Jesse didn't understand the term "born again," she spoke eagerly about receiving the Holy Spirit. When their lunch period ended, they both decided to set a time to meet later and talk in more detail.

On Saturday evening, Jesse spent hours telling Nina about his story and experiences. Afterwards, Nina was puzzled and unwilling to accept many of the occurrences in Jesse's life. She wasn't convinced that his soul was saved. She sat and spoke a great deal about Jesus Christ, the Holy Spirit, and the need to be saved. Jesse sat and listened patiently and quietly. While speaking, Nina mentioned something specific that drew Jesse's attention.

"Satan is attempting to destroy your mind," she said firmly.

"No kidding."

"Well, if you're under spiritual attack again, you can use Jesus Christ's name."

"Yeah?" he asked, becoming even more attentive.

"If you say, 'In the name of Jesus Christ, I command you to cease,' the demons must obey, because the power is in Christ's name. The demons stand at attention in fright at just hearing His name."

"I didn't know that. Thanks for the information."

They continued talking late into the night, until Nina caught a taxi for home.

I tell you the truth, anyone who has faith in me will do what I have been doing. He will do even greater things than these, because I am going to the Father. And I will do whatever you ask in my name, so that the Son may bring glory to the Father. You may ask me for anything in my name, and I will do it.

—John 14:12-14

"What do you want with us, Son of God?" they shouted. "Have you come here to torture us before the appointed time?" Some distance from them a large herd of pigs was feeding. The demons begged Jesus, "If you drive us out, send us into the herd of pigs." He said to them, "Go!" So they came out and went into the pigs, and the whole herd rushed down the steep bank into the lake and died in the water.

—Matthew 8:29-32

Jesse now lay alone in his loft at two A.M., continuously going over in his mind the information that Nina had shared with him. Eventually, weariness began to take over. As his eyelids became heavier, he glanced at the clock. "Three forty-five," he murmured. "I'd better get some sleep."

Then he heard a low, pulsating sound coming from the next room. The sound became louder and louder with each passing second. Jesse lay still as the pounding sounds seemed to vibrate through the walls, accompanied by a cluster of shrieking and growling voices. The demonic sounds now dominated the entire room.

"In the name of Jesus Christ, leave," Jesse said aloud. Immediately, the voices ceased. Afterwards, he said, "At least you could have spoken English."

He rolled over onto his side and fell into a sound sleep.

CRASH!

A gigantic beast's hand exploded through the wall. Large splinters of wood flew across the room. The enormous dark claws gripped Jesse's body and began ripping and tearing his flesh. Blood splattered everywhere.

Jesse fought furiously, his arms and legs flailing frantically. "Nooooo!" he screamed as the vicious attack continued. The crushing grip of the Devil was too powerful to break as the claws dug deeper. Jesse found himself paralyzed by Satan's grip as he was pulled into the wall of darkness. Satan spoke with an immeasurable anger and hatred in his voice:

> "I'll have to stop you!
> Because you're strange
> You're different
> You're a leader
> And I don't like that.
> People will follow you
> Because you speak the Truth.
> You speak of God and rebellion
> Of me.
> I will destroy you
> Oh, Chosen One.
> I'll try my best.
> Such a pity
> That Christ watches over you
> Or by now you'd be dead
> And the world…Mine!
>
> "Souls are all I want
> Souls are all I need.

Add them up.
How many do I have?
It's not enough.
It's never enough.
In a world of give and take
I want mine, ALL MINE!"

Jesse screamed, "In the name of Jesus Christ, help! Help me!"

The claws disappeared; the terror stopped. He sat up in the bed, sweating and quivering. Terrified, he said to God, "The Devil is trying to kill me! I know you're here, but he's trying to kill me!"

God spoke: "He's only trying to intimidate you. Don't be afraid. I am with you."

In January of 1991, Jesse met with Dale and explained the entire story to him. Dale was studying the drawing of *The Chess Game* when he said, "Jesse, look at the drawing. Pay attention to the white highlights in your eyes and on your forehead."

Looking at the drawing, Jesse discovered what Dale saw. The white charcoal highlights on his forehead resembled horns. Also, from a certain angle, only the whites of his eyes were visible, making him look ghostly. The light above reflected off his face, revealing the hooded specter's identity, which was the Devil. The second meaning of the drawing was now revealed. Satan was making a move to place Jesse in checkmate to take his soul to Hell. But, with his faith in God and Christ, he had received the Holy Spirit and made it up the stairwell to Heaven.

After Jesse explained the drawing to Dale, they both looked on, astounded.

In the month of March, Jesse met with Madame Evil at a local restaurant. After they ordered, he asked, "Lisa, what is your view on spirituality?"

"Well, Jesse, I believe we are all guided by the universe. I feel that you and I have had a past life. The power and energy within ourselves are guided by a force—"

Jesse interrupted. "What about God?"

"God?" Lisa asked, as though annoyed. She avoided the question by saying, "We have the power of the universe to influence others, and even the world. By opening our channels to—"

Jesse again interrupted. "Lisa, excuse me, but I have two more questions for you," he said in a stern tone. "Do you believe there will be a Judgment Day?"

Madame Evil gave him a quizzical stare, and, half smiling, said, "Why should I? I believe in karma."

"Do you believe there is a Heaven and Hell?" Jesse asked.

Seeming even more annoyed by his questions, she said, "Ha! Jesse, there is no such thing. We simply make the transition from one plane to the next. If you've lived a life of evil, the universe will—"

"All right, that's enough. You're a witch, and that's confirmed by God. You were sent by Satan to prevent me from completing my destiny. He was trying to use my gifts and talents from God for his purpose, to lead people to Hell. You were trying to deceive me with astrology, horoscopes, psychic readers, mediums, and New Age religion, which are all tools of Satan."

Madame Evil stared at him from across the table, flabbergasted. "That's not true," she said as her lips quivered.

"Lisa, Satan is also known as the Father of Lies."

She now seemed uneasy as she excused herself from the table. She returned moments later from the restroom with tears in her eyes, physically shaken. They soon finished their meal and departed the restaurant.

While walking through the parking lot, Lisa said, "Jesse, would you like a ride back to your place?"

"No, thanks. I'll walk."

"You know there will be more mediums coming after you, and a lot stronger than myself. Satan's hunt after you will not cease."

"I know," Jesse said flatly as he continued on his way.

A week later, Jesse met with Dale at his loft space.

Dale opened the discussion. "Jesse, what did you do to Lisa?"

"What do you mean? I didn't do anything but tell her the truth."

"Well, she came to work last week, seemingly disoriented. So I asked her what was wrong. She looked at me and said everything you spoke about her was true."

Dale sat down, eagerly waiting for a response. Jesse looked toward Dale and said, "I've told you just about everything I know about her and my encounters with the spiritual world. Again, my best advice for you is to stay away from her."

"Yeah…well, she left work early. I watched her leave, and she was crying hysterically. I asked her if she was OK, and she said that there were a few things that she needed to straighten out in her life."

"Yeah?"

"Yeah, but a few days later, she came back to work and began handing out cards to several co-workers with messages on them."

"What was written on the cards?" Jesse asked, now alarmed.

"They had each person's horoscope sign. There were also messages claiming to predict their future, and a psychic reader's phone number to contact. She also gave out flyers for a New Age bookstore."

"She hasn't changed," Jesse said, shaking his head.

"Just recently, she attempted to give me a copy of the book *Living in Joy*. She said she felt that I would find it interesting."

"What did you do?" Jesse snapped.

"I told her to get away from me and to take that book with her."

They both chuckled.

"Jesse, I'll also be going to Chicago in a few weeks to visit my parents. I'm thinking of moving."

"Cool."

Choosing his words carefully, Dale said, "Well…you know it's still hard to believe all of this."

Jesse looked away. "Yeah…I know."

CHAPTER 28

THE MISSION

But the Counselor, the Holy Spirit, whom the Father will send in my name, will teach you all things and will remind you of everything I have said to you. Peace I leave with you; my peace I give you. I do not give to you as the world gives. Do not let your hearts be troubled and do not be afraid.
—John 14:26-27

IN JUNE, JESSE made a vacation trip to San Francisco to visit Zorma Gabriel. He felt that he needed to take a break. Jesse had known Zorma for years. They had met in 1980 while in college. She was an artist, and they had many similarities. During their conversations over the years, they had always shared laughter. He figured it would be an excellent idea to get away and visit.

Upon his arrival, her husband, Sean, picked Jesse up at the airport. Sean had a calm, quiet personality with a hint of humor. When they arrived at their loft space, he was greeted by Zorma, an attractive brunette who had kept her hair cut short for as long as Jesse had known her. Zorma worked as a hair stylist and dressed with artistic flair.

Zorma immediately began showing her recent paintings. There were ten in total, and Jesse made a comment on each except one, which hadn't gone unnoticed by her.

"Jesse, you've spoken on every painting except this one," she said.

The reason he had not spoken was because she had said the painting was her "goddess." So, he had ignored it. Now he had no other choice but to make a comment.

Jesse began with a question: "Do you know anything about the Egyptians?"

"Well, very little."

"Many of the Egyptians were worshipping these other so-called gods and goddesses. They also held God's people under captivity. Eventually, God led His people out of oppression and destroyed Egypt."

To his surprise, she didn't say anything. He noticed she had several New Age books similar to those Madame Evil had attempted to deceive him with, as well as astrology and horoscope books. So Jesse began asking questions while holding several books in his hands.

"Zorma, has anyone gotten you involved in this?"

"No, I purchased them myself. I've also been involved in several Wicca sessions."

"Wicca?"

"Yes, I practice witchcraft," Zorma said calmly.

Jesse's eyes widened in surprise. "Witchcraft?"

"Yes. Wicca is an ancient nature religion. As a child, I grew up in the Roman Catholic Church. I now realize that was based on lies, and now Wicca is my religion."

"Zorma, Christianity is the true word of God."

"Jesse, that's your truth, not mine! Did you realize there were witch hunts in the Middle Ages, when hundreds of thousands of innocent people were persecuted? They suffered torturous, horrifying deaths. This all happened because the Christians felt they were saving the souls of those being burned at the stake."

"Not everyone who declares himself a Christian is one. Those people committing those killings were wrong. But God is against witchcraft. It is the work of Satan."

"I'm practicing to become a Wicca priestess. Our group holds rituals in the forest, which involve healing, casting of spells, and blood sacrifice, among other things. We do not worship or believe in Satan, even though one of our major celebrations is Halloween."

"Zorma, I met a witch in Rochester who was trying to deceive me with the books you're reading. I also had to battle against demons, evil spirits, and Satan, who attempted to destroy me." Jesse spoke with desperation in his voice, attempting to save his friend.

"I'm a witch of the light. The woman you dealt with was obviously a witch of darkness. Our cause is to try to help people find themselves through readings, magic, and healing. We worship the Goddess of the Earth and Universe."

"Zorma, there is no such thing as a good witch, just as there is no difference between voodoo, black magic, sorcery, roots, or white magic. It all falls under Satan."

"So, are you trying to convince me that Christianity is the truth? Christians believe that they know all the answers, and that everyone else is wrong?"

"Zorma, there is only one truth."

"Yeah! Yours, right?"

Jesse realized if there was any chance of sharing the truth with her, that wasn't the time. She simply didn't want to hear it.

Two days later, Jesse and Zorma entered an art gallery located on the sixth floor of a downtown building. Inside, Jesse walked around the partition and froze. Standing directly in front of him was an eight-foot sculpture of Satan. The dominating figure caused Jesse to lose his breath. He took a step back from the colossal figure in disbelief. The black creature leaned forward with its arms spread and extended, as though attempting to capture him.

Jesse's legs weakened as he stared into the creature's hideous eyes and snarling face. In terror, he turned and made a manic dash out of the gallery. In the corridor, he braced himself against the wall. Feeling faint and unable to stand, Jesse slid down the wall to the floor near the elevators. He was terribly shaken by the monstrous sculpture, knowing it was Satan displaying his unyielding attacks upon him. He sat, attempting to calm himself and collect his thoughts, when the door suddenly swung open, slamming against the wall. It was Zorma. Looking at him with excitement, she asked, "Jesse! Did you see the art piece on God?"

Jesse realized that God had used Zorma to confirm his presence, but he was too nervous to go back inside.

While leaving the gallery and walking along the streets, Jesse noticed an empty parking lot with graffiti along the wall. In the middle of the wall, one statement read, *WHO'S GONNA SAVE YA NEXT TIME?*

Above the wall was a billboard that read, *JESUS IS COMING SOON.*

That evening, while in a video store, Zorma approached him with two video tapes on Egyptians. "Which one would you like to see?" she asked.

"None."

"Jesse, pick one, and I will watch it with you."

"All right, get this one," Jesse said hesitantly.

The following morning, they watched the video tape as her husband slept. When the tape ended, Jesse said, "God led His people out of Egypt and destroyed many of the Egyptians."

Zorma replied angrily, "Jesse, that Bible you're reading was written by men and their penises. And who do you think you are? God?"

He glared at her. "You can believe what you want. And if I was God, I wouldn't be sitting here trying to get understanding from a video." He stood and walked away.

Later that morning, as emotions simmered, Zorma appeared at the bathroom door and watched him shave. They had remained silent throughout the morning.

Finally, Zorma broke the silence. "Jesse, are you angry with me?"

"No, I learned not to get angry a long time ago," Jesse said, even though her defensive, combative attitude did anger him. He was upset by her unwillingness to listen. He also knew that the deeper she became involved with the occult, the more difficult it would be for her to get out. The Devil had control of her mind.

"Well, I'm glad, because I didn't mean to upset you. I wanted you to have a good time on your visit, but it seems our differences have gotten in the way."

"Zorma, I'm fine. My trip hasn't been ruined, and you shouldn't worry." He could see that she was feeling troubled, so he spoke calmly and with a smile. He knew his battle was with Satan and not her.

"This afternoon, I'll be going out," he said. "So I'll see you later, OK?"

"Sure."

After breakfast, they went their separate ways for the day. After hours of touring and viewing art galleries, Jesse returned to the loft space late in the evening. Soon afterward, Zorma also returned with a bundle of long branches wrapped in twine. She set the tips of the branches afire and began shaking them, spreading smoke around the room.

Jesse watched with curiosity. "What are you doing?"

"I'm ridding the place of evil spirits. Late this afternoon, I met with a psychic medium and asked her about you. She said it wouldn't be a wise idea to be around you at this time. The medium said you have negative energy around you, and you're surrounded by dark influences."

Jesse stared at her in disbelief.

Seeing his expression, Zorma shot back, "Jesse, don't knock what you don't understand."

He shook his head in disappointment.

That night, around eleven P.M., Zorma and her husband were asleep in the high loft, while Jesse lay on a mattress on the floor. Unable to sleep, he imagined defending himself against knife attacks, using karate and kung fu techniques. This continued for thirty minutes. Suddenly, the mood in the room changed from blue to grey, then to black. Jesse heard loud, growling voices traveling through Sean from the loft.

"Grrrrrr!"

The threatening voice now began to circle the room. As the voice grew louder, the intensity increased. "Grrrrr! *Grrrrr! GRRRRRRRR!*"

Suddenly, it stopped, and the deep voice yelled, "Three shots!"

Jesse lay still for a moment before speaking. "So at least now we're speaking English. I also see we have a sense of humor. That's good, Satan. I didn't know you were capable."

Jesse knew Satan had said "shots" because he would attempt to kill Jesse with a gun. The reason he said "three shots" was for the Father, Son, and Holy Spirit. Jesse spoke aloud to Satan, "That's OK, talk all you want. You don't scare me! I know God and Christ will be arriving soon."

He heard a vehicle coming down the street with a loud muffler. The car sounded like an old, worn, broken-down vehicle. As Jesse lay still and listened, the vehicle stopped directly under the window. He heard static sounds, as if someone was changing the radio station. When they stopped, the song "I Want To Know What Love Is" by Foreigner began to play. It was one of his favorite songs. The song spoke about struggles in life, about loneliness and wanting to know true love.

When the song ended, static came over the radio station again. Jesse heard the vehicle being driven away from the building, and the loud muffler faded in the distance. God had just displayed His Presence.

The next morning, Jesse arose early with Sean and Zorma. While gathering his clothing for his departure, Jesse said to Zorma, "Satan was here last night."

"I felt an evil presence while asleep last night," Zorma said. "That was why before going to sleep, I chanted and surrounded myself with positive energy and light. The crystals placed around my space are also magical and absorb positive energy for my protection."

Jesse said nothing. Sean watched them both.

Jesse continued gathering his belongings, and at eight A.M., he boarded a plane back to Rochester, New York.

That night in Rochester, he walked along the street, angry that Zorma hadn't taken time to listen so he could warn and help her. He was also upset that she had mocked him and the Bible. As he walked past a vacant building, some writing on the dusty windowpane read, *Thank you and don't get angry, OK?*

The following day, Jesse found himself sitting on a bench. His thoughts were on all the current and past events in his life. Recently, Luca had moved away in pursuit of a degree in teaching, and Jesse had decided against another roommate. Now, with his debts paid and finances somewhat in order, he began wondering how he could reach the masses. The task ahead seemed impossible to accomplish. As time passed, he was overwhelmed with numerous ideas. Jesse thanked God, knowing that the creative ideas were inspired by Him. Looking back at his life, he realized God had been preparing him for his mission in life since childhood. God had always been with him and carried him through his darkest moments.

Back in his art studio, observing the 1988 drawing *The Chess Game*, Jesse realized the third meaning behind the illustration. The drawing showed that Satan was attempting to take as many souls as possible to Hell.

Having been chosen, Jesse was waging war against the Prince of Darkness in a one-on-one battle. He had been elected by God to warn the masses to save their souls by confessing their sins to God, accepting Jesus Christ as their Lord and Savior, and receiving the Holy Spirit. The steps represented those making it up the stairwell, out of the darkness, and into Heaven. The hourglass represented him running out of time before Judgment Day.

The next week, on Wednesday afternoon, Jesse sat in his studio working for hours on preliminary sketches for an illustration. He became frustrated, so he decided to go for a walk. An hour later, upon his return, he noticed a small hole through the wooden door of his art studio. After examining the hole, he thought someone may have punctured the door out of anger, but who, and why? He opened the door and noticed a small hole in his large fifth-floor window. He studied the hole and realized someone had fired a gunshot from the hotel across the street. The hole that penetrated the window was aligned with the hole in his door. The most shocking was that the bullet had passed through the area where he had been sitting an hour before. The height at which the bullet traveled through the room was at his head level. After realizing this, Jesse dialed 911.

A heavyset, uniformed policeman entered Jesse's studio ten minutes later. "What seems to be the problem?" he asked after introducing himself.

Jesse pointed out the bullet holes, and which direction he assumed the shot had come from. Surprised by Jesse's analysis, the policeman stared out the window and then back at Jesse.

"Well, what I can do for now is file a report."

"OK."

After gathering basic information, the policeman asked, "Do you have any enemies?"

"Yeah, only one."

"Who?"

"Satan."

The officer finished the form and departed.

CHAPTER 29

REVOLUTION BEGINS

Finally, be strong in the Lord and in his mighty power. Put on the full armor of God so that you can take your stand against the devil's schemes. For our struggle is not against flesh and blood, but against the rulers, against the authorities, against the powers of this dark world and against the forces of evil in the heavenly realms. Therefore put on the full armor of God, so that when the day of evil comes, you may be able to stand your ground, and after you have done everything, to stand.

—Ephesians 6:10-13

STEPHAN SAT IN the middle of the training floor, performing breathing exercises while making wide, circular motions with his arms. After several minutes, he stood and faced Jesse with his eyes closed, seemingly asleep, his arms now resting at his sides. A light film of perspiration glistened on his lean, chiseled body as he stood only in black sweatpants. Moments passed without a sound.

Then, unexpectedly, Stephan said, "Attack!" His eyes remained closed. Jesse stood frozen with hesitation and dismay. This was something he did not want to take on. He did not move until he heard the voice again, this time with more sternness.

"Attack!"

With no other choice, Jesse proceeded forward with extreme caution. While closing the distance between them, he measured his choice of attack. Stephan remained the same: motionless.

Without warning, Jesse released a crescent kick, which Stephan easily evaded. Jesse followed quickly with a front snap kick. As Stephan blocked his attack effortlessly with his arm, Jesse felt a stinging pain in his leg. The pain felt as though his leg had been struck by a steel crowbar. Jesse grimaced and clenched his teeth as the throbbing pain shot through his leg.

As Stephan slowly opened his eyes, Jesse tried not to allow the excruciating pain to show on his face.

Stephan's eyes were cold and specked with gray. A chill came over Jesse. He felt he was looking at a total stranger. They now both circled each other with a high level of intensity and anticipation. Heavy perspiration collected upon Jesse's eyebrows, some drops falling into his eyes. The saltiness burned them, causing them to sting, which forced Jesse to blink. That was a mistake.

In that brief moment, Stephan began turning, spinning, and twisting in an unorthodox manner, like a tornado in motion. This placed Jesse in a confused state and out of position. Suddenly, he felt a swift kick gently scrape against his throat, and just as quickly, a leopard's blow swept across his eyelashes. Then he received a strike to the abdomen. It felt like an earthquake, penetrating his spine, propelling him backwards.

As the fire burned in Jesse stomach, Stephan checked for further signs of weakness to exploit, but Jesse remained expressionless, showing no pain.

He quickly regained his balance, while his heart raced like a stampede of wild horses. His opponent began closing the distance as their violent dance continued. Stephan pursued Jesse with the suppleness of a snake and the patience of a praying mantis. Jesse attempted to ward off Stephan with several offensive strikes, but he felt as if he were attacking the wind.

Stephan released an echoing scream before executing his next attack. Jesse now braced himself. He responded to Stephan's offensive strikes by blocking an outside blow to the jaw and inside knife-hand to the neck. He used a crane block to deflect a forward punch to his face, which exposed his midsection to a forward thrust kick from Stephan, sending him flying to the floor. Stephan closed in on Jesse like a rushing wave. With his will and strength collapsed under the fury of attacks, Jesse lay sprawled on the polished dark wooden floor, crushed, his body slumped in defeat and humiliation.

His opponent reached out his hand and assisted Jesse to his feet. They stood facing each other, but Jesse with his head bowed and his spirit broken. He stood in silence, torn, bruised, and ragged with exhaustion.

"Be seated," Stephan said.

As they sat on the floor with their legs crossed facing each other, Jesse tried to collect his thoughts.

"You have done well, but you must understand that there is no such thing as winning or losing. You and your opponent are one and the same. In order to overcome him, you must complete his half of the circle. You must avoid and never absorb a direct attack, whether it be physical or verbal. Complete the circle, and you will stay out of harm's way. Avoid fighting at all costs; if provoked, simply walk away. You should stay clear of confrontations by not responding to them. Never insult a man's ego. He will never forget you. Be humble. Remember, this is a discipline, a study of oneself. What you have learned should be displayed in everything you say and do. You should be a man of character, integrity, and strong principles. Do you understand?"

"Yes," Jesse answered, looking him in the eye.

"I believe you are ready for the next level, but your concentration is lacking. That should improve in time."

Now, looking at Jesse in a more relaxed state, Stephan asked, "So… what have you been up to, and how is the artwork coming along?"

"Well, a lot has happened since we last met."

"Like what?"

"Do you have the time?"

"I'm all ears."

Jesse spent the next hour telling Stephan about everything that had transpired in his life, which led to Christ saving him from Hell, Jesse receiving the Holy Spirit, and God giving him a second chance in life. He also spoke of Madame Evil, Satan, and demons, and what their mission was upon this planet.

Stephan listened with patience and concern. When Jesse finished speaking, Stephan simply asked, "If I had spoken to you about the demons and evil spirits of the underworld earlier, you would have thought I was crazy, right?"

Jesse nodded. "Yep."

Stephan chuckled. "I find your experience intriguing and unique. I myself have had experience with evil. Earlier in my life, due to curiosity, I chose to test the spiritual underworld by toying with tarot cards, Dungeons and Dragons, and a Ouija board. In no time, I found myself in trouble. Strange, mysterious, and threatening occurrences began happening in my life. That's when I realized it wasn't a game. My life quickly began spiraling downward. I decided to parachute out before the crash. I threw everything away dealing with the occult, and never bothered with it again."

> *Many of those who believed now came and openly confessed their evil deeds. A number who had practiced sorcery brought their scrolls together and burned them publicly. When they calculated the value of the scrolls, the total came to fifty thousand drachmas. In this way the word of the Lord spread widely and grew in power.*
>
> —Acts 19:18-20

"Jesse, listen carefully. You must detach yourself from all your senses and emotions when dealing with this witch, or any other. You should shut down totally. Your eyes should only reflect theirs, as if you were wearing mirror sunglasses. They must only be able to see themselves, and not inside you. Do you understand?" Stephan asked with a concerned, urgent tone in his voice.

"Yes." Jesse hesitated. "I've been studying the Bible, and God states that the one within you is stronger than the one in this world. He also says, 'Why fear death, when you know of me?' Having fear shows lack of faith."

Stephan leaned forward slightly with his elbows on his knees and chin resting in his hands. He squinted his eyes and asked, "So, what religion are you?"

Without hesitation, Jesse said, "The true religion of God is Christianity, but it is written that not everyone who proclaims to be a Christian is. In all honesty, in my opinion, there is no such thing as religion. What isn't of Jesus Christ is of the Devil. Jesus Christ is separate from all the other so-called religions that do not accept Him as their Lord and Savior. So, anything that is not of God is of the Devil. Taoism, Buddhism, Hinduism, reincarnation, it's all the same—a lie, and the lie is of the Devil."

Go into all the world and preach the good news to all creation. Whoever believes and is baptized will be saved, but whoever does not believe will be condemned.

—Mark 16:15-16

Stephan studied Jesse carefully before speaking again. "It seems your journey has just begun. You have a great deal of responsibility placed upon your shoulders. We live in a world of selfishness, greed, power, and self-gratification. People have dulled their senses and are indifferent to the needs of others. Their minds are conditioned and controlled more than ever before. You must be careful.

"Don't allow anyone to discourage you. You must detect those who are deceitful and manipulative, for they will only come to cause harm to you and your mission. You must not allow anyone or anything to stand in your way."

Jesse had been sitting nervously, for he was unsure if Stephan would receive what he had to say. Now he began to relax.

Stephan continued, "You have given me a great deal to think about. I have a Bible at home that I will begin reading again. Now, I must leave because I promised my wife and children that I would take them to the movies this evening, and I'm running a little late."

They both stood and bowed, studying each other with their eyes. Stephan casually dressed as Jesse waited patiently.

As Stephan exited, he turned and said, "Many of us are given chances to correct the mistakes in our lives. With God, there is always hope. I'm sure you will take advantage of the second chance in life he has given you."

"Thank you for listening," Jesse said.

"No, thank you," Stephen answered, and with that, he departed.

But do not forget this one thing, dear friends: With the Lord a day is like a thousand years, and a thousand years are like a day. The Lord is not slow in keeping his promise, as some understand slowness. He is patient with you, not wanting anyone to perish, but everyone to come to repentance.

—2 Peter 3:8-9

CHAPTER 30

LAST SEVEN DAYS

What good will it be for a man if he gains the whole world, yet forfeits his soul? Or what can a man give in exchange for his soul?
—Matthew 16:26

ONE LATE NOVEMBER night, Jesse was in his loft space ready for sleep after a long day of working in his art studio. He lay on his side, head comfortably on his pillow as he drifted to sleep. He allowed himself to be gently carried away in the silent strength of an eagle's wings.

He began to hear the majestic sounds of violin strings whispering in his ears. The serene music was calm and soothing. In this moment of tranquility, he gradually heard other instruments accompanying the intricate melody of the violins. The music rose to a higher peak with each note performed. Hearing this elegant symphony of music, he felt as if he were lying on a bed of roses, with the brilliant sun radiating through early-morning clouds.

In wonderment, Jesse attempted to open his eyes and rise so he could see where the music was coming from, but he found himself unable to move. It was as if he were being held in place by a mother's caress on her newborn child. The delicate music now played lower, joined by trombones and tubas. Just as quietly as it had begun, the music melted away with the fading sounds of flutes and a thousand violins.

When the music ended, Jesse sat up. Not hearing any other music, Jesse realized he had just heard a symphony of music from Heaven.

The following morning, he rose and contacted a few of his musician friends, explaining his experience and what he had heard. He tried with difficulty to describe the music, but fell dreadfully short of its description. He wanted to know if any of them had heard anything similar, or possibly had it in their possession. None did. For days, he searched and spoke with others. In disappointment, he finally gave up.

The following week, while purchasing CDs in a downtown record store, he noticed the double CD from the original motion picture soundtrack, *Jesus Christ Superstar*. He hesitantly picked it up and considered whether to purchase it. He remembered one of his teachers playing the reel-to-reel tape in fifth grade class, and the songs had mesmerized him. So, he placed one of the CDs that he had in his hand back in the rack, and purchased this one instead.

Back at his art studio, he played the song "Jesus Christ Superstar" on his CD player as he worked on a drawing. Jesse had a habit of playing one song for hours, but this time, he allowed other songs to play from the CD. After a few minutes, he heard the song he had heard days before while half asleep. It was exactly as he had heard it. He was astounded as he sat at his drawing table. "John Nineteen: Forty-One" was the song title.

Nina arrived at Jesse's art studio the following week. The two had been hanging out frequently. Nina shared the word of God with him, while Jesse kept his head buried in the Bible, encyclopedias, dictionaries, almanacs, and study books. He was trying to learn as much as he could on his own. Jesse was like a big brother to Nina, and the two of them got along well, even when Jesse pushed her buttons and irritated her in a friendly way. Usually, they were a challenge for each other, with laughter often in the air.

"Jesse, what are you working on now?" she asked, looking over his shoulder as he worked diligently on a cartoon illustration.

"What does it look like?" he asked comically.

"Oh, boy! Here we go. I got it. I'm going to shut my mouth and sit over here in the corner and stare out the window and leave you alone. I see you're in one of those moods."

Jesse turned to look at her. "Moods? What mood?"

"Everyone knows how moody artists are, and you're no exception."

"Well, you just happened to ruin my deep concentration. That has nothing to do with being moody."

"Yeah, right!" she replied as she sat down in a cushioned chair, propping her feet on the windowsill. She looked out the window at the snow-covered city below, listening to music from her headphones.

She was wearing a purple beret, combat boots, rolled-up jeans, a black military jacket, a red polka-dot scarf, and pink mittens.

After five minutes, with a mocking tone, Jesse asked, "Well?"

"Well, what?"

"Aren't you going to ask what I'm up to?"

"I thought you were in deep concentration."

"I finished, so now I can talk."

"You're kidding me, right?" Nina asked, turning around in her chair.

"Naw, come check this out." He motioned for Nina to come over.

"You're a basket case," she said as she walked over.

"Well, that makes both of us," Jesse said, laughing, which caused Nina to laugh just hearing his booming voice.

She punched him lightly in the arm before looking at his sketches. "These drawings are nice. What do you plan on doing with them?"

"There's going to be a festival next year," Jesse said with excitement in his voice. "I'm planning on saving my money and having these illustrations and cartoon images placed onto T-shirts with messages of God's word on the back. Hopefully, I'll make enough money to afford to keep the process going and produce more T-shirts. I'm also planning on printing and copying some of the illustrations and giving them away."

"Isn't all of this awfully expensive?"

"Yeah, but what else am I going to do? What I need to know is would you be willing to be at the festival? It's only for one weekend. I would like you to be there, since you're well read in the Bible. If people have questions I can't answer, they could speak to you."

"Sure, I'll be glad to," Nina said. "Just remind me when the date arrives." She looked at another drawing taped to the table, covered with an oversized sheet of paper. "What's under that paper?"

"Oh, that's a drawing I've been working on for a while. It's almost completed. Would you like to see it?"

"What do you think?" Nina joked.

Their eyes met, showing respect and admiration for each other. There was a communication between them where words were not necessary. They enjoyed kidding each other as they both shared their unusual sense of humor. They broke out in laughter as Jesse pulled the sheet of paper from the drawing.

"Wow!" Nina exclaimed. After several moments of studying it, she asked, "How long have you been working on this drawing? It looks like a carousel of life, but it's obvious this isn't a normal carousel."

"I started it soon after I completed the drawing of the chess game. But after my traumatic experience, I stopped working on it. Now I'm ready to complete it, and I've added quite a bit more."

"OK, now explain it," Nina said, placing her hands on her hips and leaning forward to stare more intently at the artwork.

"My, my, I thought you'd never ask," Jesse replied.

Nina giggled as Jesse began his elaborate explanation of the drawing, which was drawn in graphite and charcoal on a 43" by 32" gray illustration board.

"To the left of the carousel is a beautiful woman praying. While in a euphoric state, she's asking God if she should marry. Around her neck is a small cross attached to a simple silver chain as a symbolism of her faith in Christ. The woman is also wearing an intricate face mask, because she doesn't know who she is. The bird whispering in her ear represents wisdom. She ignores the answer she receives and marries. Beneath the bird, I've drawn the bride and groom. They're wooden figures because there isn't any love between them. They're wearing blindfolds because they are the blind leading the blind. They have no idea what marriage is. Their wedding bands enclose them because now they have imprisoned themselves after giving their vows. The groom has a wind-up attached to him because he has been conditioned by society.

"Moving further to the right along the carousel, I still have her as a wooden mannequin, dressed up as an unsmiling clown. She is unhappy because her life is being controlled by her new husband. He's next to her, smiling, because he's content to manipulate, control, and dominate her. The horse breaking away from the carousel symbolizes her life going out of control. Located above and attached to the carousel are several clown faces with flowing ribbons. The smiling faces rotate from left to right. Midway, the clown's face changes, displaying disappointment and indifference within their marriage. As the faces rotate to the extreme right, you see anguish.

"Now, moving back to the center on the floor of the carousel, the ball, block, and white swan symbolize the birth of a child. The woman's cross is now lying on the floor because she has lost her faith.

"The silhouette of a white dove flowing from left to right represents peace in their marriage. But by the time it reaches the center, showing years have passed, the bird changes to a hawk, jumping off this page of their life. The giant piranha that I've drawn off-center to the right represents destruction in their marriage, as the scenes from the left change from light to dark. Inside the fish, where there is normally the seating area, the husband wears a black mask, which displays the anger and darkness within him. The tortured souls within the fire symbolize the mental and physical torment women go through at the hands of their predators. He's punishing her because she was found committing adultery.

"Looking to the upper left of the carousel near the clown faces are several showcase windows displaying her life. The first window is wrapped in chains. In the second, she's tempted by Satan and removes her ring. In the third, she's a puppet being manipulated by the strings of the puppet master. Her father sexually molested her as a child. In the fourth mirror, she appears in a lesbian relationship. The fifth involves sexual exhibition.

"As we continue to the right of the drawing, you can see that the cracks in each window display have increased. Upon the sixth window, anguish escalates to a peak level. The seventh window explodes. Devastation."

Jesse glanced at Nina and asked, "Are you following so far?"

Transfixed by the drawing, Nina said, "Yeah, continue."

"Well, moving back to the piranha, where the torment is taking place, I drew a skeleton. Everyone has skeletons in their closet, and this one represents his, which is on fire. Here, above the fish to the right, I've drawn the bride again. Her face mask has fallen off, and she witnesses her husband also in the act of adultery. Behind her is a gravestone symbolic of the death of their marriage, and the two plates of stone represent the Ten Commandments. This is another image of her, here, in the upper right corner. Her mask is dropped, and she isn't blind anymore. She's reading the Bible and finding her true self as a child of God.

"As we return back to her in the wedding gown, she is wearing a necklace of sparkling pearls with matching earrings. A cross is marked on her forehead, symbolic of her having received the Holy Spirit. The woman's exquisite wedding gown is dazzling, with a brilliant light shining behind her. She is smiling because she is born again in Christ. Christ is the groom, and those having the Holy Spirit are his bride in marriage. She is a new person."

Jesse paused and looked at Nina again. "Are you ready for more?"

"You'd better speed it up; you know my attention span is short."

They laughed.

"OK, moving back to the fish one last time. I drew his mouth wide open with small, sharp teeth. Inside its mouth is a radiant, shining cross. Christ's glory was magnified on the cross, due to completing God's will of saving souls. Jonah, at first, was a reluctant prophet until he was swallowed by a large fish at sea; there he stayed for three days and three nights. Christ was resurrected on the third day.

"I drew Satan snarling, displaying his fierce rage because he hates to lose one soul. But then, to the right is the mask of Satan, and he's laughing because he has deceived the masses. The caboose on fire behind him is those captured as 'slaves of sin,' running off the track into the torments and darkness of Hell. Jesus Christ said that he came to give sight to the blind, but, since you say you see your sins remain, you shall die in your sins. Above, the bubbles symbolize souls going to Heaven. The crosses represent the saints.

"Here, in the high upper right corner, I've drawn a diagonal light, which is symbolic of God piercing the darkness and putting a stop to all the madness in this world. Surrounding the 'Carousel of Life' is a metal gate, and the carousel itself is slowly sinking in water. To the lower far left is a little girl, and near her feet is a boat, symbolic of Noah's ark. The innocent little girl is peering over the gate at the circus, with fear of possibly having to partake in this evil generation."

"I'm speechless," Nina remarked. "What's the title of the drawing?"

"Last Seven Days."

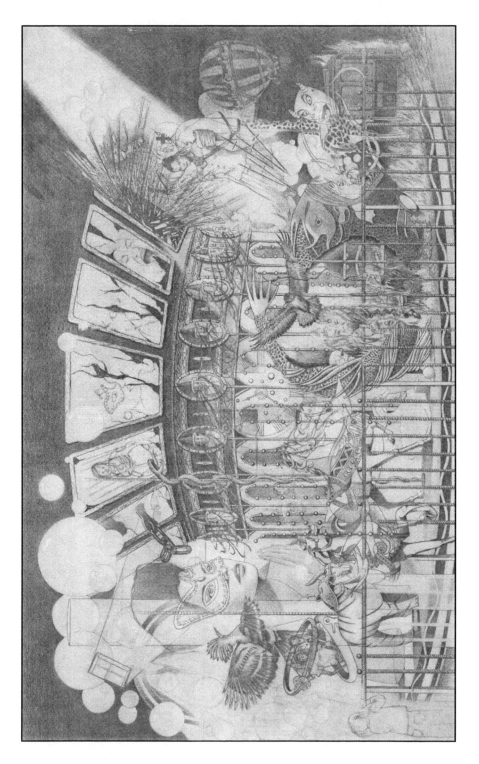

CHAPTER 31

RISE AND FALL

The god of this age has blinded the minds of unbelievers, so that they cannot see the light of the gospel of the glory of Christ, who is the image of God.
—2 Corinthians 4:4

IT HAD BEEN several weeks since Jesse and Nina had met together. One evening they decided to meet at a local restaurant. Their conversation usually consisted of Nina doing most of the talking, while Jesse listened. Nina appreciated his attentiveness when she spoke of her personal struggles. For some reason, however, during this meal, she remained quiet.

Suddenly, she said, "Jesse, I don't know how to bring this up to you, because I'm sure you're going to fight me about it."

Jesse looked at her. "I'm listening."

"You'll have to be baptized by water," Nina said.

"Why? I've already received the Holy Spirit."

"Baptism by water is a requirement by God. It is a symbolic act of repentance." Nina placed her fork onto her plate and looked directly at Jesse.

"Will I need to stand in front of everyone and give a testimony?" he asked.

"No, the pastor will ask you a few questions and then explain to you what's taking place before the baptism, and that's it."

"All right, just say when."

"How's next Sunday?" she asked. She seemed excited and surprised that Jesse hadn't given her a difficult time about it.

"What time?"

"Ten A.M. I'll pick you up at nine."

"OK," Jesse answered, feeling slightly hesitant. He watched a group of people leaving the restaurant. The last person in the group glared back at him with a stare of hatred. When their eyes met, he waved his clenched fist in the air toward Jesse, then turned his back and left the restaurant.

"That was weird," Nina said, surprised, after watching the incident.

"Not really," Jesse replied, and continued eating his meal.

The following Sunday, Jesse was in the car with Nina, traveling to church down a deserted road surrounded by trees. As Jesse looked down the road, a vehicle abruptly turned onto the road in front of them. Jesse looked at the bumper sticker, which read, *Welcome Home.*

As days passed, Jesse continued speaking to employees at his job about his experience and the need for them to save their souls before Judgment Day. The responses varied. Some did not give his experience any consideration, but he continued talking regardless of their responses. Many were astonished because for years, he had been quiet and aloof. Now, he was talking with everyone about salvation.

Needless to say, he now had even fewer friends. Those he spoke to away from his job did not want to hear what he had to say. He was mocked or watched from a distance. But some knew his character and had great respect for him. They listened carefully as he led them through scripture, although they may have felt sympathy for him and thought he had finally snapped. So, out of respect and concern, they listened, expecting the worst had finally come true.

Late one night, weary, disappointed, and feeling a sense of failure, Jesse made a plea to God. "Father, I'm doing what you've asked me, but they're just saying I'm crazy! Could you send them a sign to prove I'm telling the truth?"

Soon afterwards, he fell asleep, and God spoke: "Do not allow those who are indifferent to discourage you. You must continue speaking the truth, and never compromise yourself. Many eventually will listen."

Jesse woke the next morning and arrived at work. While sitting in the office at the security desk, he worked on several cartoon illustrations. He also searched through the Bible for an appropriate scripture for the illustration. He was excited to see his plans beginning to develop.

Suddenly, he glanced at the floor near his feet and noticed an area where fluid had been spilled earlier and had dried, leaving a dirty stain on the floor. The liquid had formed into a cartoon image of a demon. The demon's mouth was open wide in a devious smile, with its tongue lashing out. It was laughing at Jesse in his attempt to draw cartoons and add scripture in hope that people would become more aware of the need to save their souls.

Jesse stared at the image for a moment and then looked further under the desk, where he saw another image above the demon's head: an image of Christ laughing. Jesse knew Christ was watching over him and encouraging him to continue with his project. Jesse became so excited that he brought several employees into the office and began telling them what had happened and showing the images to them.

As they looked at the images on the floor, two other separate images surfaced. One of the images was on the employee's monthly in-house newsletter. In the foreground was a photograph of a coworker laughing at the hotel's picnic. In the picture, a serpent demon sat on his shoulder. Just beyond and above the demon and farther in the background was an image symbolic of Christ, clothed in white, with his arms outstretched. Above the photograph, it read, *Hello Sunshine - Goodbye Rain.*

Jesse had been looking at slides he had recently made of his art. One of the slides wasn't a representation of any of his art pieces. As he looked closer at the abstract image, he saw a picture of himself falling, while Jesus Christ dropped down and saved him from an oncoming demon.

As his coworkers viewed the images, many were surprised and afraid. Some rushed away quietly; others said that he was a prophet.

"I'm not a prophet!" Jesse argued. He explained that his only purpose was to let them know they should save their souls. Actually, he had no idea what a prophet was. In his mind, the heroes in the Bible were extraordinary human beings called by God.

As time passed, more people suggested that he was a prophet. Jesse's response was always the same: "I'm not a prophet!"

In early spring of 1992, Jesse finally accomplished the goals he had set for himself. The silk screening on hundreds of T-shirts had been completed, and several illustrations had been printed. After working constantly for several months, he was satisfied with the results.

As the weeks passed, Jesse continued receiving signs from God, along with attacks by Satan, and the thought of possibly being a prophet weighed heavily on his mind. So, he gathered research material in hopes of understanding who a prophet was.

After flipping through several pages, he read aloud: "A prophet was chosen by God to speak His unbending truth to the masses. He warned the people of God's judgment against sin and led them to repentance. Prophets also spoke against injustice, oppression, establishments, and immoral societies. Few people listened. They were rejected, hated, attacked, tortured, and cast into prisons. Because of their message, many prophets dealt with extreme loneliness."

After the completion of his reading, Jesse felt that the position of a prophet wasn't something he wanted to take on. He couldn't see himself welcoming this burden with open arms. To put it bluntly, he didn't want the job—not realizing that he already held the position.

Several nights later, with his mind in a state of confusion, Jesse began speaking to God. "People are saying I'm a prophet. Well, I really don't care what they say or think. That's why I'm here to ask You. Am I a prophet?"

God spoke, "I have chosen you and only you. You are the Last Chosen Prophet."

Stunned, Jesse felt even more weight on his shoulders. He felt that sharing his experience and telling people to save their souls was one thing. Now, to tell them that he was the "Last Chosen Prophet" seemed overwhelming.

He answered God, "People are going to try to kill me, and nobody's going to believe me. I don't have anything to show them that I'm telling the truth!"

God spoke again. "I have chosen you to warn them. Yes, they will hate you. They won't listen or do as I say, but you still must warn them. Do not fear them. I am with you."

In his mind, Jesse still couldn't accept what he had heard, even though he knew it was true. He said to himself, "Why me? Who am I? I'm nobody!"

As weeks passed, Jesse continued telling his story and stressing that people should save their souls. Upon offering scripture and information to them, he would stutter and hesitantly state that God had declared him the Last Chosen Prophet. The response he always received was silence. This led to even more people whispering behind his back. In time, he began ignoring all the mockery and distant stares.

On a warm summer afternoon in June, Jesse stood nervously at a small local church function, displaying his T-shirts. He had decided to participate after someone's request, feeling that being involved would help prepare him for the Cornhill Festival later in the fall.

He was dressed in cuffed, torn blue jeans and untied black boots covered with splashes of paint. Under the reflecting rays of the sun, the white T-shirt shone brightly against his dark complexion. The short sleeves had been rolled up above his shoulders, exposing his lean, muscular arms. He also wore dark sunglasses with earphones. He was listening to a cassette tape on which he had recorded a wide range of music from some of his favorite artists. He felt out of place in these conventional surroundings. To expel his uneasiness, he focused on listening to his music while shaking his head and tapping his feet. He closed his eyes for long periods and became lost in his thoughts. This happened often throughout the afternoon.

"Hello, um…Hello, excuse me!"

As though being disrupted from a sleep, Jesse looked down at the gentleman standing directly in front of him. The gentleman wore a brown suit, white shirt, conservative tie, and round, wire-rim glasses. He also wore a pair of two-tone polished wing tips. He was leaning forward on his toes, attempting to look through Jesse's dark sunglasses, with his black leather-cased Bible clenched at his side.

Jesse removed his sunglasses and earphones and greeted the gentleman with a smile and handshake.

"Hi, I'm Jesse."

"Oh, I'm Marvin."

"Nice to meet you," Jesse said, smiling.

Maintaining eye contact, Marvin said, "You're not to have the Lord's work for sale!"

Jesse's smile disappeared. He replied, "It is also written that you are not to criticize."

Marvin stumbled back a few steps, at a loss for words. He flipped frantically through the pages of his Bible. Having found a scripture to retaliate, he took a step toward Jesse with newfound confidence.

Jesse, however, put his earphones and sunglasses back on, ignoring him. An invisible wall rose between them. Still, Marvin stood looking up at Jesse with Bible open in hand, barking scriptures like a drill instructor giving orders. Jesse slowly turned away, continuing to ignore the gentleman. Marvin began stuttering, as if unsure of himself, while taking steps backwards. He eventually departed with the disappointment of not having an audience.

The church function was unsuccessful, because Marvin was the only person who approached him all day. But Jesse didn't allow it to discourage him as he packed his things to leave.

Once back at his studio, Jesse paced back and forth, angry about the gentleman who had approached him and placed judgment on him and his intentions. He thought of ways not to allow anger to overcome him. So he decided to play music and noticed a CD that someone had given him weeks earlier, which he had never played. He figured then was the best time.

The song began with the sound of time traveling through a galaxy. A youth's voice spoke, unsure of who he was. Immediately, an evil voice confirmed who the youth was. The evil one's intention was to destroy everyone. The youth's voice spoke again, this time accepting who he was. Finally, the last voice that spoke was authoritative, assuring, and calm. It instructed the youth to maintain his composure as best he could and to face obstacles and adversity with a smile. He also added that others would not accept him because they were unwilling. The title of the song was "In The Beginning" by the Moody Blues.

Time passed, and it became late. Jesse was worn and tired. The day had taken its toll on him. Lying down with his eyes closed, he saw something in the darkness approaching him. A creature's menacing eyes peered directly into his. Its head was covered with scales, and its forked tongue slithered back and forth. The demon waited, as though expecting a response from Jesse. It then tilted its head down, lifted its enormous black wings, and vanished.

Jesse's eyes flashed open for a brief moment before he fell asleep.

Hours past midnight, darkness had overtaken his room. Outside, the sky was moonless. A stale breeze snaked its way through an open window, disturbing the pile of papers on the desk by scattering them onto the floor. Dark shadows flooded in and hovered near the ceiling, surrounding him. Jesse sensed something standing over him. Its haunting presence had been above him throughout the night.

Suddenly, the gray sheets under which Jesse slept transformed into a straitjacket. He found himself bound and strapped, unable to move as he struggled in fright.

Then, *BAM! BAM! BAM!* His head and face were pummeled by the hooves of the creature that towered above him. The merciless stomping upon his face continued as he struggled to free himself. Jesse screamed for help, but seemingly in vain. His voice was suffocated by the drowning sound of gurgling blood through his damaged mouth and broken teeth. The heavy force of the pounding continued. *BAM! BAM! BAM!*

The blows became heavier upon each delivery. The dark figure above seemed to enjoy torturing him and dancing upon his face. Now, barely speaking above a whisper, Jesse said in a weak voice, "Please…Please help me."

His blood-spattered face had been battered into a gruesomely disfigured state. He peered through his damaged eye sockets as the beast continued stomping and smashing his head.

The Devil screamed in a violent rage,

> "Ball of confusion
> That's what I want.
> Faster! Faster! Faster!
> Even though your mere little minds
> Could never keep up
> Though you think you will.

"Man, always think you have power.
Power to do what?
You don't know what power is
But I do.

"Me fool you?
Of course not, you're too smart for that.
You know it all.
Pride.
So I welcome you to Fools' Paradise ... HELL!"

Lucifer paused for a moment. The pounding had nearly sent Jesse into a state of unconsciousness. With his eyes barely open, he gazed into Lucifer's transfixed stare. Satan continued pulverizing him as he screamed, like someone gone mad.

"I'll meet your every pleasure
Your every desire
I'll serve you, only if you serve me
In Death.

"Choose your weapon
Oh, intelligent man
Funny you always seem to choose the wrong one
OOPS! Deceived another one
And you thought you knew it all
Oh, well, welcome home
HA HA HA!
BURN, BABY, BURN!

"Oh, sorry
Here you don't need a suit and tie
Here we're spirits
Those days of pleasure are over
Now you'll suffer with me
FOREVER.

"You should've never listened in the first place
HA! IDIOTS!
You say you should have known
But you did, you did."

Now, leaning over, the Devil peered into Jesse's eyes for signs of fear and weakness.

Jesse's thoughts raced. *The only thing to fear is fear itself...Faith without action is dead...The one within you is stronger than the one in this world.*

Scowling, Satan twisted his head, leaned in closer, and examined Jesse in his morbid state. Now seething and taunting, he said, "Oh, Chosen One, huh? You're *pathetic!*"

Satan continued a fury of attacks upon Jesse as he lay paralyzed, unable to respond. Jesse said with what felt like his last breath, "In the name... In the name of Jesus Christ..."

Before he could finish the statement, the assault upon his body ceased, and Lucifer vanished. Jesse immediately sat upright and faced the large windows, where he saw a flash of blinding light. In the midst of the luminous light stood a hooded male figure in white. After an instant, the figure disappeared.

Jesse quickly removed the sheets, frantically searching his face and body for damage. There was none. He glanced at the clock along the wall. It was 3:45 A.M. Jesse approached the wide windows and stood motionless until daybreak.

I am the light of the world. Whoever follows me will never walk in darkness, but will have the light of life.

—John 8:12

CHAPTER 32

MASTER OF DECEIT

One day the angels came to present themselves before the Lord, and Satan also came with them. The Lord said to Satan, "Where have you come from?" Satan answered the Lord, "From roaming through the earth and going back and forth in it."

—Job 1:6-7

IT WAS NOW mid-June and only weeks before the New York State Cornhill Festival in July, an annual weekend event attended by more than 200,000 people. Thousands of artists displayed their crafts at the festival. There was also a wide variety of music, food, and entertainment.

On Saturday afternoon, Jesse sat with Nina, explaining his plans and ideas about exhibiting his work at the festival. Nina was overwhelmed with excitement and anticipation.

"I'll be more than happy to assist you," she said. "Don't worry, I'll be there to help. Jesse, I also need to tell you something. I've taught you all I know. God has placed it on my heart that I should lead you on to someone else."

Jesse looked at her reluctantly, because he trusted very few people.

"What's his name, and who is he?" he asked.

"His name is Mark Grossman. He's twenty-four years old, and he's well read in the Bible. He's an instructor in one of the classes at the church. I think he'd be an excellent teacher for you."

"How do I know that God is telling you that he wants Mark to instruct me?"

243

"Well, Jesse…" Nina began, but Jesse interrupted.

"I'll give you my answer after I speak with God," he said. "Then I'll know." Nina agreed.

Several days later, they met again, and Jesse confirmed with Nina that what she had said was true. Nina was delighted and quickly made plans for him to meet Mark.

The following week, during their meeting, it became clear to Jesse that he and Mark had two extreme personalities.

They were at Nina's apartment and settling down for dinner.

"So, what brought you to the Lord?" Mark asked.

Jesse briefly spoke of the events that happened in his life. He said that God and Christ had declared him the Last Chosen Prophet. Mark quickly dismissed this claim, while Nina said that he should listen. As Jesse continued, however, Mark still considered his claims to be impossible nonsense. Finally, after being ignored for the last time, Jesse decided to remain silent.

It was an uneventful night. Jesse listened to Mark talk in his authoritative tone while driving him back to his studio. With the vehicle parked in front of his building, Mark continued speaking. "It's been nice meeting you, but I must be honest. At this moment, I'm privately teaching two students, along with taking classes, which have become overbearing. I will not be able to teach you, but there is someone I can recommend. I'll take everything you've mentioned in prayer, and I'll give you a call with my answer."

Jesse stood outside the vehicle, staring at him with what was obviously a disturbed look on his face.

"Are you OK?" Mark asked through the partially open car window.

Arrogance, Jesse thought. He shook his head and turned away.

It was late, and the alley he walked through was extremely dark. Suddenly, he found himself surrounded by demons. He ignored them as he spoke to God. "Father, I know you wanted me to learn from Mark, even though we have our differences. But he is such a self-centered person. Believe me, I tried, but I can't tolerate him."

Jesse fell quiet as he continued walking. After a few steps, he said, "I also know that you departed from Samson when he disobeyed you and revealed his powers to Delilah. If you leave me, I'll be finished. Satan will destroy me!"

While walking through the alley with his head lowered, the demons multiplied. At the end of the alley, he stood on the corner in dismay. A vehicle drove to the intersection and stopped, even though the light was green. Through the windows, he heard the song "I'd Rather Be With You" by Bootsy Collins playing before the car pulled away.

The music surfaced above the festival noises. Throughout the day, thousands of people passed by. At the Cornhill Festival, Jesse set up his artwork and placed flyers and T-shirts on the tables. He also played jazz music through the speakers of his stereo system to attract those passing by.

Kids were everywhere, along with balloons, clowns, and musicians. Babies were pushed along in carriages, while some children with gleeful smiles on their bright faces smothered themselves with cotton candy. Some children pondered the best approach to eating their glistening red candy apples, while others just marveled at the syrup-covered apple sitting upon the stick in their tiny hands.

The day was filled with giggles and laughter among the elderly as well as the young. There were even several small marching bands and a man on stilts wearing a tuxedo with a top hat. Several clowns stood in the midst of a crowd of smiling children, while they created all sorts of shapes and sizes of animals with colorful balloons. Little girls paraded around with pink paper crowns upon their heads, and the boys had painted faces.

The festival was a rainbow sea of people. There were as many nationalities as there were foods, with an overabundance of hot dogs, hamburgers, sodas, frozen Kool-Aid® cups, and corn on the cob. Dogs darted in and out of the crowds with their tongues dangling, looking for handouts, lost from their owners as their leashes dragged behind them.

The blue sky wore shades of red and pink as birds joined in on the festivities, gliding through the warm air. It was a perfect day.

Jesse sat in his booth, observing the crowd. Some glanced over at his work but continued walking, while others rushed by, ignoring him. As the day wore on, more people stopped and collected flyers and other material. Many of them departed with smiles after reading the messages and realizing that most of the items were free or for sale at a low cost.

Early in the afternoon, Jesse was approached by a young girl and her mother. The little girl showed interest in one of the T-shirts, but after reading the verse on the back about being "born again," the mother placed the T-shirt down, gave Jesse a wicked stare, and snatched her child away. Jesse acted as though he hadn't noticed the look of disdain.

By the end of the festival, as the crowd became sparse, Jesse began to break down his display. He felt satisfied with the response and turnout for the first day, but there was one disappointment. Nina hadn't arrived. He thought, *Maybe tomorrow.*

As he wrapped the last box of items, he felt someone watching him. When he looked up, he noticed the same little girl standing there. She wore a pink polka-dot dress, red shoes, white ankle socks, and ponytails.

"What's your name?" he asked, kneeling down on one knee.

"Tiffany!" she replied with sparkling, innocent eyes.

"How can I help you, Tiffany?"

"I would like…I would like to buy the T-shirt," she said, smiling, as her mother stood in the distance.

"Which one?"

"That one!"

"This one?" Jesse pointed to the same T-shirt from earlier.

"Yes…how much is it?" she asked, her voice filled with excitement.

"For you, free!" He smiled, happy that she had come back, as he pulled the shirt from the box and handed it to her. "Is it the right size?"

The little girl stood speechless for a moment, then said, "Yeesssss!"

"Well, do you like it?"

"Like it? I love it. Thank you!" She turned away and ran toward her mother, who remained expressionless.

Jesse's smile became even brighter as he continued packing.

Let the little children come to me, and do not hinder them, for the kingdom of Heaven belongs to such as these.
—Matthew 19:14

The following day, Jesse was met with an even greater response from the people. Everyone seemed delighted to receive the cartoons and illustrated flyers with scripture. He received numerous positive comments and even unexpected occasional hugs from those who were extremely grateful. At the end of the day, however, Jesse once again felt disappointed because Nina had not come to assist him. He thought for sure she would have come.

Now, back at his studio, he wanted to relax and take a break from his busy weekend. He turned on the television, grabbed a quart of orange juice from the refrigerator, and flipped open a magazine. He froze as he stared at a full-page ad featuring an image of Satan. The Devil was bent over, clenching his stomach, with his head arched back and eyes closed in gut-wrenching laughter. He seemed almost in tears from laughing. The heading on the page read, *A Little Ain't Enough*. Satan was saying the small number of people Jesse had reached was a joke, and he was laughing at his minimal accomplishments, compared to the massive number of souls he was collecting.

Doubt and disappointment entered Jesse's mind. He thought of the millions of people he might never reach. His mission seemed impossible to achieve with his limited ability, resources, and income. It was a mountain he didn't believe he could climb.

At that moment, he looked up from the magazine and toward the television. A cross flashed briefly in the center of the television screen, symbolizing Christ's presence. Jesse knew that he must continue in his work no matter what the odds.

On Monday, Jesse was sitting behind the security desk when Nina arrived to work.

"Nina, why didn't you help me at the festival?" he asked.

"Jesse, I prayed to God, seeking His advice in asking if I should go and assist you. I was in prayer for a long time, and God told me not to go. I was told you're being deceived, and everything you're doing and attempting to do is wrong. What you are doing is not of the Lord. You're misled and misguided. Jesse, you need to wake up, or you're the one who's going to Hell."

Jesse stared at her in disbelief as she hurried away to her office. The following morning, on his way to work, he was in deep thought, wondering what had caused Nina to turn away. He was extremely disturbed by her statements. He continued walking until he came to a concrete wall. Looking up, he saw words in black scrawled on the surface in bold letters: *GOT THE BITCH OUT OF THE WAY.*

Nina later admitted that she had indeed been deceived by Satan.

Be self-controlled and alert. Your enemy the devil prowls around like a roaring lion looking for someone to devour.

—1 Peter 5:8

CHAPTER 33

RAIN

Welcome to Disney World

CHRISTMAS HAD ARRIVED and gone. Jesse entered his parents' home late at night after putting in long extra hours at the hotel. Everyone was asleep, so he kept quiet to avoid disturbing anyone. He had spoken earlier in the day to his mother, who had sent a home-cooked meal to his job. She also informed him that all his family members and friends had arrived, and everyone was enjoying themselves. Jesse had planned to visit the following day to spend time with his family and play with his niece and nephews. But for now, the house was still and quiet from all its earlier activities.

On the living room floor, Jesse found a large wrapped present labeled for him from his mother. He sat at the kitchen table unwrapping a dish of food she had set aside for him.

When midnight arrived, he departed quietly. Once outside, while walking along the snow-filled, ice-covered street, he noticed the arrival of several police cars in the area. In order not to arouse suspicion, he decided to walk in the middle of the street. At that time, a police car whizzed by, stopping several feet ahead. As Jesse walked past the vehicle, the police officer looked out the window at him and yelled, "Merry Christmas!"

Jesse glanced over at the officer and replied, "Merry Christmas."

As he continued walking, Jesse felt someone grab him from behind by his shoulder and spin him around.

The officer yelled, "What's your name? Where do you think you're going?"

Alarmed, Jesse said, "Take your hand off my coat." Glancing over his opposite shoulder, he noticed dark figures beginning to circle him as the yelling continued.

"Where are you coming from? Answer me. Can't you talk?"

The officer's grip tightened as the others in uniform closed in. Mass confusion, yelling, and screaming surrounded him.

WHAM! The officer slammed him atop the hood of the patrol car.

Jesse lay still with his head pinned against the cold metal hood of the vehicle. After frisking him, the officer yelled, "What's wrong? Can't talk? George, where do you think you're going?"

Sharp metal braces were clamped tight around his wrists as blinding red and white lights flashed across his eyes. Now, looking forward, he saw three other officers rushing toward him. As the officers came into view, Jesse recognized one of them. They both had lived in the same neighborhood and attended the same high school and college. His name was Jerome Radcliff.

As their eyes locked, everything became still and quiet. The chill of his breath escaped his mouth and settled in front of him. Shouts in the background became muffled voices. Even the falling heavy snowflakes seemed to stop in time, before continuing their fall to the earth. Jesse remained silent and frozen in anticipation of a response from his friend.

Nothing. Radcliff didn't say a word. He ignored Jesse and continued walking away.

Jesse blinked in disbelief as the angry screams returned. A single sharp voice rose above the rest as the officer held up Jesse's Christmas present from his mother.

"What's in the box, George?"

"You have it, why don't you look in it?" Jesse replied. "Maybe it's a present for you." He glanced over his shoulder and into the officer's eyes with an unyielding stare.

"I guess we have a smart one here!" another officer yelled.

The car door was yanked open and Jesse was shoved inside. The officer slammed the door on his foot as it dangled out the door.

"George, get your foot in the door. We don't have all night!"

Laughter came from other officers.

After being humiliated and handcuffed, he sat with his head lowered. Outside the car, he heard bursts of more laughter. He glanced outside the back window, where he saw several officers laughing hysterically. A police officer had opened his shoulder bag and taken his Bible out, lifting it in the air, while they all laughed and mocked him.

At that moment, the passenger door was yanked open. "George, where do you live, and where are you coming from?" the officer screamed into the car.

Jesse hesitated before speaking. "I don't know why you're addressing me as George. That is not my name. But I also have a question for you... What do you know about God?"

Surprised by Jesse's response, the officer barked, "Who are you to ask me about God? Who do you think you are?"

BOOM! The door slammed shut. After a few minutes, the officer opened the driver's door and sat inside. While closing the door, he said to Jesse, "I'm taking you down to the precinct for booking, and you'll be spending your holiday behind bars."

"Well, if you do that, you'll be making a big mistake," Jesse replied.

"Mistake? You tell me how I'm making a mistake!"

Silence.

"All right, where do you live?" the officer asked, now speaking in a calmer tone.

"I'm not going to tell you where I live, but my mother lives in this neighborhood. I was walking from her home several blocks away before you arrested me."

"Look, I don't have time for your games. I'm taking you to jail."

"You're making a mistake."

"OK, where does she live?"

"A few blocks in that direction. Drive, and I'll show you. She'll verify who I am."

After giving Jesse's statements consideration, the officer said, "Look, you'd better not be lying to me."

Jesse remained silent while gazing out the patrol car's window.

"OK, let's go," the officer said as he started the engine. While driving, he continued with further questions. "Why did you ask me about God? I was raised Catholic, and I've received communion. I know who God is."

"Jesus Christ never started the Catholic church. It was started by man to control the people. Jesus Christ is the founder of Christianity. It states that in the dictionary, encyclopedia, and almanac."

"But the Roman Catholic Church is a part of Christianity," the officer said, sure of himself.

Jesse remained quiet for a moment. Sensing the officer's interest in what he had to say, he proceeded cautiously. "In Matthew, chapter twenty-three, Jesus spoke against the religious leaders. He states, don't call anyone on earth 'Father,' for only your true 'Father' is in Heaven. The Catholic priests are called 'Father.'

"Jesus also spoke of Heaven and Hell; there is no such thing as Purgatory."

The officer had fallen quiet as Jesse spoke.

"Confession should be made to God, not to the so-called priests. They're no different from you and I. We're all sinners. Also, in the Catholic church everyone 'hails Mary.' God says to worship him and worship him alone, and Jesus Christ is God. Everyone bows down to the Pope, but he is the biggest lie. The Roman Catholic Church is an institution that is brainwashing the masses."

In the pride of your heart you say, "I am a god; I sit on the throne of a god in the heart of the seas." But you are a man and not a god, though you think you are wise as a god.

—Ezekiel 28:2

These people honor me with their lips, but their hearts are far from me. They worship me in vain; their teachings are but rules taught by men.
—Matthew 15:8-9

Every plant that my heavenly Father has not planted will be pulled up by the roots. Leave them; they are blind guides. If a blind man leads a blind man, both will fall into a pit.
—Matthew 15:13-14

The officer slammed on the brakes, causing the vehicle to come to a screeching halt in the middle of the street. The officer whipped his head around, looking over his shoulder to glare at Jesse through the cage. Hate and anger filled his eyes, as though they would burst from their sockets, and veins spread across his flushed red face.

"Who in the hell do you think you are?" he screamed. "I should have busted your head open on the concrete back there, rammed my fist down your throat, and ripped out your damn heart!"

Jesse was stunned but not surprised. He sat wondering if it had been the officer who had just spoken to him or the Devil himself. The remaining ride to his mother's house was quiet.

A hot-tempered man stirs up dissension, but a patient man calms a quarrel.

—Proverbs 15:18

After being directed to park in front of Jesse's mother's home, the officer continued yelling, "Look, I'd hate to wake and disturb these people and find out you've been lying to me. So far, you've been speaking in riddles. You're a liar, and you're trying to speak to me about God."

"I've only been telling you the truth," Jesse persisted. "God, Christ, and the Devil speak to me just as I am talking with you. God has declared me the Last Chosen Prophet. My only concern is that you save your soul."

Dead silence.

Slowly, the officer tilted his head to listen carefully to what Jesse might say next. After a moment of not hearing anything, he asked, "So, what is the Devil saying to you now?"

He spoke like a psychiatrist questioning a deranged patient.

"Chain, chain, chain…chain a fool," Jesse sang. "And right now, he's laughing."

The officer peered hesitantly at Jesse before stepping out of the car and onto the enclosed porch of his mother's home. Minutes later, he arrived back to the patrol car.

"That's it," he said. "I'm taking you to jail!"

Jesse looked at the officer and shook his head in frustration. The officer started the vehicle as Jesse said, "You're making a mistake. I want your name and badge number, along with the other officers."

"Look, George, I'm tired of your nonsense. The woman I spoke to said all her children are adults and they don't live with her. You've been lying all along."

"I don't know why you continue calling me George. My name is Jesse."

"So, you say your name is Jesse, huh? Well, the name on the package is Tim!"

"Tim is my nickname."

"OK, well, what is the woman's name who lives here, and what's the phone number?"

"My mother's name is Grace Thomas. The phone number is 716-428-6924. I also know one of the officers who was present when you arrested me. His name is Jerome Radcliff. We went to school together. He can verify who I am."

"Why didn't he speak up, if he knew you?"

"That's a good question. Only he can answer that."

After calling the phone number and speaking with Jesse's mother again and with his fellow officer, the officer realized Jesse had spoken the truth. He sat a moment in his car, apparently upset, before speaking. "Well, listening to you speak and watching how you carry yourself, it's obvious you've got your act together. I suppose now you're going to turn this into a racial issue?"

Jesse listened without speaking as the officer continued.

"I get sick and tired of blacks blaming everything on whites for their problems. They feel whites owe them because of what happened during slavery and the Civil Rights Movement. Why don't they get over it? That was years ago. My wife is black. She's also Catholic."

"And?" Jesse asked.

"Well, I'm not prejudiced," the officer declared.

"One thing I must admit," Jesse said, "is that many blacks today are their own worst enemy."

The officer, surprised by Jesse's response, started his patrol car and drove back to the area where he had arrested Jesse. Stopping the vehicle, he opened the door, assisted Jesse from the car, and uncuffed him.

"Well, like I said earlier, it's obvious you've got your act together. Would you like me to give you a ride to your place?"

"No, thanks." Jesse turned and walked away as tears swelled in his eyes.

"Listen, thanks for the information," the officer shouted. "I'll be sure to look up everything you've said."

Jesse continued walking as the snow gently fell, mixing with rain.

Do not repay anyone evil for evil. Be careful to do what is right in the eyes of everybody. If it is possible, as far as it depends on you, live at peace with everyone. Do not take revenge, my friends, but leave room for God's wrath, for it is written: "It is mine to avenge; I will repay," says the Lord.
—Romans 12:17-19

CHAPTER 34

WHISPERING WIND

The Lord saw how great man's wickedness on the earth had become, and that every inclination of the thoughts of his heart was only evil all the time. The Lord was grieved that he had made man on the earth, and his heart was filled with pain.

—Genesis 6:5-6

THROUGHOUT JESSE'S DAY at work, he was involved in discussions, attempting to prove that Jesus Christ was God. Several co-workers denied this, having many different beliefs themselves: some Muslims, Jehovah's Witnesses, agnostics, and even those labeling themselves Christians.

After work, feeling frustrated and walking to his studio, Jesse decided to bring the issue up with God. As he approached the building, he noticed an old rusted van parked along the curb. Bumper stickers covered almost every inch of the vehicle. The stickers read, *Jesus Is Lord* and *Jesus Is God.*

Once inside his studio, Jesse opened the Bible and flipped through the pages of scriptures. He found an overwhelming number of scriptures declaring Jesus Christ as God. One of the scriptures, Revelation 1:8, read,

"I am the Alpha and the Omega," says the Lord God, "who is, and who was, and who is to come, the Almighty."

Later in the night, he decided to read the book Ezekiel. Several hours passed before he finished. Puzzled by what he had read, Jesse said to God,

"I just finished reading Ezekiel, and I have no idea what that book was about." He continued asking God about the book before falling asleep.

He found himself in a place enclosed in darkness. Lying on his back, above his head he saw a fiery red-hot cattle-branding iron flying down toward him at a high speed. Flames engulfed the iron as it sped closer and closer to its destination. Then, *WHAM!*

The branding iron pounced on Jesse's chest, the powerful impact causing his body to jump up. Upon his chest was stamped:

IDOLATRY

Jesse sprang up from his sleep, overwhelmed by emotions of fear, panic, and desperation. While he sat breathing heavily and sweating profusely, he touched his chest. The marking had disappeared.

Turning on the lamp, he picked up his Bible and located the book of Ezekiel. He read several passages aloud.

> *Some of the elders of Israel came to me and sat down in front of me. Then the word of the Lord came to me: "Son of man, these men have set up idols in their hearts and put wicked stumbling blocks before their faces. Should I let them inquire of me at all? Therefore speak to them and tell them, 'This is what the Sovereign Lord says: When any Israelite sets up idols in his heart and puts a wicked stumbling block before his face and then goes to a prophet, I the Lord will answer him myself in keeping with his great idolatry. I will do this to recapture the hearts of the people of Israel, who have all deserted me for their idols.' Therefore say to the house of Israel, 'This is what the Sovereign Lord says: "Repent! Turn from your idols and renounce all your detestable practices!"'"*
>
> —Ezekiel 14:1-6

> *They will throw their silver into the streets, and their gold will be an unclean thing. Their silver and gold will not be able to save them in the day of the Lord's wrath. They will not satisfy their hunger or fill their stomachs with it, for it has made them stumble into sin.*
>
> —Ezekiel 7:19

By 3:45 A.M., Jesse found himself constantly dozing and unable to stay awake. He turned off the light and lay his head upon the pillow to rest. Then he heard a faint whisper: "I alone am King."

Jesse immediately jumped up and looked about the room. Thinking he had imagined hearing the voice, he lay back down, and again, the gentle, calm voice spoke: "I alone am King. I ruleth over…"

Frantically, Jesse rose one final time and stumbled through the darkened room in search of a writing pad and pencil. He began scribbling as the voice continued speaking. The voice paused several times before continuing. Whenever the voice paused, Jesse assumed the voice had finished speaking, but the voice would continue in a calm, quiet, deliberate pace. After several minutes of scribbling in the dark, he realized that the statement was concluded.

Jesse immediately fell asleep in the chair until morning, unaware of what he had written. He awoke late in the morning and worked to decipher the scribbling on the several pieces of paper. After rewriting the statement, he was astounded as he read it.

I alone am King
I ruleth over the land, sea, and universe
And everything in it
I control its elements
And keep them in balance
Everything stays in suspense at my command
Nothing disappears without my knowing of it
For I Am God, God Almighty.
Almighty over everything
As far as you can see or think
No mind can comprehend
Or see My existence
Yes, since the beginning of time
Time for Me, there is none
But yours is limited
Yet you question of My Existence
Question yours, not Mine
Your time has come
It is just about over
You've dominated long enough
I, ruler over all
Will now dominate you

You will do as I say
No more, will you crush My people
Enough is enough
Gone at last from the face of the earth
No longer, shall you sicken Me
I've seen and heard enough
Enough of you and your vile things and statements
Statements of Christ my only Son
No more you laugh
Laugh in Hell forever, or will you
Your time has come
It is gone
Gone where everything will perish
Even your own soul
For you did not want life, so you have death
Death indeed
Be gone, By gone, It's over
Said and finished
My word is My word
Goodbye, farewell to you all
And your accomplishments
Nothing
Nothing in despair of nothing
Wasted time
All gone away, to nowhere
Now can you see, can you hear?
What I'm telling you, what I'm saying to you
No, and you won't
Because you continuously refuse to listen
Listen to me, not them
Those who chose to steal, lie, and hate
But you trust them
And I am trust
But trust not Me, oh feeble-minded beings
And I created you, what a waste of your time

And Mine
You could have done anything
But you chose not to
The stars, the sky, they're all Mine
Yet you think you own them
Need a license, Ha!
License to do what, steal and kill
For that's all you do
That's all you're good for, sad but true
So have your own way
Oh worthless few, pity you
You dominate no more
Jimmy Crack Corn and I don't care
You sing no more, good night
I rule over night and day
I see you in the night as well as in the day
You can't hide from Me
You and your crimes of sin and passion
It's over, all over gone
You have been forewarned
By My Chosen One
But yet you still won't listen or obey
Obedience to Me or yourselves
Fear Me or yourselves

Hell, you laugh about it
As though it doesn't exist
But you won't when you're there
You'll cry then and I won't hear you
Not one word
You'll listen then to the cries and screams
Of pain and anguish you set upon yourselves
But then it will be too late
Though you cry so anxiously
It will be the end

But the beginning for those
Who listen and obey

AMEN
GOD AND CHRIST

The message was given to him by God to deliver to the masses as a
warning and a call to reconciliation.

CHAPTER 35

REGENERATION

IN FEBRUARY OF 1995, Jesse received a phone call from his mother early on a Tuesday morning.

"How's everything going?" she asked.

"Hi, Mom. Everything's working out fine."

"Well...I just called to tell you Caesar is in Strong Memorial Hospital... with cancer."

"Cancer?" Jesse said hesitantly.

"Yeah, and the doctors aren't giving him much hope. I've been praying and—"

Interrupting, Jesse asked in an urgent voice, "Did he save his soul?"

"Well, he always has said his prayers every morning and before going to sleep, and he has always believed in the Lord."

"That doesn't mean his soul is saved."

"I know when he was a child his parents forced him to go to church every Sunday. They made him stay from sunrise until sundown. After that, he didn't want anything to do with church. Everyone has spoken to him about saving his soul, but he won't listen. He just gets angry."

"I'll stop by the hospital and speak to him."

"He won't listen to you."

"Yes, he will. God is with me. Mom, I gotta go. There's a knock at my door. I'll stop by and see you later this week."

"All right."

"Love you."

"Bye."

Jesse walked through his art studio and opened the door. He was surprised to see the person standing in front of him. He hadn't seen him for quite a long time.

"What's up?" Jesse said, more of a statement than a question.

Eric seemed uneasy. "Well, I was in the neighborhood and decided to stop by."

"Well, come on in," Jesse said, trying to make him feel comfortable.

"Did you know Caesar's in the hospital?"

"Yeah, I just finished talking with Mom on the phone."

"I saw him yesterday. You should stop by to see him as soon as you can."

"All right."

"So, what have you been up to? It's been a while."

Jesse showed Eric the projects he had been working on and briefly explained his experience involving the chess drawing. He went on to explain to Eric the need to save his soul. Eric listened patiently and said, "I was recently invited to a church service, and the pastor was preaching on exactly what you've just spoken about. At the end of the service, he said for anyone who wanted to receive salvation from the Lord, to walk up to the altar."

"Well, did you?"

"No, but now standing and listening to you speak, I know this isn't a coincidence. Everything has a purpose. I plan on attending the church this Sunday. Actually, I know now I'm going to accept Jesus Christ, receive the Holy Spirit, and be baptized by water there. I know God is calling me, and I would be a fool not to respond."

"All right!" Jesse said, happy for his brother.

Eric moved toward the door. "I'd better get going."

"I'll see ya around," Jesse said, knowing his brother wasn't one for words.

Before leaving, Eric turned and said, "I've seen your T-shirts and artwork throughout the city. A lot of people are talking. Your message about God is spreading. Keep it up."

Jesse gave him a few T-shirts and several prints. "Here, take these. If you need more, let me know."

Eric nodded his head in thanks while leaving.

Wednesday evening, Jesse sat thinking about visiting Caesar in the hospital.

What would we talk about? he thought. They were worlds apart. Caesar had provided a stable household for their family when he married Grace. He had come along during their hardest time. Jesse wondered how their family would have survived if he hadn't. It was also a blessing to have his younger sister, Crystal. Even with the harsh treatment Jesse had received as a child, there was a side of Caesar that was caring and supportive. Jesse thought maybe some of Caesar's mistreatment of him may have stemmed from his past upbringing or traumatic experiences he had faced in his own life. Some things will never be understood or answered.

Jesse spent time in prayer, wondering if he should go visit Caesar in the hospital that night. God spoke to him immediately and said, "You're waiting in vain. Go and renew his spirit, and do it now."

At that moment, Jesse grabbed his leather shoulder bag and jacket and rushed out the door. Once outside, he hopped on a bus going to the hospital.

Arriving at the hospital, he nervously entered the darkened room. The only light came from the television above the bed.

"Hello, Tim! Come on in," Caesar said eagerly, with a smile upon his face.

Jesse froze for a moment; he felt that something strange was in the room. Turning, he saw a demon lurking in the corner, below the windowsill. The creature was glaring at Caesar with a sullen expression. After Jesse discovered the creature, its seething anger became focused on him.

Jesse turned toward Caesar, who lay in the bed. "How's everything?" he asked, ignoring the demon.

"Well, they've got me all tied up in bed here with all these tubes. It doesn't look good, but hopefully I'll be all right."

Caesar had always taken adversity and difficulties with a sense of humor, but this time seemed different.

"So, what have you been up to?" Caesar asked.

Jesse thought for a moment before answering. Caesar was very fragile and weak, so he kept his response brief. He said that his soul was saved and wanted to know if Caesar had saved his through Christ.

Caesar asked, "How do I save my soul?"

Surprised, Jesse answered, "Before you go to sleep tonight, say to God you're sorry for your sins and that you accept Jesus Christ as your Lord and Savior."

Caesar looked at Jesse and said, "OK."

They continued watching television. Moments later, Caesar turned down the volume with the remote in his hand. He slowly leaned toward Jesse and gripped his arm. Looking into his eyes, Caesar asked, "Can you repeat that again? I want to make sure I get it right."

Stunned, Jesse stuttered with excitement, "You...you...can repeat after me."

Jesse repeated what he had said moments earlier, and Caesar repeated each word after him. They both turned again to watch television. Jesse silently asked God if his stepfather was saved. At that moment, a commercial appeared on the television advertising Listerine. The Listerine bottle wore a suit of armor with a sword in hand, while a dark, demonic shadow attacked. Eventually, the Listerine bottle stabbed the demon with its sword, and the demon died, withering away against the wall. Jesse had received his answer.

He looked at Caesar and said, "Your soul is saved; you're going to Heaven."

Caesar replied, "I'm not ready to go yet!"

Jesse chuckled.

"Jesse, you know...I'm sorry that..."

"Don't worry about the past," Jesse said. "Many of us do things that we regret and feel sorry about, and I'm no different."

"Thank you."

"Don't thank me, thank God."

"You're right. Thank you, Lord, but I still also thank you."

Caesar died several months later and went to live in Heaven with Christ. Jesse shared his experience with his family members and advised them to save their souls through Jesus Christ.

The word is near you; it is in your mouth and in your heart, that is the word of faith we are proclaiming: That if you confess with your mouth, "Jesus is Lord" and believe in your heart that God raised him from the dead, you will be saved. For it is with your heart that you believe and are justified, and it is with your mouth that you confess and are saved. As the Scripture says, "Anyone who trusts in him will never be put to shame." For there is no difference between Jew and Gentile—the same Lord is Lord of all and richly blesses all who call on him, for, "Everyone who calls on the name of the Lord will be saved."

—Romans 10:8-13

CHAPTER 36

CHOSEN 1959

Dear friends, do not believe every spirit, but test the spirits to see whether they are from God, because many false prophets have gone out into the world. This is how you can recognize the Spirit of God: Every spirit that acknowledges that Jesus Christ has come in the flesh is from God, but every spirit that does not acknowledge Jesus is not from God.

—1 John 4:1-3

IN APRIL OF 1995, God opened the door for Jesse to continue his mission in New York City. On a Tuesday night, he met with Grace before his departure. They sat talking after a meal of chicken, cornbread, peas, rice, gravy, and collard greens. Grace served Jesse his favorite dessert dishes, chocolate cake and banana pudding, topped with ice cream. They sat through the evening laughing and joking about his childhood and teenage years.

After Grace cleared the table of dishes, they continued talking over a glass of Kool-Aid®. Sentiments of love and admiration were felt, even though they were seldom spoken.

"Are you sure you're going to be OK?" Grace asked.

Jesse nodded. "I'll be fine."

"Well, here, take a few dollars with you."

"Naw, Mom, I really don't need any money."

"Please, here, take it. You never know what might happen."

Jesse reluctantly placed the money in his pocket.

"Are you sure you had enough to eat?"

"Yeah, the meal was great."

"You know…with everyone now gone, I've been wondering if I should move back to my hometown in Alabama. I've been thinking about buying some land and building a house there."

"Sounds like a good idea. You've always said that you missed the land, the quiet, and the warm hospitality of the South."

"Yes, I have," Grace said hesitantly, still seeming unsure.

"I think you should do it."

"You know what, you're right. I feel it's time for me to go back to my roots," she said with a smile. "All right now, it's getting late, and I don't want to hold you up any longer. You just make sure that you call and let me know you're all right. New York is a big city, you know."

"Don't worry, Mom. I'll be OK."

"Now, if things don't work out, you know you always have a place to stay," she reassured him.

"I'll be fine, Mom. God's with me."

"Yes, I know He always has been."

They held a long embrace before saying their goodbyes.

The next day, Jesse met with Nina outside his building just before departing. He held his large black duffel bag over his shoulder. There was happiness and sadness between them, and, as usual, laughs.

"So, this is it, huh?" Nina said. "You're leaving me here all by my lonesome?"

"Yeah, this is it."

"Well, I've got to admit I'm going to miss you, even though you are a nut."

They laughed.

"I'll miss your wacky self, too," he retorted.

More laughter.

"I'm not comfortable with goodbyes, so give me a hug and get out of here," she said. After their brief hug, she added, "Complete God's mission."

"God has already—"

Nina interrupted him. "Jesse, I know who you are."

They both smiled as Jesse hailed a taxi cab on his way to the airport.

After arriving in New York City, Jesse immediately continued delivering the Lord's message of salvation. He found many receptive to what he had to say. Others said he was schizophrenic, a sorry excuse for a prophet, or simply confused and a liar. Jesse continued on just the same, ignoring the comments.

After two months, he moved to Newark, New Jersey, for better living conditions and rent. He commuted back and forth to his security job at a major hotel, while continually delivering his message in Manhattan. Every week, he gave out thousands of flyers in Grand Central Station and Times Square.

One evening, after leaving Grand Central Station, he stopped to purchase something to eat. At a newsstand, a gentleman lingered nearby with his back to Jesse.

Turning to face him, the man said, "You're making things very difficult for us. You're making it very difficult." He walked away.

Satan, Jesse thought.

Later that evening, while in his apartment, Jesse received a visitor from a neighbor named Douglass Sherman. Douglass had been raised in Newark as a child. They both looked out from his large apartment windows over the city. Jesse was disturbed by the poverty, darkness, and despair he saw throughout the city. So, he asked Douglass, "What happened to this place?"

Douglass's body slumped, and he said, with sadness in his eyes, "The city never recovered after the riots during the Civil Rights Movement. Heroin and cocaine were introduced in the late sixties and early seventies. Then, in the eighties came crack."

That night, Jesse felt deeply saddened by the destruction, devastation, and the effects of crack in the inner-city black communities. He hurt, having seen mothers turned into prostitutes, fatherless homes, abused and homeless children, crack babies, and the rise of violence in the homes, neighborhoods, and streets. The horror of it all was beyond words. Jesse felt a system had been methodically placed to condition, manipulate, and control the minds of the people. He also thought about how the characters in the Bible had been changed from black to European to deceive the masses, especially blacks in America, and rob them of their true biblical heritage. He wondered why most of the angels depicted in paintings were Caucasian.

He found himself angered by the lies of the Europeans and Americans to willfully misinterpret, misuse, and misrepresent the Bible to justify slavery, racism, and prejudice. He also found it outrageous that many whites believed that blacks were cursed by God, to justify their own greed, power, and need for supremacy. Jesse began to be consumed by the pain that he felt, so he began to write to release his hurt and anger.

> For only if you could see, hear, feel and touch
> From my eyes
> By now you'd probably be on crack
> Cracked right out of your mind
> For that is just what they wanted, control
> Control of the masses
> The Black Race

After finishing the first few lines of his thought, he stopped for a moment, and that was when the Devil spoke. Jesse wrote down what he heard:

> Put them to sleep, so they can't think
> One way or the other
> Genocide, been doing it for years
> It works one way or another
>
> Who cares, no one
> Not I, kill 'em all
> Murder them, the more the better
> Hated them from the beginning
>
> God's people, Ha!
> Chosen, get outta here!
> I hate you all
> AFRICAN AMERICAN
> Ha! You've accomplished nothing
> Actually, you've gotten worse
> Keep the movement
> what movement

There is none
You're dying by the thousands, can't you see
Of course not, you're too busy trying to please me
Fashion, Merchandise, Money
Are all my tools to rule over you
It works every time, old and young alike
SLAVERY
I invented it, everything comes back to me.
For I rule thee
Your mind, body, and soul are all mine
Too bad you can't see me, which helps serve my purpose
But you do know me
You all do
You always did
But still I was able to control your minds

Be more concerned about the white man than me
He's never done anything and never will
Just the same, but make my claim to fame
For he doesn't know of me
And doesn't even believe I exist
Oh thee intellectuals, all the same
Ignorant.

Tick Tock, Tick Tock
Time runs off the clock
Isn't it grand the howlings
And killings every night
That's what you wanted
That's what you have indeed

Oh the heat, don't worry about it, it's always hot
More than you can bear
You thought it was hot there
You haven't experienced anything here

Torment...Believe it, constant and forever
If only you could imagine
Then maybe you might change...Your mind
But please don't
Because I need you
With me in suffering
Can't do it alone
And don't want to be alone
You're my friends
And I need my friends indeed
Black, white, it's all the same here

Capital punishment, I love it, I love it
Bring them home to me
I'll show you what punishment is
For I created it
Murder, deceit, killings

More, more, more
Chain, chain, chain
Chain a fool

Race riots, I started all that
And I'll never end it
It works for you, and it works for me
You're on top of nothing, I own you all
Who chose to be mine
Which are many unwilling but able

Fooled you, huh?
That's what I'm all about
Deception, deception of the masses
Those who do the same follow me in vain
FOOL'S PARADISE.

Jesse placed his writing pen on the desk and focused on an abstract
print on the wall across the room. It was a lithograph he had purchased

earlier in the week. For some apparent reason, he found himself drawn to the painting. After studying it for a short time, he noticed a black angelic figure emerging through the vibrant colors.

As time passed further into the night, Jesse found himself wearisome. His very tired eyes soon took over. His heartbeat and breathing slowed, spiraling him down into a deeper stage of sleep.

At three A.M., his eyes opened, while being awakened by a calm voice. Jesse began writing as the voice continued speaking.

Death waits at your door, and I AM knocking. You owe a debt you can never pay, America. You knew me, but I never knew you. Blood flooded the streets, screams unheard. My people cry no more. No more will you speak of "Glorious Days," this evil generation. Your weeping shall be forever; theirs for a moment. America, your time has come.

Land of the Free, you don't know what freedom is. I will crush your "Statue of Liberty," for only I give it. I alone am justice, and when I speak, you will listen. I have listened to you enough, and I have heard the cries of my people whom you ignore. Peace, love, harmony, and justice is what they ask, and you give them murder, but you call it justice. Justice for your cause. What is freedom? Souls you snuffed out like a candle light, which now suffer damnation because of your expedient cause to justice. Now you stand before Me in trial, for you've shown no mercy, and neither will I give thee. You call these people animals. You are the animals, and you shall die the worst way—eternal damnation for all you have done to my people. They wanted freedom, you gave them hell; now you have yours forever, even though theirs was just momentary before death.

Death—do you know what death is? Death is eternal. Death is my sentence on you in judgement, not yours to silence my leaders. You killed them to silence the people, but no more. Your time has come. No more will you dominate my people with your intimidation and brutalization, and this you call justice. I am sick of your lies. No more loving your children while others suffer, and then going to church on Sunday. The year has arrived in 1959, and you shall know I AM the Lord.

God

CHAPTER 37

ALONE

Many people spend their lives going up the down escalator.

YEARS LATER, IN May of 1998, Jesse found himself surrounded by doctors. He had arrived in the emergency room at the hospital one morning, overcome by dizzy spells and insomnia. The doctors examined him thoroughly, but could not account for his dizziness and inability to walk straight without focusing on the floor.

After being released, he took a taxi back to his place. While in his apartment, the room seemed to constantly spin. He sat on the sofa, feeling lost and hopeless. He knew his constant dizziness was because of lack of sleep, not eating properly, and exhaustion. He had overextended himself for years in his constant battle against Satan to warn others to save their souls. His body was breaking down from the demands he had placed on himself. His greatest fear was that the dizziness would remain permanently.

During his trials, God had continued flashing the word *Job* before him. Jesse was trying with difficulty to figure out the message that God was sending him. He kept wondering why God would constantly speak to him about employment during his time of crisis.

To take his thoughts away from his worries, he placed a recently purchased CD into his stereo and heard the song "Feelin's Gotta Stay" by Rick Ocasek. The song was about not giving up, even when everything seems hopeless.

Later in the evening, Jesse decided to attend a church service. The church was small. The sanctuary could hold two hundred people, and everyone sat on folding chairs. There was a small stage with a wooden podium upon it and a few musical instruments positioned to the right for the band members. The interior appeared to be kept in spotless condition. That evening, as Pastor Andrews led members through the daily hymns before delivering his sermon, Jesse sat quietly three rows from the front. After the last song of praise and worship, everyone sat down, and the young pastor began speaking while pacing back and forth. His voice boomed as he spoke with vigor and commitment, oblivious to the congregation. Several words spoken by Pastor Andrews drew Jesse's attention as he listened more closely.

"Dreamer, dream on! Dream in the day as well as in the night. Never stop dreaming!"

The members remained quiet as he continued, with some probably wondering what he was speaking about. Jesse paid even more attention after hearing the word "dream."

"The animals, trees, and birds know who you are. Joseph, no matter what difficulties you go through, you must never stop dreaming!"

Jesse sat up farther and leaned forward, hearing the Bible character's name "Joseph." Joseph was his favorite character in the Bible because of all the disappointments and hardships he had overcome. Jesse was beginning to accept that God was speaking through the pastor to communicate to him, but he was still unsure. He leaned even closer as the pastor continued speaking.

"Joseph!" the pastor shouted. "Your mission will be completed in New York City. Nothing and no one can stop you. Read about Job in the Bible, and remain strong!"

The pastor's tone changed, his pacing ended, and he addressed the congregation, as if unaware of what he had just spoken. Jesse had received God's confirmation and words of encouragement through Pastor Andrews.

After church, Jesse stood at the bus stop. At that moment, a vehicle drove by with the song "Dream On" by Aerosmith blaring through its windows.

Once home, with an uplifted spirit, Jesse fell asleep. Once again, he was awakened in the early morning hours by a whisper. He scribbled what was spoken and then fell asleep on the sofa. The writing read,

ALONE

I will right your wrongs
But some of you will bear arms against me
You bear arms against yourselves
For you fight against the wind and sea

I am the wind and sea
No one dominates me
I dominate you, if I choose to
But I don't, I choose to give freedom over domination
Again freedom you wish not to receive
Freedom which is everlasting love

Love above all else
Love one another
But you wish to hate each other
And you call yourselves civilians
Citizens of the universe
What universe, yours
You've created none
Yet you doubt me
You doubt my existence
You doubt even your own
I have no doubt at all
Of your condemnation of Hell
You have chosen
Freedom in Hell?
There is no freedom
Ha! Are you kidding me?
Hell is for suffering, not freedom
Only my children will taste freedom
Freedom which they so wish to have
I ordain thee
Because you are mine, but a handful
All else is gone
Gone to oblivion
Gone to waste
Acknowledgement of me

THE ENDLESS HOUR

You chose not
Acknowledge yourselves, you chose to
Superstars of no one
I know you not
Egos abroad, self-satisfaction
Hordes, whores, pimps, war mongers, rapists, killers
all shall perish
You are the sick ones
No mysteries.

For you are damned
Your time is short
Theirs everlasting
Joy, Happiness, and Salvation
I love them and they love me
We shall abide in happiness forever
Thanks to Christ My Only Begotten Son
Whom you still mock to this day
Well, your mockery has ended
Ended unto Hell where you will
Weep and gnash your teeth forever
Your time has come
And I've waited so long

Give it time, you say
He won't listen, he'll go away
But I did listen and I didn't go away
I hear my peoples' cries, mourns, and pains
And I'll never go away
I'll never leave them
But you will perish in Hell
You've conquered and beaten them enough
Your time is over
I have finished my work
It is done in advance
A long time ago, from the beginning
The beginning was the end

ALONE

I knew you, But you knew me not
Now you are alone in darkness
For I am the light among my people
Who chose to reverence, obey, and love me
And they are the light
Of the world of darkness
But in Hell there is no light

For I am not there
But you shall be enslaved forever
Forever in Hell's domain
Turn while you can
Now, before you face the Wrath of God
None will survive
For I am King
And I sit on my throne
And do whatever becomes me
And you shall listen then
Idiots, your courts are a joke
I'll show you how it's done

'Cause you chose not to listen
To what I say and do your own thing
When I placed you to rule
You rule not on my accord but your own
And they laugh
Laugh no more
For I will judge you
Judges, Judges, Judges
Judges of what?
Nothing.

Captivity and violence
Roam the streets
While you sleep so peacefully
Condemn the poor, free the rich
Is your law not mine

Enjoy.
Pleasure principle
Just don't get caught, you say
Believe me when I say
I watch your every move
And it sickens me
You're all for show
Show them, but you won't show me
For I know you, I made you

You may sing and dance with them
But you'll cry with me
Thee condemned of my courts
Where truth and justice rules and domains
My people will jump for joy
And be of great chorus
When truth reigns over death
Reign with power
Aghast, hope is here
And has conquered all their doubters
For I am hope to my people
Believers of my word
And proven unto me
I love you so stay strong
And don't give up
The war is over and I have finished it
Just continue in your doings
For you have peace
Peace and unafraid of the wicked
Yes, I watch over you
In jealousy and tender mercy
For you are mine and I yours.

For I rule forever and ever
Peace be unto you all
Laughter and jumping for joy
Will be all the same in the hereafter
Hallelujah!

ALONE

I with you, you with me, forever
Forever in the everlasting glow of love
Which I AM
So stay strong and keep up with the battle

For I am with you
No one shall conquer you
There is no defeat
Victory is yours
Amen

Amen, to those who know what it means.
Yours Truly, God

CHAPTER 38

BABYLON

EVENTUALLY, THE DIZZY spells ceased. Jesse moved back to New York City in the spring of 2000. He moved into an art studio in SoHo, where he slept on the floor at night and worked on his art during the day. In the month of October, after handing out flyers on the streets, Jesse began walking along a darkened, isolated area. He saw a homeless person and gave him a flyer. After studying the illustration and reading the message of salvation, he stared at Jesse with discontent in his eyes.

"I don't want this crap," he snapped as he began to throw the flyer to the ground. "I need a dollar!"

"Go ahead, throw it down," Jesse said. "I'll see you on Judgment Day."

Hesitating, the man looked at Jesse and stuffed the flyer in his pocket while walking away.

Jesse began crossing the street. As he glanced over his shoulder, he noticed a vehicle speeding directly toward him. Without hesitation, he dove between two parked vehicles as the oncoming car swerved, passing close by and barely missing him.

Music blared from the windows of the vehicle as it continued down the street. The song was "Dead or Alive" by Bon Jovi.

Jesse stood up from the pavement. While dusting himself off, he noticed a bumper sticker with a cross on the parked vehicle.

Physically shaken, he returned to his art studio and worked on his paintings into the night. When it became late, he cleaned his brushes, set his easel aside, and placed his jacket under his head for a pillow while falling asleep. In the early morning hours, he was again awakened by the calm, gentle voice.

> "Babylon over the storm which wagest by the sea
> The storm wagest over the sea, Babylon O Babylon,
> King of Babylon shall fall."

Without hesitating, he found paper and began writing as the voice continued speaking.

> For Babylon has forsaken me, chosen death indeed
> Death by sea which take no heed
> For I continuously warn thee, to no avail
> Aghast, you shall have yours
> For you chose not to reverence the Lord, but yourselves
> So continue so, you scavenger and pulpit bearers
> Yours you shall have, condemnation of death I hear you no
> more
> Cry to yourselves, for those you have chosen to worship
> And see what they can do for you, not I but them, they're yours
> Take them, follow them, have them lead you to death
> Your chosen ones
> Massacred by the thousands
> Leaders of no one, the lost souls of Hell
> Judgeth by day, traveleth by sea
> Which of thee will survive the storm, I see upon thee
>
> None.
> For none have listened to me but yourselves
> Idiots all
> For all have forsaken me
> Ruler of earth and all its domain
> Pity no one listens
> For if you did, you would live and none should die
> Yet you won't listen, and you never will
> Let alone do the works of God

Because to you, yours is more important than mine
But what is works
Works which beareth fruit or works which beareth death
To be thrown in the lake of fire
Wasted, futily wasted
Yet you work so anxiously, to do nothing
Rather than do the works that endureth forever, mine
But that's not important to you
Because you consider yourselves first over me
What a pity, for I created you

Shall the Maker ruleth over the Master?
Shall the pot complain to the potter?
No, but you do
Fools, you have no sense to understand the heavens above
And the earth below
But shall you listen, shall you ever…of course not
Due to your silly plans of life, and you don't know what life is
Let me tell you, you will never know
Know-it-alls, you know nothing
Washed minds, wasted into oblivion
Gone with the mist of the sea
The sea turned and you turned
And you turned the sea sat and sat
Now the sea turns no more
For I rule the sea and all its inhabitants
And now you shall die
With it and all its evil ways
For which you have adopted and even strive for

For your minds are lost, valley of lost souls
Which was of no importance to you, until now
Now in the everlasting, burning flames of Hell
Reverence who, reverence the Lord
You don't know what reverence is
You reverence each other in death
I AM I

If you choose to reverence me you shall live
Take heed, for you have been forewarned
And if only you would listen, and turn to life from death
But you won't and you never will
Now your cities lie in ruin, with butchering shops for my sheep
Thousands led to the slaughter of Hell
Now listen, listen to me and you shall live, now is the time
Sex, adulterers, you have no pity, you have no shame
And oh how you worship in vain
Your needs will never be met
Mine, which of course you won't do;

Oh chosen few
You love your tendencies too much
It is like a delicatessen, you never get enough
Taste buds always craving for more sin
Die you want, so death you have it
For I am the Ruler over death
Death beyond your comprehension
Heroes, there are no heroes, but one and he belongs to me
But you will choose to hate even him,
The one I chose to warn you:
The one I chose for reconciliation
But again still you won't listen
Let alone do as I say
You choose not to reverence the Lord
So the Devil is your master
Amen
You shall serve him like a puppet on a string
Free will, you had it but now you've chosen to give it away
Given away to the pleasures of the world

Rather than seeking the Kingdom of Heaven
Where all everlasting treasures live,
Your time was spent collecting treasures of the world
Which are totally destructible.

Jesse was later informed by God that Babylon is New York City.

Then the Lord said, "The outcry against Sodom and Gomorrah is so great and their sin so grievous that I will go down and see if what they have done is as bad as the outcry that has reached me. If not, I will know."

—Genesis 18:20

CHAPTER 39

FREEDOM

A FEW DAYS later, Jesse woke again after spending another tiresome day being mocked and rejected by others. He felt discouraged by the indifference of those he met.

At 3:45 A.M., the voice spoke quietly and patiently, and he began writing.

> You never will
> See the dawn of the day
> See the spring of the night
> What a surprise
> You had my advice
> You neglected to listen or do
> You never will see
> The spring of the day
> What a shame
> You had it your way
> You never will survive
> All has gone by
> Now is the time
> Farewell
>
> You never will understand why
> So go now, it's over twice in a day

You were special once
But again, goodbye
You were special then
But now it's gone
You say it's OK, but it isn't
Too bad you wanted it your way
Your way, not mine
From life to death
Farewell
To all your friends and family
Which once were
Which are no more
Because you chose to have it your way
Love, I am love
I loved you once, but now no more
I knew you, but you never knew me
So, farewell
I cried for you, but you laughed at me
me and my Son.

So laugh no more
In the oblivion of souls
Which dwell forever
As none
None in time, none in space
None into existence.

The message was for those who continually rejected God's message of salvation through Christ Jesus.

Jesse was tired, but he spoke to God about those who said they had died and gone to Heaven and were brought back to life to spread the Lord's message. Others said that they had witnessed a light after a death experience, and others spoke of witnessing the depths of Hell itself.

Their visions are false and their divinations a lie. They say, "The Lord declares," when the Lord has not sent them; yet they expect their words to be fulfilled. Have you not seen false visions and uttered lying divinations when you say, "The Lord declares," though I have not spoken? Therefore this is

*what the Sovereign Lord says: "Because of your false words and lying visions,
I am against you," declares the Sovereign Lord.*
—Ezekiel 13:6-8

*For such men are false apostles, deceitful workmen, masquerading as apostles
of Christ. And no wonder, for Satan himself masquerades as an angel of
light. It is not surprising, then, if his servants masquerade as servants of
righteousness. Their end will be what their actions deserve.*
—2 Corinthians 11:13-15

Jesse lay in bed, asking God what Heaven and Hell were like. He
continued his requests until he finally fell asleep.

Suddenly, he found himself screaming while being overtaken and
dragged down into a thick mass of darkness.

"Please...Noooo!"

The powerful pulling force dragged him down toward the chamber of
death. He continued screaming in anguish, even though his voice echoed
off the walls unheard. Now, in a wild frenzy, Jesse fought frantically, kicking
and clawing in a desperate attempt to prevent himself from plunging into
the bottom of this blackened tunnel. His struggle only accelerated his
downward motion, causing even more trauma. The walls were covered
with slick black sludge, which made it impossible for him to brace himself
and prevent reaching what awaited him. His eyes were now dilated with
the thoughts of horror bellowing through his mind.

Faster...Faster...Faster!

Fear accelerated. As he sped closer to the end, his thoughts of terror
increased. It was as though his heart had been ripped out of his chest due
to the amount of anguish and pain he felt as he continued screaming.
Agony. Hopelessness. Despair.

Down.

Down.

Down!

Into the deepest inescapable blackness ever known. It all became
unbearable, and he unleashed an agonizing scream.

He suddenly found himself afloat. Euphoria. Within his soul was a
sense of peace and serenity. He remained still, as though listening to a
butterfly in flight, while surrounded by a silent blue sky.

Then, in an instant, he awoke. He sat up with his heart pounding, bathed in sweat. Jesse realized that God had allowed him to feel the horrors of Hell, and also experience the stillness of Heaven.

CPSIA information can be obtained at www.ICGtesting.com
Printed in the USA
BVOW03s1856201013

334042BV00003B/19/P